SACRED
MANHOOD

SACRED
EARTH

SACRED MANHOOD
SACRED EARTH

A VISION QUEST INTO THE WILDERNESS OF A MAN'S HEART

JOSEPH JASTRAB

WITH RON SCHAUMBURG

HarperCollins*Publishers*

Copyright acknowledgments can be found on page 212.

HarperCollins books may be purchased for educational, business, or sales promotional use. For information please write: Special Markets Department, Harper-Collins Publishers, Inc., 10 East 53rd Street, New York, NY 10022.

FIRST EDITION

Designed by Alma Hochhauser Orenstein

Library of Congress Cataloging-in-Publication Data

Jastrab, Joseph, 1950–
    Sacred manhood, sacred earth : a vision quest into the wilderness of a man's heart / by Joseph Jastrab with Ron Schaumburg.—1st ed.
        p. cm.
    ISBN 0-06-016945-1
    1. Men—United States—Psychology. 2. Masculinity (Psychology). 3. Men's movement—United States. I. Schaumburg, Ron. II. Title.
HQ1090.3.J37 1994
305.32′0973—dc20   93-37813

94 95 96 97 98 ❖/HC 10 9 8 7 6 5 4 3 2 1

CONTENTS

FOREWORD: THE DESTRUCTION AND RECLAMATION OF MEANING

During his time, Plato protested the loss of respect for tradition. Shakespeare showed us all hell broke loose among kings and queens who no longer cared for any other souls, including their own. Ibsen's works revolved around the loss of spirit through overcodification. Thousands of artists, politicos, theologians, and philosophers have described, and still do, the ubiquitous human cycle in which loss is followed by seeking. This matter is an old, old story. Therefore, a modern person's endeavors toward reclamation of spirit are not, as one might first suppose, a mere "fashion," or "sign of our times." Rather they are one of the most common and driving symbolic endeavors of *any* time, past or present.

Even though we may wish otherwise, it is predictable that the life of the spirit—in both individuals and in groups—will at some time, and in rather regular cycles, suffer from what you might call "a wearing out" of numinousness. Spiritual symbols that once had immense impact and ability to move people become diluted. Note that I did not say that what stands behind the symbols wears out—the numen can never be worn out—but rather the representations that humans make of it are eventually put forth in more and more colorless and deadened ways, so that eventually a body is no longer attracted through those representations. When this occurs, the images become wilted rather than fresh. They lose their strongest nutrients, and therefore their strongest affects and effects.

But, as disheartening as this may seem, I observe, from having spoken with large groups in some forty cities in the past two years, that there is today not only a painful decline in some sectors of culture, but also a strong renaissance of spiritual feeling at many levels and among many different kinds of people. For example, the Mexican *mestizaje* movement in the churches, the renewed emphasis on Jewish *midrash* by Jews and non-Jews alike, the awakening of various Euro-Americans to the rituals and stories of their own ancient pasts.

There is also the recent and glorious first-time ordination of women priests by the British Anglicans; the rather sudden decision by the Roman Catholic church, not so many years past, to return Christ's mother, Mary, a feminine power, to the ontological hierarchy after several hundred years of inference that she was just a poor Jewish girl in divine trouble; the Maori from New Zealand and the native people of Hawaii, among others, are continuing to reclaim ancient ritual and make up the rest, fresh and anew, according to "a kind of old dreaming memory"— all these represent an intrinsic drive in individuals toward a psychic wholeness that includes meaningful practices.

The patterns for these practices are innate to humans and are already intact in the layer of the collective unconscious in the objective psyche. These universal patterns can, in effect, be "dreamed up," by those who care to, or who are charged to look into the far corners of the psyche. Though their faces, costumes, songs, dance steps, foods, and rituals be all of somewhat different configuration, at the bottom, human beings utilize the same symbols and means for the development of their spiritual natures. This is a brief excerpt from a poem-chant called, "The Six Gifts of the Seven Day Creation."*

> The Drum: On the first day, we were given the drum. The
> great Taiko drums of the Japanese, the tiny hand drums of

* Copyright © 1980 by Clarissa Pinkola Estés

Tibet, the oil drum of the steel band in Kingston, the five tier
trap set, the drum of the old Korean woman who lives in the
alley, the African goat-skin drum, the bone drum from the
Caucases, the body itself used as drum by the hill people
from Tennessee and Kentucky, the tin cans, canisters, bowls
and floors drummed upon by children, even very young
infants, in their usual play— there have always been drums.

Bells: On the second day we were given the bell. Be they
the chimes of Westminster, the bells of high Mass, the bell
of Godwyn that spoke not only in tones but in words as
well, the bells on the knees of the Hopi snake dancers at
Walpi, the silver ankle bells of Sita, the golden finger cym-
bals of middle eastern dancers, the wooden bell of the
alpine farmers, or a child looking for something to tap with
a stick so that it will ring, ting, chime—there have always
been bells.

Chants. . . : We were given the chants, the sounds and
the words. Be they the monastics and cloisters singing the
Requiem dirge, the Dineh lullaby chant sung by the grand-
mother, the red-ant chant of the southernmost people, the
Hebrew chant that is not words but only sounds that open
the heart inexorably, the steaming chant of the *cantaora* in
Flamenco, the "chant for the foot," sung by the Maidu
hunters, the natural song of the breath of lovers, the chant
of the Magyar grandparent singing over the newborn child,
the chants that are created on the spot by children as they
walk, skip and dance—there have always been chants.

These, and more, are aspects of ritual that manifest in human
beings even before they can speak or walk. Hold the five-month-
old baby by its hands, and it will do a fine high-stepping dance to
music. The child will name itself, often many names and none
having to do with the child's given name. The child will name
others, these names often being based on a physical characteristic,
or according to the way the child feels about that person. When a
little older, the child will spend much time trying to escape from
all adults, often venturing farther and farther from home in order

to find perhaps a new world, but more likely, in order to find how and "what one becomes," when confronted with an unknown part of the world.

The child will find ways to become brother and sister to others who are not blood kin. They will cut the flesh somewhere on the body and become blood siblings, or show affiliation and sorority by wearing the same red thread around the waist, or by like tattoos, by like scratches behind the ear, or by some other means they will symbolize their love and affinity for another. Children love fire and big water and the tallest of everything and smallest of anything, and objects that shine, and rocks of a certain kind, and bones. They put shards and strips and parts and particles of everything into their pockets. Anyone who has ever seen a child guard this collection of knobs and pieces knows that, to the child, these matters are holy.

Afterward, the children tell stories about all that they have done. They are renewed each day by their ritual, and no doubt, many go home and sleep deeply from having done such intense work. The spirit of the child, regardless of class, gender, or ethnicity, is kept rich by such play. This play is not diversion, it is practicing for the more sophisticated forms of renewal of spirit that naturally grow out of all people—if they will allow them.

In the spiritual practices of adults, what is innate in the child is called by the grown-ups these names: chanting, drumming, singing, dancing, rhythms, naming ceremony, clan affiliation, talisman making, departing for deserted places in order to find an answer or oneself, scarification, the retelling of epics, and so on.

All these rise up not only out of groups who live in isolation far away from so-called modern culture, but these rituals arise in all humans, children and adults alike. All for soul's sake. All to either express or move a person to a psychological aperture, through which one can hear the proscriptions of and see the patterns for spiritual renewal with clarity.

This is what used to be called *religion* in the truest sense of the word. Religāre: to bind together, as in the idea of sheaves for instance: the binding together of one's senses, the binding together of one's mind, body and spirit, the binding together of the community, the binding together of all these with one's world and all things in it, from the tiniest flower growing through a crevasse in the rocks to the greatest and the oldest.

I came to understand these essential matters through my work as an ethnoclinical psychologist whose training, in part, is concerned with the anthropology of groups, tribes, and communities, and as a certified psychoanalyst who has practiced and been heavily involved in grass-roots social justice work for more than two decades. I've witnessed firsthand the sufferings of the psyche and spirit in those who have survived torture, those who have endured forced resettlements, and other spiritual and cultural devastations.

One might expect a person who has lost meaning in life, through whatever circumstances, to perhaps give up and that would be the end of it—and them. It is true that some who have lost much do in fact choose for some length of time, bitterness as a kind of shield against future pain. Some attempt to dismantle their own as well as others' hopes and callings in an effort to exert a kind of imaginary control over life: as they see it, this secures protection against having to yield, or be uncertain, or be inspired and then disappointed ever again.

But most do not take up residence in these psychic stances, for they draw too deeply on one-sidedness and invective and not enough on renewed love of people and of life. Most stop and look, perhaps converse for a bit, but then, as in the metaphors of the mythos of old, they pass by the hooded stranger selling poisoned apples. And in doing so, they advance to the next vendor who has what they truly desire, who in the English medieval mystery plays was sometimes named, "Lifefull," or "Full of Life."

Here is *the observable miracle*. People who are attempting to maintain body and soul in a destroyed culture, or in a situation where there has been, for whatever reasons, immense loss of meaning in one's life, do not—as some erroneously speculate—crawl away for eternity, suffer endlessly, die off, or else live forever in silence. Quite the opposite. In even the most devastated human beings there remains a pristine archetypal pattern for the regrowth of spiritual life, and this impulse toward renewal of spirit, when harassed, forbidden or tortured, will, instead of dying, dive directly underground in order to preserve itself.

Therein it lies in an incubation, in a hiatus or in a long darkness, waiting for *the* moment, the right idea or the chance rich enough, permeable enough for it to reemerge. That is its work, that is what it waits for, a chance to send its shoots upwards from its root again, to rise above ground once more.

This drive to spirit that is incubated in the devastated heart during a time of psychic darkness is called the archetype of *Return.* It is a renaissance, a reknowing, an often at-first-awkward rebirth upward from the grave. Its purpose is to quicken a return to cycles, to nature, to spirituality, to the seeking, finding, reclamation, and repair of worship and ritual. In all, it is an *absolutely necessary reconvening* of the spiritual meanings that underlie all of life.

I have seen this regrowing of spiritual self after a long devastation in refugees from Guatemala and El Salvador, I've seen it in the African American pride movement, I've seen it in those who have left religious life, I've seen it in those who have lost their family traditions, those who have entered too deeply into the melting pot until they were faceless, voiceless, and completely stripped of the renewing ideas and rituals that support inner life first and action in outer life second. I've seen it in my own families as they gradually made their ways back from their own cultural devastations. All have striven to remake, to reconstruct spiritual life—from their bones upward. New ritual was devised and incorporated along with the old. New ways were created for recognizing that the old life was over. New life required that each one in some way begin again from the beginning, as well as from all that was left of the end.

Here, let us note that there are several stages to reclamation and repair of spirit and self. From an empirical stance of noting the behaviors of many persons who have struggled with these matters over long periods of time, I would briefly list them in this order: the admittance or recognition that one has lost something of great import; the grieving of that loss, that is, feeling its full effect; the anamnesis, that is, the recalling of all that occurred to effect such a loss—both the external and internal factors; the first awkward reconstruction of what is known from the psychic shards that have been left behind; the creation of a stronger structure that is self supporting; the creation of an even stronger structure that is supporting of self and one's inner circle; the creation of the most integral structure that is supporting of oneself, one's primary relationships and begins to move supportive action in the larger community and world.

For personal reasons, Joseph Jastrab felt strongly that he too must begin at *aleph*, at the beginning, in order to find out for himself: What is spirit? What is *religāre*? What is it that binds him together in a way that has *meaning* for him and for those he loves?

His work and others of similar genre, are, to my mind, a part of a large and ongoing body of personal writings that have canalized upward into print in various parts of the world, particularly over the last five hundred years. By these lights, Mr. Jastrab's work does not belong so much to any "gender" category, but rather to the body of work that renders personal stories about the reconstruction of spiritual culture in those who have surrendered it or been stripped of it. His work is most assuredly an ethnological self-narrative; one person's pathway to the meaning of a life lost and found. Like others in the narrative genre, Mr. Jastrab's style is firsthand and honest. At times his language suggests an earlier form, that though no longer in common use, is still applied for poetical, liturgical, and oratorical purposes. His book is in his own voice, and as such is a worthy biography of part of the world soul.

As with other psychological epics, both ancient and modern, I am less concerned with the content of the endeavors than I am with the psychological meaning of them and the initial catalysts for them and what, in the end, they have to contribute to understanding the many aspects of the psyche's ongoing ways and needs. Mr. Jastrab's latter-day epic begins with a worthy and desperate attempt to return to full senses. Over time, he and his fellow travelers make the time-honored effort to reconstruct something that might only be recalled in night dreams, or through being visited in the forest by a herd of owls, or while alone where nature and human beings are not separate or at war with one another. This book, in essence, is a document that strives in its own way to tell what happens when a bunch of men go out into a wilderness and try to dig up the living God.

—CLARISSA PINKOLA ESTÉS, PH.D.

AUTHOR'S NOTE

The stories presented here emerged from a series of Men's Quests that took place in the Adirondack Mountains of New York State from 1982 to 1993. Our work was based on the ancient practice of the Vision Quest. The term "Vision Quest" was introduced by nineteenth-century Anglo-American anthropologists to identify certain Native American rites of passage, and later used as a generic term to describe a truly native human practice. Though the world-wide expression of the Vision Quest is diverse, it commonly involves self-purification rites, solitude, prayer, and a journey into the wilderness. In its most essential form, the Vision Quest is a template of rites and myths that support the soul's longing for wholeness. In the Vision Quest, the myths that animate human life are replenished and made new.

The work presented here is part of a larger movement to revitalize this practice in modern times. This contemporary quest work rests on the foundation of ancient practice, yet our intent is not to re-create the past. The task before us is in serving the rebirth of the sacred that is true to the particular challenges and opportunities of our present age. In times of cultural flux and transition, our identities as men and women need to be continually reinvented. I envision the Men's Quest, and other events of its kind, as breeding grounds for the new story. Much of this work is necessarily experimental in nature and must necessarily take place beyond the eyes of the culture. The men who have returned from the wilderness to share their stories in this volume do so in the spirit of the Giveaway. We offer these glimpses of our experience with hopes they may elicit more of the insight, compassion, and good humor of your own quest. This book is dedicated to all men and women whose longing for wholeness returns them to the sacred earth.

There is a story about a Nez Perce Indian who went to study anthropology with Franz Boas at Columbia University in the early part of the century. When his studies were completed he returned to his tribe with the intention of recording all their stories. He found, however, that when translated into English they had little spirit or humor. They were, he said, "nothing but cold corpses." Throughout the development of this manuscript I continually felt more like a translator than a writer. These stories were given in the language of experience. I have translated them here into English. I have done my best to stay close to the original language, but I must admit I share the same concern as the Nez Perce man. Your willingness to bring your experience to this text is required to bring this translation back to life. These words mean little unless you can find them living within your own body. What follows, then, are stories from men who have journeyed beyond the border of culturally defined manhood—stories from the deep woods of the heart.

—JOSEPH JASTRAB

INTRODUCTION:
THE WORLD
NEEDS A MAN'S HEART

> *I have a feeling that my boat*
> *has struck, down there in the depths,*
> *against a great thing.*
>   *And nothing*
> *happens! Nothing . . . Silence . . . Waves . . .*
>
>   *—Nothing happens? Or has everything happened,*
> *and are we standing now, quietly, in the new life?*
>   —JUAN RAMÓN JIMÉNEZ
>   *TRANSLATION BY ROBERT BLY*

I'd grown too big for my skin. For some time, I'd felt a deepening restlessness, an itch to get on with my life. There wasn't anything particularly wrong with my life, yet I knew that there was something more to be lived than I had as yet allowed. The old story had run its course and had given me all that it could. Now I was being called to give myself over to a larger story—one I couldn't yet name, but could feel as a deep longing moving through every cell of my body.

This longing has drawn me here, to these canyons in the Utah desert. Others have gathered here too. I know very little about these people, except that we all share symptoms of some divine disquiet. We have come to this desert encampment to honor the spiritual restlessness that our culture often fearfully diagnoses as a problem to be fixed. Yet when the soul stirs with such insistence, it is calling our attention to some new life inside that wants to be recognized. This calling instinctively lures us away from the cares and distractions of everyday life and toward the outermost fringes of the world. On such a fringe, I find myself tonight.

I am taken by the auspicious beauty of this night. A fully ripe moon bathes the landscape in a hauntingly cool light. Long shadows heighten the relief of the pebbled ground. There is an uncommon radiance here that gives shadow an added dimension of life. The dark forms appear as real as their lighted counterparts. I look down at my own shadow, faithful companion, saddened by how much of myself I find there. It invites me to walk with it. I accept.

I wander out of camp. Instinctively, I seek a place that knows nothing of my past, a place that will not hold me to my name or speculate on who—or what—may emerge from this old, dry skin. Like an animal seeking a nesting place to give birth, I hunger for the nonintrusive silence of the desert night. As I draw farther away from camp, the voices and trailing laughter of the others die away. I continue walking, stopping to look back only after the night has taken all sounds, except the low pulse of my beating heart, fully into itself.

Looking back I notice my tracks. They resemble those of a coyote, wandering here and there, seemingly without reason. Coyote, I've come to learn, is rarely reasonable though always curious, and his nose never fails to unearth something interesting. By now it is clear I need a medicine more potent than reason alone. So I continue to let my way be guided by whatever draws my attention.

My imagination, relishing such freedom, plays on distant canyon walls. Their surfaces are awash with mineral stain shadows of mythical beasts and gnarled faces that shape-shift, the way images in clouds do. Small clumps of sagebrush offer up a heady fragrance. The smell conjures up ancestral memory: vaporous images of native dancers, their songs mingling with the intoxicating smoke of the burning herb. Red sandstone boulders, scoured by eons of wind and fire, hold a strong presence here, as if placed with the clear intent of a Zen rock garden.

I walk among the stones until I come on an entrance to a large curved canyon. The terra-cotta walls rise abruptly from the desert floor to encircle a patch of the northern sky. The seven bright stars of the Big Dipper are prominently displayed within this frame. Out of habit I follow the Dipper's pointer stars to locate the North Star: Polaris, the true-star, the axis around which all others turn. As I set my gaze on this still point, the restlessness that led me here suddenly returns like a comet, blazing through my heart before it bursts into conscious thought: Certainly, all life moves in relation to a center. What, then, is my center? What does my life revolve around? What matters to me—really matters?

Polaris continues to twinkle in silence as I become lost in thought. Impatient to get this matter settled, I surmise that the answer to my question *should* have something to do with "saving the planet" or some other noble service. But before my mind can settle the matter, I am drawn back to my senses.

Inside the sheltered walls of the canyon I notice a small cluster of plants that seem to glow with a phosphorescent radiance. Moving closer I see that this light emanates from a group of datura flowers. Flowers in full bloom, in the middle of night! The trumpeting white blossoms seem to be enjoying a secret courtship with the moon. I'm aware that native peoples of this region ingest datura, or jimsonweed, to induce vision. Tonight, though, simply being in this plant's presence is enough to free up my perception. Intent on savoring this delicate mystery, I sit on the damp sand facing the blossoms and I fall into a penetrating stillness.

As I attend more fully to the blossoms, they seem to recede into the wall behind them, then emerge once again, back and forth. The wall itself is alive with images of faces and bodies: men, women, animals. There seems to be neither rhyme nor reason to what I'm viewing. I simply relax and enjoy the flowing, dancing forms.

I then realize with overwhelming clarity that I am surrounded by images of feminine power: the full moon, the night-blooming datura, even the womblike walls of the canyon itself. The Earth Mother, I fancy, is making herself known to me, filling my senses with her presence.

My reverie is broken when I feel the landscape turn toward me as if to say, "Who are you?" I'm startled by the aware presence and acceptance I suddenly find myself surrounded in. My longing to be seen runs headfirst into my terror of being seen, and I quickly blurt out, "How can I best serve the planet?"

In the answering silence I grow self-conscious and uneasy. I begin to suspect that offering myself so readily to service may be merely a distraction, just another way to avoid looking deeper into my heart. Rationality then charges in, judging my question to be grandiose, pompous, too big to allow any satisfactory reply.

I struggle a while against these swirling cross-currents before I finally let them be. I take a deep breath and plunge beneath the surface foam of my chattering mind. This time, my heart does the asking: How can I best serve the planet?

There's no sound, yet I hear the whisper:

The world needs a man's heart. . . .

The words drop like so many pebbles into still waters. The ripples lap against the canyon walls of my inner landscape. Again I listen, and again I hear the echoing words: *The world needs a man's heart.*

I was expecting something different. This answer confuses me. I try to whisk the words away, hoping to receive a more reasonable response. Yet doing so is like trying to extinguish a glowing ember by blowing on it; the harder I blow, the brighter the ember.

Again the whisper comes: *"If you wish to serve, forgive . . . forgive your heart . . . your man's heart. The world needs a man's heart. It all starts with forgiveness."*

Then everything is still. I notice I'm alone in a canyon, sitting on the cool sand, draped in a mantle of moonlight.

After a time I leave the datura feeling both grateful and troubled. My mind grapples with the words. Was this the voice of the Earth? The voice of Self? Whatever the source of the invitation, I feel I have been impregnated with something alive and meaningful, something only partly of my creation but which is now fully my responsibility.

The essence of the communication, however, resonates clearly within me. It is time for me to come home to explore myself as a man in a new way.

>>   <<

My experience in the desert occurred in the summer of 1981. At the time I was thirty-one—old enough to "be a man" by most standards. Yet more than three decades of trial and error left me more confused than confirmed as a man. This was the first experience I'd had that held any promise for me attaining the elusive status known as manhood. It was my wake-up call, one of a series of such tappings of the soul.

Like all boys, I received my culture's prescription for the path to manhood: Don't be a sissy, don't admit defeat, don't depend on others, don't reveal what's really going on inside, don't trust any feeling that touches your vulnerability, and so on. Such a program not only is based entirely on someone else's truth but, as I realized later, runs against the soul's most primitive instinct, the expression of wholeness. Who could claim any real victory in attaining that?

When I was young I was consumed by two seemingly contradictory passions—my curiosity about the natural world and my love of the mysteries of religion. School guidance counselors made it clear, early on, that I must choose one path or the other. I got the idea that a man of science and a man of faith were mutually exclusive callings. I concluded that it must be so, because I hadn't met anyone who stood outside these rules. All of the priests I knew rarely journeyed beyond the walls of the church, and all of the scientists I knew treated the inner life as something one eventually grows beyond—like playing with toy trucks. Everyone I talked to seemed to be happily in agreement with this breakdown. I too agreed and was miserable.

In retrospect, I realize this was my first conscious experience of the fundamental split held sacred in our culture: heaven and earth, body and soul, heart and mind—cleaned up, set apart, and neatly laid out. I nonetheless continued to experience a spiritual radiance and mystery in nature, even in the places I was taught were furthest from such potential—in rocks, bones, dried leaves, and such.

One day, when I was about seven years old, I was rummaging through an old soil bank searching for some cast-off treasure—the secret discipline of boys of that age. I found a rock that attracted my curiosity. On the outside it was ordinary and nondescript, yet something about its unexpected lightness told me this stone possessed a secret. I broke the rock open and found a tiny cavern inside lined with glittering quartz crystals. It was as if I had stumbled on a jewel mine, hidden millions of years, waiting for me to find it. In an instant, my entire body shook with joy. I had opened a rock and discovered a living, radiating presence inside! I had opened up to an aliveness I had not felt before. I rushed to share this discovery with others. In a way, I was crying out, "Look at this miracle, look at this joy, look at me and confirm these things are true!" Yet none to whom I turned saw the divine revelation that I could see. And no one was able to reflect my joy with the intensity that my child's heart demanded.

Like the young Fisher King, who burned his fingers on the roasted salmon, I stumbled too soon on a source of spiritual fire. I had a taste of its nourishing beauty and wisdom, but I found no one with whom I could apprentice to learn how to integrate such discovery. My experience was too hot to handle, so I left it alone and eased the pain of self-betrayal by numbing myself as best I could.

It would be many years before I would be able to accept these events, painful as they were, as essential to my development as a whole man. In that stone, I caught a glimpse of the place where the spiritual and the material worlds came together. I longed to encounter that place again, and I knew that nature would show me the signs I needed to find it.

For most of my adolescent years, I felt frustrated in my efforts to explore and express this spiritual desire inside me. I was raised Roman Catholic. I remember sitting in church when I was a boy, staring at the dazzling stained-glass windows that depicted Christ's Passion, known as the stations of the cross. I felt inspired by Jesus' example of walking that road, of staying true to his calling despite the suffering that brought. And I secretly enjoyed the pageantry; the spectacle; the music; the sensual stimulation of light, color, sounds, and smells; the miracle of transformation symbolized in the Communion wine and wafer; even the mysterious and incomprehensible rhythms of Latin—in rare moments, all of these worked to evoke the spiritual realm and draw me toward it. I remember, too, fixing my eye on the priest, watching his every move as he conducted the Mass. In private moments I played with the idea of entering the priesthood myself. After all, if the goal was to get to heaven, why not choose a profession that maximized the possibility! It took just one meeting with a deadly serious theologian for my instincts to alert me to the likelihood that only half of me, and probably none of my friends, would ever be allowed through the pearly gates. Besides, my goal wasn't to become Roman Catholic, it was to explore the mysteries of life. So my quest to unite God and nature steered me away from the seminary toward a bachelor of science degree program in earth science. I thought surely I would find what I was seeking there.

From the frying pan into the fire! What I discovered was the mystery dimension, subjected to scientific method, was trivialized even further. My geology professors referred me to the "biology people" who referred me to the philosophy department, who finally hinted there were services at the school's counseling center that I might find useful. The problem was clearly identified, and I was it. These were four of the loneliest years of my life. For years following graduation, I had nightmares of being imprisoned in institutional buildings, walking down empty hallways in a maze of existential despair.

I left college and began working full-time for a wilderness survival school. The idea of renouncing the world and immersing myself in nature with groups of people for weeks on end felt like a healing balm for my weary soul. Some of our trips were thirty days long. I would return from a trip, spend a few days in base camp, then be out again for another thirty days. One year, I spent more than two hundred days in the field with various groups. We would begin the trips with packs full of modern camping gear and practice such skills as lighting fires without matches, foraging for food and medicinal plants, and building shelters from natural materials. By the end of the trip, we would have gradually relinquished such conveniences as matches, cooking utensils, knives, tents, and sleeping bags, relying instead on our skills to meet our basic needs and using only what the forest provided.

I remember one bivouac experience in particular that took place in late March in the Adirondack Mountains of northern New York State. The task I gave to the participants on this expedition was to go out on their own and build an emergency shelter, to sleep the night without a tent or sleeping bag, with nothing but the clothes on their backs. The sky was steel gray and threatening rain that day, and about three inches of crusty old snow lingered on the ground. I smugly declared these as perfect conditions to put our survival mettle to the test and eagerly joined in the adventure myself.

There I was in my shelter, sitting like a devout ascetic, settling in to practice his disciplines. I was gaunt and hungry, yet committed to endure the night without the distracting indulgences of food, fire, or human companionship. Unlike my students, I was confident I would survive the night. No, my goal was not survival, I had done that dozens of times before in conditions more demanding than these. I was stretching for something more, something I couldn't quite name. I could only feel a compulsion to seek out these extreme and austere experiences.

A steady cold rain fell that night. As I lay there, a chill fell on me that penetrated into my bones and even beyond. I felt alone, abandoned, and bitter. I had traveled for years on a path that seemed now to end in nothing but a cold emptiness. Resentment finally gave way to sadness. My tears joined with those falling from the night sky. In that joining I experienced those tears, not as mine alone, but as the tears of all of us who were trying to return to our roots, a sense of belonging here on earth. This deepening communion of myself with the larger Self of earth, sky, and humanity sparked a heartfelt insight that changed the course of

my life: Much of my work as a wilderness guide was really nothing less than a search for God. That same longing that once led
me to religion, and then to science, had resurfaced. I realized that
I saw in nature my best shot at contacting the divine source.

It seemed no matter where I turned in society, there was a prefabricated design waiting to consume me. In the natural world,
though, I felt no such threat. I didn't have to agree with the
experts, star in Little League, confess past sins, or worry about
future damnation—in nature I was simply invited to celebrate my
life, here and now. And yet, the path I had chosen had no celebration at all. I chose the survival route, and this was the deal: I
would seek physical hardship and devote myself to self-denial,
and then God would take pity on me and save me. Didn't work.

There I was in my survival shelter, demonstrating once again
my commitment—but once again God hadn't shown up. I finally
had to admit that, no matter how well I idealized this desolation,
it had not led me to the sublime union I was seeking. I had
become as deadly serious as the theologians and scientists I formerly judged. I then realized my hidden agenda: I wasn't really
looking for God, I was searching for perfection. And no matter
where I turned, perfection was not there.

My next act was one of the most liberating in my life. I reached
into my pack for food and ate until I was satisfied. I then began
picking twigs from my shelter to start a small fire. By sunrise the
skies had cleared, my belly was full, and my shelter lay before me
reduced to a pile of ash. A body and soul that had begun the
evening at odds had discovered a newfound tenderness with
each other. God never felt so close.

It wasn't long before a friend introduced me to some of the
teachings found in Native American cultures. Through reading,
and study with a small group of American Indian teachers, I
learned all I could about such practices as the Sweat Lodge,
Medicine Wheel, and the Vision Quest. I later went on to study
rites of passage and questing traditions from around the world,
paying close attention to traditions that emphasized our vital
spiritual ties to the earth. My quest to unify priest and naturalist
was being confirmed through this apprenticeship and study.

>>   <<

Like many of the men of my generation, I had struggled to absorb the messages of the women's movement. The conventional John Wayne image of manhood that prevailed in the 1950s had crumbled during the social tremors of the 1960s. As women launched their struggle to reclaim their share of human rights, they began to voice strong social and philosophical viewpoints on gender issues. Women were speaking with passionate conviction, the older men of my generation weren't saying much. I sided with the women.

In my relationships with women I found positive reinforcement when I was yielding, when I was able to avoid confrontation. I learned to choose sadness over anger, water over fire, receptivity over assertion. I concluded that my personal salvation, indeed the salvation of the entire planet, lay in denying masculine qualities and cultivating feminine ones. And so I took up the finely honed chisel of self-betrayal to chip away at what I judged to be the crude aspects of my being. And to guard against a relapse, I successfully severed most of the threads of connection with my male community as well.

But in the canyon that night in Utah I was confronted with a new perspective. I was given notice that it was now time for me to take the next step. I could no longer be the "good boy," trying so desperately to squeeze into someone else's definition of manhood. I needed to stand as a man and relate to the Earth, to women, to other men with the fullness of my being. A conscious goddess energy moved toward me, saying, *"Well now, where's the God in you? Find that, embrace it, and then we'll talk further."*

I returned from the canyon lands with more questions than answers. What is a *man's heart?* If we men haven't been offering our hearts to the world, then what have we been offering? How does a man walk a path with heart?

Though it seems obvious to me now, at the time I was a man blind to the most natural source of support for my Quest. It eventually dawned on me that what I needed was a larger context, like an ongoing group. But not just any group—a group of men.

And I thought, God help me!

At that time I had little regard for men as companions, except perhaps in the realms of sport and idea polishing. Sure, I loved a vigorous game of pickup basketball with men who could challenge my abilities. And I enjoyed joining them in heroic projects to "save the planet." But to be with men and talk about what's deep in our hearts? Frankly, that was about the most boring thing I could imagine. Women seemed to be the ones who could draw the best out of me. Like many men in that era, I had tried to open my heart, so to speak, by cutting off my balls—or at least pretending they weren't there. Yet, as I continued to test the waters of male community, I began to realize how nearsighted our vision had become. Many of us were looking to the Great Mother for salvation, but nobody I knew was seeking right relationship with the Great Father. We all seemed to be reacting against the "Terrible Father," the one who sires reason cut off from love, truth hardened into static form, law void of compassion. But there was no mention of any *positive* masculine alternative. What a revelation to sense for the first time that masculinity might not be intrinsically evil! And it was within this possibility of the masculine and feminine living as coequals that I found the courage to let go of fixing my heart in favor of finding it. I stood at the gateway to a world of manhood that appeared like a vast wilderness. I wondered if there were any other men who were glimpsing similar territory.

I decided to find out. I had been guiding wilderness Vision Quests, with groups of men and women, for several years. The quests were based on the pan-cultural spiritual practice of spending time alone in nature and seeking renewed vision and power to live wholeheartedly one's destiny. The autumn following my experience in the canyon, I began to plan for the following year's Vision Quests. As I did, the echo of the voice in the canyon returned to spawn the idea of offering a Vision Quest for men alone. And so, in late autumn 1981, I mailed a letter and descriptive brochure to more than five hundred men, whose names I had accumulated over the years from my experiences as a college instructor, quest guide, and workshop leader. The response, to put it mildly, was underwhelming: a total of two replies. One was from a friend named David who enthusiastically accepted the invitation. The other was from a man who, without a word of explanation, demanded that I remove his name from my mailing list immediately. Yes and no—my own ambivalence, perfectly mirrored. I wrestled with the question of whether I should abandon the enterprise. But in the end, the questions that arose in the canyonlands proved stronger than my concerns of failure.

In the summer of 1982, David and I hiked to a spot along an isolated river valley in the Adirondacks. For five days we simply headed off in whatever direction our spirits took us. We camped, tested our endurance with long hikes, held council, howled at the night sky, and created spontaneous rituals that evoked both wildly playful and tender expressions of our hearts. Our agenda was simply to meet each other as friends—as men—and to seed the possibility of future men's quests.

On our last afternoon together, we built a sweat lodge: a dome-shaped structure, covered with tarps, that was just big enough to sit in. A fire outside the lodge heated a number of rocks for several hours. When night fell we placed the rocks in a pit at the center of the lodge and entered. Pouring water over the red-hot rocks, we were enveloped in waves of moist heat. Our purpose was to sit in communion with the Earth and follow our hearts' lead. We sang and prayed to become open to the guidance of the Old Ones, those who had come before us and had kept the spirit of the Quest alive through the generations. I prayed for the courage to stay true to this new vision that was pulsing in my heart. Within the darkness of the sweat lodge I could feel how my manhood longed to be an expression of selfhood and how my selfhood longed to be an expression of the sacrament of Earth.

When our ceremony was complete, we opened the door flap to our cocoonlike lodge. Steam billowed from our bodies as we crawled out into the night to plunge ourselves into the cold waters of the mountain stream. Overhead, the sky sparkled with stars. Yet off to the north the sky was ablaze with shimmering, iridescent color. I rubbed my eyes, fearing they had been affected by the scalding steam inside the lodge. But the waves of color remained. Suddenly I realized—the northern lights! The primal beauty and mystery of this event were the first gifts given in response to my prayer. I felt my heart touched once again with the blessing to continue with this Quest into the wilderness of men's hearts. Beauty and mystery would be our guides.

PART ONE

〰〰〰〰〰〰〰〰〰〰〰〰〰〰〰〰〰〰〰〰

THE HOLY LONGING

It is good knowing that glasses
are to drink from;
the bad thing is not to know
what thirst is for.

—ANTONIO MACHADO
TRANSLATION BY ROBERT BLY

1

THE CALL TO QUEST

This thing we tell of can never be found by seeking, but only seekers find it.

—ABU YAZID AL-BISTAMI

In order to arrive at what you do not know you must go by a way which is the way of ignorance.

—T. S. ELIOT

The first day of the Men's Quest finds us gathering at a roadside camp for what is known as a "Hudson's Bay start." During the fur-trading days in the late eighteenth century, expeditions launched by the Hudson's Bay Company would set up their first camp a short distance from headquarters. That way the traders could get set bearings for the trek to come. They shook down their gear and made sure everything was on hand and working. There was time to sort out what was essential for the journey and what should be left behind. In the same way, we spend our first night near the road. Some of the men here are experienced campers who could trek the Himalayas in style and comfort. But many have been raised to think of "outdoors" as that untamed interval between the front door and the car door. Today we will sort through equipment, expectations, and fears. Tomorrow we will move to our base camp deeper in the wilderness.

The journey we each make to our meeting site is rarely easy.

There is a significant amount of outer preparation required before we can leave our day-to-day life behind. We must select appropriate gear, clothing, and food; get in shape physically; and attend to last minute personal and business demands that inevitably pop up before a journey such as this. Yet these challenges are just the beginning.

Our inner world is likewise stirred by our yearning to follow the call to adventure. The conscious intention to quest charges the psyche with the promise of change. And there is not a man among us who will fail to find a voice within that welcomes change *and* a voice equally determined to resist change. Sometimes these voices are reflected in conflicted dreams and memories. Sometimes our inner ambivalence is mirrored in the concerns of friends: You're going to the wilderness to do what? What's gotten into you? Quite often the solitary pilgrimage to our meeting site is enough to unmask superficial consent.

One man's journal recorded it this way:

> The car is packed, bills paid, good-byes said—my preparations are finally complete. I make my way north to the mountains, alone in the car, yet with the crowded company of my thoughts. A "Vision Quest" . . . all the voices chime in: Who will I be questing with? Will I be up to par? What if they're all jerks? Aren't there better ways to spend this time? What if I don't get a vision? *What if I do?* All those voices compete with one other voice, one that says: God, do I need this now!

This man discovered something else along the way:

> Preparing for this quest has awakened all the selves I ever created and discarded. In greeting those selves now, I see them as everything from charming rogues to tortured souls. That's what they had to be, so as to guide and protect me through all the different journeys my life has taken.
>
> Yesterday, in a suit and tie, I chaired a business meeting. Now, on the drive to the Quest I wear jeans and a T-shirt. Around my neck are the mummy beads I wore almost eighteen years ago, during the

most turbulent and dangerous years I have had on this earth. At the highway rest stop, I look at myself in the men's room mirror. I recognize the person on whose neck those beads hang. We are old friends and I am surprised to see him again.

Another man straggled in late after driving halfway across the country. His road was a long one, and not just in miles. Five months earlier he had been fired from his job. The week before the Quest, he and his wife had finally confronted the deep rift in their marriage. She got sick on the day he left and could barely speak when he called from the road. He himself got walloped by a bout of diarrhea that forced him to pull over every fifty miles. As he later recalled:

There were moments when I felt it was useless to continue on. I'm going to be late and I'll screw it up for others if this gets worse. Then I remembered the warning from the Men's Quest preparation guide that we may find our lives falling apart the day before the Quest and allow fear to interpret that as a sign from the universe that we should stay home. Too much of my life has been spent afraid of leaving home. So I determined to press on come hell, high water, or a shit flood. Thus I arrived, late, somewhat worse for wear, but I was there!

The men park by the road, unload their gear, and hike the short quarter mile to our first camp. It takes a while, however, for most to "arrive" fully. Bodies are all present and accounted for, but the presence in the eyes flickers in and out. One man expressed it this way:

Gather at the road
No Guarantees
Keep-away-from-me-asshole-till-I-find-you-out handshake
Enough water purifying tablets to last three years
Enough to put out the "Water Fear Fire"
Only 9,999 places for fear to hide
Looks like a busy night.

You discover a lot about a man's story by watching him go about the business of finding and establishing his tent site in the forest. About how much trust he has that there will be ground enough for him. Whether he has been allowed to fail or whether success was demanded of him the first time. What the nature of his personal boundaries are. Whether he favors isolation or enmeshment. How comfortable and skilled he is in creating a home for himself in the world. His entire existential state is revealed within the first hour of being in camp.

A man who chooses a site closest to the center of camp appears to be in a daze, waiting for direction that doesn't come. His every hesitant act is attended by a furtive glance over his shoulder. He has not felt many hands of confirmation on his shoulders, he will tell us later.

His neighbor has been scurrying about like a hypercaffeinated squirrel since he arrived. His camp is up and in order in just a few minutes. He paces around his finished work hoping to find a loose thread, a rope that needs tightening—anything to keep himself occupied. His identity has been built around constant activity. He later admits that he has been busily preparing for this Quest for weeks. He half-expected to be greeted with blaring trumpets and bouquets and to be handed the key to the forest along with a detailed schedule of activities. The relaxed atmosphere of these woods, he says, is already driving him crazy.

Then there's the one at the far end of the campground, moving slowly in his own world, which is impeccably neat and serene— that is, until another man starts setting up his tent just a few yards away. If looks could kill, this one would earn multiple life sentences.

Some of the men's packs are prepared so skillfully they look like photographs from the L.L. Bean catalog. Others are shapeless blobs that ride their heavy-breathing carriers' backs like obese equestrians. These packs, crammed with tents, sleeping bags, clothes, food, journals, and drums, weigh sixty pounds or more. What can't be weighed, however, is the expectation, anticipation, and fear they also carry.

A man from New York City comes with two giant suitcases

packed beyond limit. When opened they explode to reveal a jumbled confusion of mittens, gloves, sweaters, hats, jackets—and more sweaters. He has had no experience in the wilderness and wears his fear and innocence openly on his face. An accomplished teacher and leader at home, he is here now risking intimacy with a small group of men away from everything he knows of the city and its ways. His hands moving like scared birds, he erects the largest "one-man" tent I have ever seen: a baby blue nylon Taj Mahal with a cupola-like dome on top. Here is a tent as unaccustomed to this forested wilderness setting as its owner. But the man is game. He is here and his feelings are displayed for all to see. He has packed his ignorance and his longing. And, truly, one could not hope for a better start for a journey such as this.

At the other end of the spectrum is the man who arrives totally equipped. He carries a magnificent knife handed down from his grandfather. He has camped, trekked, bicycled, climbed, and otherwise negotiated a demanding variety of wilderness environments and is at home in them all. His body, hardened from years of pushing himself to extremes, has scars that bear witness to close encounters with physical challenge. But the texture of feeling is missing from his face. His eyes show that he prefers the erotically charged intimacy of being face to face with a sheer rock wall hundreds of feet above ground to facing the aching abyss that lies between himself and another human being. He has come here to open some door of connection that until now has been closed to him. He has mastered the elements with the concentration and zeal of a mountain climber but is now being called by life to descend into a cavern of feeling that does not succumb to strong will alone. He must find another way to negotiate this terrain. A bone-chilling loneliness has finally brought him to his knees, and to this Quest.

The flurry of activity quickens and the camp springs to life. Group tarps are erected, the camp kitchen established, sitting logs are placed in a ring around the fire pit, and the men put finishing touches on their tent sites.

I scan the faces assembled here. These are eyes of men ready to set sail on an unknown ocean, eyes that hold both fear and unbearable excitement, eyes of men ready for pilgrimage. All of our sophisticated modern camping gear stands in stark contrast to the overwhelming sense that we are answering the call of some very ancient native human practice.

I scramble atop a nearby knoll to take in the camp as a whole. The Quest reveals yet another face. The atmosphere feels charged with the anticipation of a great hunt—men allied in pursuit of food for themselves and their people. Though each hunter gathered here somehow senses that his quarry is none other than himself.

>>   <<

What would compel these men to join a quest? Why would anyone leave the comforts of home to spend a week and a half with a group of strangers in the wilderness, drumming, chanting, fasting, praying for vision? What are these men responding to that would bring them to an experience like this?

If we set reason to the task of following this trail, we'll discover the secondary tracks and conditions of these men's lives—reflections of the real thing. We would learn, for example, that the majority of these men are white, middle-class, American males ranging from age sixteen to sixty-nine, with a predominant cluster between ages thirty-five and forty-five. Their tracks reveal many to be seekers without a particular religious affiliation, though there are a good number of followers of Judaism and Christianity on this trail as well. About half of the men are currently married, and many of these are fathers. They are self-identified straight men, and gay men. They are carpenters, clergymen, computer programmers, and unemployed. They are lawyers and artists, businessmen and teachers, students and nurses, medical doctors and psychotherapists.

These tracks can be fascinating to follow. But if we never lift our eyes from the trail, we'll never find what we're looking for. Over the years I've had the privilege of looking deeply into the eyes of hundreds of men who have found their way into this camp. What I've experienced in these eyes is more of the nature of poetry than of scientific fact. Yet those feeling-toned images convey more information than any of the facts of their lives I have been privy to. What these eyes reveal is a great hunger—a hunger that cannot be eased by bread alone. No matter the size, shape, or history of the man, there is always this great hunger. It calls our attention in different ways, yet it is the one thing that all of the men in this camp share in common.

For some, the hunger is felt as a vague restlessness, a longing for renewed passion, purpose, or meaning in their lives. Some are called by the unsettling discovery that no amount of worldly success truly comforts the gnawing emptiness they feel inside. Others experience the call through provocations from people and events in their lives—the desire to become a parent, the invitation to write a book, the dream of world peace, the possibility of marriage, or other such invitations to manifest more of their self-potential. And for many, the call comes through a demanding crisis that wounds deeply—a friend dies, a lover leaves, we lose our job, our health, or our youth. Those gathered here have been called to quest through circumstances that range from gentle tappings to violent rendings. Men often wake up in such circumstances painfully aware of how isolated they are from their heart's wisdom, from other men, and from the living earth. Bringing the pain of this isolation out of hiding is a courageous life-affirming step.

Such times of transition present us with the opportunity for growth. If we stay present to the sunset dissolution of the old certainties, victories, and identities, we may eventually notice the first rays of a larger identity and destiny breaking the horizon. These leading rays of the new story are what we call vision.

But between sunset and sunrise lies the dark wilderness of night. This wilderness will not be conquered, nor will it be saved. It requires a more courageous response: This wilderness asks that we *experience* it *as it is*. It asks us to open our hearts to the sorrow we find there, to the joy, to the emptiness, to the primal energy and movement, to the dreams, visions, and imperfection—open to all that is there. The world needs a man's heart. It needs a heart that is not afraid of its capacity to suffer pain or bliss; a heart that knows its tenderness not as weakness, but as generative grace. The men who have gathered here have made the choice to follow their wounds and spiritual longing into that wilderness. And, risking their former allegiance to isolation, they choose to do so in the company of other men, in communion with the Earth.

Traditional societies enact rites of passage to recognize and honor our many passages into extended identity: from conception to birth, from adolescence to adulthood, from adulthood to elderhood, from elderhood into death, and from the ashes of death into rebirth. These rites also attend the transforming moments of marriage, separation, prophetic vision, or other significant changes in one's relationship to life and community. They exist to ensure that times of great change are celebrated as times of great opportunity. This Men's Quest is a contemporary expression of the pan-cultural need to encourage the process of transformation by celebrating it.

Those who have studied this process closely commonly recognize a threefold rhythm in these rites. At the beginning of our passage, we are involved in the first phase of separation. Here we stand in place acknowledging as honestly as we can the joys and sorrows of where we are here and now. And we work to touch and embody the deepest resonance of our soul's longing; for the soul's longing for wholeness is the most fundamental urge in our lives. All else follows. And so, at the beginning, we engage in a series of ritual enactments designed to strip away the misconceptions and resistance we might have to following this holy longing. These rituals also prepare us for leaving our known world behind; for once free, our longing invariably heads for the hills. It has an insatiable hunger for the wild unknown.

Separation is not really about traveling to a new location. That alone changes nothing except the scenery, for we carry the world inside us. To leave the known world is more a leap of faith into an immediate abyss than a well-planned trek to some distant land. Leaving home to enter the wilderness is primarily a symbolic act that fosters a deeper leave taking. We're asked to let go of any ideas whatsoever of who we think we are, what we can and can-

THE CALL TO QUEST

not do, what is possible, what is right or wrong with the world. This, then, is the primary focus of our initial days together.

In a few days we will begin the second phase of initiation by entering the threshold world of solitude. For three days and nights, each man will stand alone before the mirror of nature, surrounded by beings that make no demands on him except that he be true to himself. It is in this threshold world that initiation into the next order of living is possible.

Following that, we will move to the third phase of reincorporation. In that phase, we work to reform our being around the virtues and direction that we will have contacted during our visit to the threshold world. We prepare, too, for the road home to our daily lives.

Separation, initiation, reincorporation—the three phases that help us negotiate the cyclical path from the known world to the threshold world and back again to the new world. Viewed three-dimensionally, this path is really a spiral that has height and depth, for we never do return to the same home once we've truly left it.

For centuries these rites have given guidance and meaning to the transitions of human life. Much of contemporary society, however, tends to focus on instant results rather than on the gradual stages of transformation and growth. As a consequence, there is little continuity of relationship between the individual, the culture, and the planet. And so, when a man undergoes the changes that are a natural part of his life progression, he often does so alone. No confirming hand is laid on his shoulder to support him and guide him into the next phase. Over time he becomes more and more cut off from deep and essential parts of himself and from the continuum of relationship with the Earth. His becomes a life of "quiet desperation," as Thoreau aptly described it—quiet, because society accepts the hollow shell he presents to the world; desperate, because his heart struggles alone. There is a shadowy part of culture that wants to keep him there. Quiet and desperate, he will not rock the boat.

Living in such a disempowering context we might be inclined to greet the call for change as cause for tribulation rather than celebration. We will be tempted to treat the pain by finding its cause and fixing it as soon as possible. For a plumbing problem, the "find-and-fix" approach is useful. But for a heart in crisis, such a technique simply confirms the fear that keeps us imprisoned in the old life. And the desperation deepens.

No wonder, then, that when we hear the call to the Quest, we often ignore it, ridicule it, anesthetize it, or treat it with a fragile fantasy of a perfect life after death. Many are called but few choose to follow the calling.

Not surprisingly, then, the quest myth is commonly associated with the figure of the hero. By *hero* we don't mean a culturally appointed individual or someone with supernatural talent. The hero is that natural part of all of us who refuses to be satisfied with prefabricated answers to life's questions. And he lives inside each one of us waiting to be given permission to act. The hero's precept was best summed up by the poet Kabir: "If you have not lived through something, it is not true." The hero is sure of his questions, but not so sure of his answers. The questions he asks are much too precious to bury under a pile of foregone conclusions and superficial answers. For whom and for what do I live? Where do I find meaning, purpose, and passion in my life? What is my relationship to myself, my people, my world, my God? In short: *Who am I?*

The challenge of the hero, and of each of the men assembled here, is to go beyond merely *asking* such questions to *living the questions.* Rainer Maria Rilke was quite adamant about this in his mentoring of a young man: "Have patience with all that is unresolved in your heart and try to love the questions themselves. . . . Live the questions now. Perhaps then, someday far in the future, you will gradually . . . live your way into the answer."

"The point," he said, "is to live everything."

Our Quest, then, is informed by the questions we are willing to embody and is propelled by our courage to live into the unknown.

Seen from the broadest perspective, all stories of quests and questing contain many interconnected themes. Joseph Campbell identified the common thread that ties all these legends together. That thread, which he called the monomyth, runs as follows:

> A hero ventures forth from the world of common day into
> a world of supernatural wonder: fabulous forces are there
> encountered and a decisive victory is won: the hero comes
> back from this mysterious adventure with the power to
> bestow boons on his fellow man.

In these few lines, Campbell conveyed the essential story of the hero's quest. This story suggests that in our longing to know ourselves and our relationship to God and to the world, we must embark on a journey. We must take leave of the familiar shores of our known world, with its local customs and beliefs. We must then enter a world of mystery and uncertainty—a world that we perceive as dangerous—and test ourselves against the onslaught of powers that threaten to destroy us. We may be called in spirit to join the Grail knights, whose passion for wholeness led them directly to the pathless forest. We may be invited, like Odysseus or Jonah or Jesus, to journey into the underworld—to die in order to be reborn. Or we may find ourselves like Jason trying to navigate between the treacherous clashing rocks, looking for true passage through the challenging currents of duality. We must understand, though, that the clashing rocks, underworlds, and pathless forests we meet "out there" are, in truth, a reflection of unexplored territories of conflict, darkness, and mystery within our own minds and hearts.

Facing such challenges, we quickly learn the limitations of the secular hero who attempts to conquer by force of will alone. For the challenges encountered here can only be met as the hero surrenders in communion with a larger spiritual identity. *On a journey of this sort, every decisive victory is born out of an equally decisive defeat.* And paradox is more often the rule than the exception. Every gift of empowerment on our Quest comes through the full acceptance of our weakness. Every illuminating vision is born out of a "dark night of the soul." And every endowment of love is regenerated by our dying to the raging abyss of hate. Passing through these cold nights and refining fires encourages the hero to draw on resources he may not know he possesses but that have been lying hidden within from the very beginning. He may be gifted with renewed vision, vitality, equanimity, or remembrance—consolation prizes given to those who first give themselves to life as it is.

Transfigured by these courageous acts, the heart then naturally guides the hero back to the world he left behind. We return to share the fruits of our labors for the good of all our people. "A vital person," Campbell observed, "vitalizes the world." On this journey, whatever you do for yourself, you do for all of us.

All spiritual traditions recognize the urge that flows beneath the everyday doings of our lives—the urge for a pilgrimage that will pierce the veil of illusion of our separateness; a pilgrimage that unites the disassociated, disowned, and rejected parts of ourselves and our world; a pilgrimage that will carry us Home by way of a path with heart. Perhaps this is the calling that the men in this camp all home in on.

Or perhaps we are responding to nothing less than evolution itself: the impulse that courses through the green-blooded veins of sun-seeking plants, the calling that draws clay up from the Earth to walk with two legs, the spirit that changes seawater into blood.

Whatever its circumstances, whatever its source, the call to the soul's high adventure has lured us from our separate lives and brings us together in a vessel of brotherhood dedicated to transformation—and invites us now into its simmering midst.

2

THE COMMUNITY OF SEEKERS

You see, I am alive.
You see, I stand in good relation to the earth.
You see, I stand in good relation to the gods.
You see, I stand in good relation to all that is beautiful.
You see, I stand in good relation to you.
You see, I am alive, I am alive.

— N. SCOTT MOMADAY

Near the end of his life, a wise and noble teacher was approached by his disciples. The prospect of their teacher's impending death had caused them to be afraid. Seeking the distilled essence of his wisdom they asked, "Dear Father, what are the most important things we should remember after your passing?"

And the teacher said,

You may take refuge in these three truths:

Remember that the state of enlightenment and freedom which you so readily recognize in me belongs to each one of you. Look inside yourself to find yourself.

Remember there are many paths, but the only one that matters is the path with heart. Stay true to its lead, and walk its full length.

And remember to be in good relation to those who walk with you; to the community of seekers devoted to truth.

Hearing this, the disciples felt their fear lessen, but it didn't take long for concern to creep back in. One man then asked, "Dear Teacher, of these three things, which is the *most* important?"

And the teacher said, "That I cannot say, but do consider this: The true path is not an easy one. It demands great effort. And though you each must find your own way, your journeys will be graced and eased by the communion of spiritual fellowship. Stay true, stay in your heart, and stay together."

A fundamental creative tension exists in the Quest: the dance between solitude and community. In many ways the search for vision must be a solitary pursuit. When the seeker or the hero undertakes his journey, he must leave behind the world he knows and strike out on his own. He alone must face the challenges he meets along the way. In seeking vision, no understudies are allowed.

The image of the hero's journey commonly calls up scenes that spotlight a solitary figure battling against all odds to win a prize of some sort. This image fits our culture's fascination with the rugged individual. Yet the solitary individual and his renunciation of the world is only half of the story. Equally important is the community of relationship within which this questing is taking place. If we applaud only the hero's departure, and fail to celebrate his return, our lives are thrown out of balance. Balance returns only when we are willing to live this paradox: Our journey is a solitary one that must be undertaken in good relation to all life.

In fact, this communion with all life—inner and outer—is precisely what a sacred manhood is all about. It's hard to go beyond cliché when discussing this communion, because we so readily acknowledge it intellectually. But so few of us today actually *experience* the mystery of this communion as a daily reality. The recovery of sacred manhood begins with noticing that we've turned our backs on selected parts of ourselves, others, and the Earth. And the recovery proceeds as we are willing to forgive ourselves for doing so. Perhaps we've turned away from anger, or from sadness, or from the need for beauty, or from spiritual longing, or from wildness. These are not just human desires and behaviors, *these are acts of nature.* If we close our hearts to those parts of creation that are painful to be in relationship with, we become more and more isolated from ourselves and from the source of life itself. We will have to live our way back into that way of being wherein we feel our own bloodstream diminished in the poisoning of a river or our own longing aroused in the falling of a star. William Barrett stated it simply: "We shall have to find ourselves within nature before God is able to find us."

From a truly ecological perspective, the individual exists *only* as the local expression of a greater whole. The pine tree is that being through which the forest realizes and expresses its pine-tree-ness. The forest is an opportunity for the earth to express a unique aspect of its life diversity. The earth is a particular expression of the life of our solar system. This perspective eventually leads us through galaxies, the realms of gods and goddesses, and ultimately to some Great Mystery. This Mystery is known to some as God, to others as Divine Universal Intelligence. By whatever name, the pine tree is an expression of that mystery—as is every "individual" human being.

Valuing isolation and solitude at the expense of community not only distorts the truth of the hero's journey, it is also dangerous. Isolation may not kill us outright, but it will dry up the wellspring of the soul. The fire of our solitary spirit is no longer tempered by the waters of community. Exposed to such heat, our inner landscape becomes dry and brittle. In isolation, we tend to become very serious and lose the buoyancy of humor we need on our Quest. Eventually, we will burn out, consumed by a quest that is out of relationship with the whole.

Relationship is the fabric that gives both meaning and identity to the individual. Relationship calls on us to be responsive to life, to touch and be touched by our world. When we are out of touch with community, even the spiritual search becomes a solitary, mechanical attempt to "get the job done." This is the "pop-the-hood-and-fix-it" approach to enlightenment. The fundamental objective is to arrive at some ideal of perfection as soon as possible with as little feeling as possible. And all of the wild and native voices of the heart that will not conform to that directive must be silenced.

Yet a greater part of us knows that the vitality and integrity of any community—be it an ecosystem, a corporate board, a spiritual fellowship, or the domain of the heart—lies not in the conformity of its voices but in its diversity. Diversity provides a collective ability to respond to changing conditions. And the only way we may receive the gift of diversity, and contribute to it, is through relationship. The poet Rumi didn't beat around the bush:

> You know, the jackass doesn't have much sensibility,
> But even he gains spirit from the company of his own kind.
> But when the jackass crosses the desert alone,
> How many more blows it takes to get him there.
> Now, this is what this poem says to you:
> If you're not a jackass, don't cross the desert alone!

And so, not wanting to be more of a jackass than I already am, I sound the drum that calls us together for our first formal meeting since arriving in camp. Now we stand face to face with all of the men with whom we'll be spending the next—and, who knows, perhaps the last—ten days of our lives.

We are like animals venturing into strange territory; all our senses are tingling at full alert. The air is alive with anticipation, with a primal tension you can almost smell. We size each other up: Who are these guys? What are they capable of? Is it safe to be me here? These questions are more active than normal because each man present has agreed to leave behind many of the details of his personal history. We refrain from revealing last names, ages, occupations, addresses, sexual identifications, political affiliations, taxable income, number of gold credit cards—any "zip code data" that might stereotype us in a static way. Our intent is to look beyond the measured history, to the evolving mystery of each man present, including ourselves.

Much of our work during this early phase of separation is in identifying the ways we overlay direct experience with concepts

that pretend to be the life they stand for. Our personal names are a prime example. Our names are probably the one word we hear and pay attention to more than any other word in our lives. That word becomes a symbol for our identity, an identity anchored in what Rilke called "the sum of all misunderstandings that collects itself about a name." Static names certainly have their uses, yet we mustn't fool ourselves into thinking we truly know someone or something just because we have a name for it.

And so we play with our names to encourage us to look behind the label and see who's really there. We often use a simple ritual in which we share our lineage: "I am Paul; grandson of Henry and Sarah, and John and Maude; son of Paul and Susan." In this way we honor those who gave us a start within the circle of human society. We might then embrace a larger circle of relation: "I am Paul, great-grandson of Sun and Earth; great-great-grandson of some Great Mystery."

The next step in the ritual is to cast our names to the winds and stir them up a bit. We do this by sounding our names as a chant. Each man draws a deep breath and lets his name out, stretching the contours of the vowels and feeling how the consonants provide containment and rhythm. The sustained resonance and altered cadence of the sound helps free the name from its usual moorings. The group then reflects the song back to the man who offered it, and he gets a chance to hear his name with some mystery breathed into it. Perhaps now, or at some later time on the journey, he will be ready to ask for a name that more faithfully reflects the nature of his soul. Many do, and in my thirteen years of leading quests, no two men have received the same name from this wilderness.

And so, for now, you are . . . , and I am . . . , and it will be that way until something else comes; not from memory, not from the corpse of yesterday, but from something true within the heart of this moment that wants to live and be seen.

The watches are the next to go. As is true of our given names, the overlay of clock time on the timeless rhythms of the uncivilized world can serve a useful purpose. Yet that limited purpose too often claims full dominion over our lives. But we are here to remember that the map is not the territory, that *Paul* is not who I really am, that *three o'clock* means nothing to the ocean and its inhabitants or to the Earth traveling through space.

On the Quest, then, we ritually divest ourselves of the power of this overlay by surrendering our timepiece bracelets for the duration of our journey. We will now mark time by rhythms that can be felt: by the rising and setting sun, by the rising and falling breath, by the beating heart, by the rhythm of hunger and fulfillment. The rising inbreath becomes a time of rebirth; the falling outbreath, a time of dying. Outside the concept of clock time we are born and die many times each day. For some of us, this act of separation from the clock is truly more threatening than any other during this phase of the Quest. It's like asking a man to shift from the programmed steps of a march to an improvised dance with an unpredictable partner—life.

Given these restrictions, the conversation during these early moments together is guarded. We are challenged to discover each other without falling back on the cocktail-conversation strategies that have served us in the past.

Some of the men are noticeably eager, even impatient to get going. Others hide behind fearful eyes that betray the pain they've experienced before in such meetings. Standing before us is all of our history of relating to men—our fathers and other elder males; our brothers, friends, and sons. With this in the way, it is difficult to be present to what is actually happening here and now. One man confides to his journal:

> I enter this group with a friendly smile that barely conceals the churning in the pit of my stomach. I've been wounded enough times by a blow or a cutting remark from other men to know that each one of these guys carries a sword. And until I know what their intentions are with that sword, and how skillful they are at using it, it's going to be hard for me to relax here.

This business of community is not easy for a lot of men. An ancient current of competition charges men's nerves and must be dealt with whenever we gather in groups. Community brings us face to face with all of the images, misconceptions, fears, and wounds that come from our experiences with competition and conflict. Community demands that we face these different parts of ourselves. There's the part, for example, who feels that he will be secure only if he emerges from competition as the total victor. He enters the fray bearing a banner that reads, "There can be only one—and I'm the one." Another member of our inner tribe may feel more comfortable submitting to such authority; his banner reads, "Yes, there can be only one truth—and let it be *his*." Still another part deals with competition by feigning indifference: "Only one, two—who's counting? Please, I'm beyond all that."

The Quest values competition; in fact, it relies on this powerful interaction. The Latin root of the word *competition* means "to seek together or with others." This root honors the co-creative power of true competition. It's not competition that we need be concerned about. The real question is, "Whom, or what purpose, does our competition serve?" When we compete out of service to fear, we inevitably split ourselves and the world into warring factions, and nothing changes. When we compete in service of wholeness, we engage in dynamic conflict that enhances each member and the community at large.

So, our first communal act on the Quest is to dance with these polarities of individuality and community—literally dance them, in an opening ritual movement known as the Welcome Dance. Tradition has it that this dance was used as a form of worship in the Greek mystery schools and later as a means of greeting among twelfth-century Knights Templars. Upon returning from their solitary exploits, the knights would seek communion not through talk—though there were certainly many spirited tales to be told—but through dance. With their arms clasped in a circle and their bodies moving in unison on the Earth, they established the common ground necessary for receiving the diversity of each other. The competition and conflicts that followed could then be held within the life-affirming metaphor of the dance.

The dance form is simple: Together we take a step toward the center, the feet come together, and the knees bend twice as we bounce slightly in place. Then a step back out, feet together, and again bounce twice. Then a short step to the left, feet together, bounce, bounce. The circle slowly turns sunwise around the center as the pattern repeats over and over.

The movements reflect our dance with duality: stepping in and stepping out, breathing in and breathing out, celebrating unity and celebrating diversity, contracting and expanding; pain and pleasure, light and darkness, me and you—all life moves between these poles. And the Old Ones say that when we are willing to accept both poles, when we stop taking one side of life against the other, then a third movement enters our lives. Our lives begin to turn in beauty and integrity. We leave the quest for instant perfection behind and we slowly begin to grow in wholeness.

And so we dance: stepping in . . . stepping out . . . to the left. . . . The porous forest soil yields to the collective intention of our feet. To help us stay together, we sing a sacred chant I learned years ago from an old shaman. He said, "This chant has power— remember it and you will never again question where you stand in life or what time you stand in; you will never be lost again."

And so we sing its steady cadence:

> Here and Now,
> Here and Now,
> Here and Now. . . .

Eventually, each man carries the chant in his own way, all contributing to the rich, deep chord of our collective song that rises from the forest floor and echoes over the treetops. I lift my eyes to meet the faces across the circle. A few easy smiles begin to surface, reflecting the delight of a body carried by the rhythm of life. On other faces the brow is knit in deep concentration. Those who cannot give themselves over to the rhythm struggle, their steps calculated and unsure. These men dance now with conflict: The powerful pull to surrender to the dance is countered by rigid muscles that protect some deep cellular shame.

The chorus of voice and movement rises and falls as the dance turns through delight, through fear, through resistance, through surrender. *It's all Here, right Now . . . right Here, right Now.* . . . The dance whirls like a great storm with a life of its own, pushing against the "normal" time limit for such things, and then stretching on until it's clear that the only place to relax is in the eye of this growing tempest. . . *right Here, right Now.* . . .

More men have now announced their presence. Eyes meet across the circle. I look past the surface features, the mask that we all present to strangers. I welcome the sadness that hides behind one man's fiercely guarded features, the rage that burns behind another's resigned look, the longing that begins to bleed through pride, the courage that lies behind fear, the desire masked by hesitancy. . . . *It's all Here, right Now.* . . . I can feel the eyes of the man directly across from me tracking the contours of my inner world; eyes intent on welcoming whatever they uncover. It's startling to be met with such presence—like the dangerous excitement one feels meeting a wild animal eye to eye.

Slowly, the dance winds down, steps shorten, voices trail off. Only the faint pounding of feet on this dance-tempered earth remains. The heart drum inside the chest beats a strong cadence. And as if our dance had awakened some presence in the ground, an invisible hand of desire from below reaches up and draws us to our knees. I pat the ground hard with my palms, a gesture of reverence for the Old God I imagine sleeping there. "Father Earth," I whisper, and slap the ground again. A resonant thud issues forth. And within seconds, twenty-eight hands begin striking the ground, drawing forth its visceral, hollow tones. Our rhythm finds a strong, steady groove—and an old joy returns. Soulful solemnity mingling now with spirited play. Mature men embracing their boyhood, bringing it forth to leaven the present with playful abandon. For a graceful moment, we who quest forget we are searching for anything. The world stops, and we are here with it, not trying to cure it, change it, save it, but simply celebrating it.

It is finished, and we give the dance away in beauty, to the Earth, to all the peoples of the Earth. We have danced on soil made of our ancestors' bones. We pray that, one day, our bones will be danced on as well. Our bodies, our soil—very close now.

What an energized peacefulness this dance instills in me—like the warm afterglow of slow, deep lovemaking. A passionate, powerful current of male energy moves inside me. The chant has taken up residence in my bones. . . here and now, here and now, right here, right now. . . . I continue to feel the pulse and its liberating invitation. I take up residence in my bones. I stand on sacred ground. A good place to live from.

>>   <<

Our Quest community includes not just us men, but the forest that serves as our home and all the beings who live here. The first humans of this land recognized these beings as people in their own right: the Four-Legged (animal) People, the Flying People, the Swimming People, the Tall-Standing (tree) People, the Stone People, the Star Nation, the Plant Nation, and so on. Each of these communities live within an interpenetrating web of relationship with the Two-Legged (human) People. Our modern science of ecology returns us once again to the edge of this world of extended kinship. It reveals a landscape wherein the only place we stand separate from our animal, plant, and mineral kin is in a defended state of mind. Among the living, however, such distinctions are not true.

To live in integrity here in this forest we must be in good relation to this place and to the beings who serve as our hosts. We must learn to see beyond our cultural indoctrination so we can greet all of our environment as being alive and spirited, and recognize all natural cycles as sacraments. We must learn to live in beauty.

With that in mind I ask the men to make a solemn procession to the first of many shrines we will visit on our journey. Located a couple hundred paces from our camp, this shrine at first appears to be little more than a hole in the ground. In fact, though, this is the altar on which we will daily place holy offerings: the material that our digestive tract refuses.

This revelation attracts some affirmative nods of recognition and an equal number of puzzled expressions. I meet these faces of doubt with a preacher's zeal. The sermon goes something like this:

Yes, this shrine is also known as a latrine. I ask that we bring our attention fully to the act of shitting because it is one of the most primary connections we have with the life cycle, one that in our culture is normally closeted. At home you take a shit, turn a lever, and your offering magically disappears to who knows where. That's the problem: Most of the time we don't know where it ends up. There's a break in our awareness that plucks us out of the food cycle. Our lives have become sanitized to the point of pathology.

Living in wholeness means living in accord with all phases of the circle of life. American Indian peoples call this practice walking in beauty. The Beauty Way empowers us to find beauty in all that we are and to create beauty in all that we do.

Our culture's bias runs against the primitive, the primal, the primary processes of the cycle. We call our soil "dirt" and we associate dirt with things that are unclean, scandalous, or obscene.

But what does our direct experience tell us? Pick up a handful of soil—smell it, look carefully at it. Look at the forest about you and at all of the life this soil nourishes. We could just as well call this stuff the placenta of life. Within each handful of this dark, rich forest soil live approximately five billion microscopic plants—as many plants as there are humans on the planet. There are also close to a million animals and over a hundred miles of tiny root hairs in just one handful! When buried in the soil, our shit becomes food for many of these beings. It helps to grow trees. And each inch of this precious topsoil is the result of two hundred years of growth, death, decay, and rebirth.

There's an old Jewish saying that goes something like this: "The reason no one can find God any more is that no one is willing to stoop so low." If there is a God, then it would make sense that God lives everywhere—in this soil and in the stuff of our bowels. Many people today proclaim "God is dead." In truth, our Industrial Age notion of the sacred has sanitized God to death. We've done the same thing to God that we've done to our bread and sugar—we've taken the germ and dark molasses out. The God of modern people has got all the vitality of Won-

der bread and cotton candy. It's no wonder that so many people are leav-
ing the churches looking for a square meal.

So, when we're called to visit this shrine, let us stoop low. Let us look
up at the sky and proclaim "God lives here" and then look down at the
soil and say "and here as well."

My friends, this ain't just dirt!

Our service closes after a comprehensive demonstration of user-
friendly squatting techniques. No white porcelain throne here.

Having begun to explore our relationship to elemental earth and
soil, we now turn our attention to our water nature. We walk to
the river.

It is easy to forget that our bodies are mostly water. Close to 70
percent of what we commonly call "me" is pure water, twelve
gallons on the average, with just enough skin to keep us from
spilling over. "No water, no initiation," say the Old Ones. The
passage from a limited experience of self to a more expansive one
requires our willingness to dissolve. And so, anyone who chooses
to grow will need to establish a good relationship to fluidity.
Water is our teacher here. Every birth is accompanied by blood,
sweat, and tears. The call to the river is an invitation to return to
these liquid mysteries of our origins.

The river that flows through our camp is a thoroughfare of
water-smoothed rocks and boulders, a playground that the child
in me finds hard to resist. So, I invite the men to play.

The group descends the bank and makes its way toward some
downstream pools. The man in front of me leaps like a cat from
his perch and lands surely on a small rock about four feet away. I
apprentice myself to his graceful movement. But before long, he
is off again, hopping from boulder to boulder, well on his way
downstream.

I glance behind me and notice men who are more cautious on
this terrain. Using hands and knees, they gingerly negotiate the
more challenging traverses. They move like toddlers, surprised
and relieved to find themselves upright, their tentative steps
unsure of each landing. For these men, this crossing triggers

memories of similar moments in the past when they confronted the limits of their physical abilities. Perhaps they suffered defeat in a contest of athletic skill. Perhaps they were chosen last for the team—or not at all. The ghosts of humiliation live in a dark closet somewhere deep inside our hearts. A simple event like crossing a stream can open that closet and allow old ghosts to reassert themselves.

It is not easy to bear the weight of shame around other men, for our histories record little understanding, compassion, or acceptance for such a state. Shame is not usually something that a young boy brings to his father or that one man easily discusses with another. As boys we colluded to sign an invisible pact, in which shame is declared to be the antithesis of manhood. If the need to deal with the shame is too strong to contain, we might take that need to women. But at all costs, the old pact says, keep that shame out of the house of men!

So, what do these men do with the shame that is invariably uncovered on a journey such as this? Some honor the old agreement and try to keep the shame hidden. Others have learned that humiliation is a stepping-stone to humility, which itself is a prerequisite to transformation. And they struggle to allow themselves to wear their shame on their faces. They recognize that to acknowledge shame is to release it from the harsh hand of fear. Once touched with compassion, shame begins the slow metamorphosis into a humble and empowered vulnerability. There is much going on inside these men as they negotiate this river passage.

Eventually, we all gravitate to a couple of small water holes. We shed our clothes as if they were the old skins of molting animals. In this naked state a primordial return to the waters of origin begins. The water is cold and not all bodies present are enthused about such a surrender. Some men yelp as they contact the brisk and bracing waters. Others ease themselves in inch by inch, feeling the sensation spread through the body and explode in every nerve. Some men seek the shelter of privacy, shy about revealing their white, neglected bodies to the elements and to the eyes of other men.

Across the way a totally brown body with full bushy beard and low-riding balls flashes into the stream. No marks of whiteness on this sinewy specimen of animal manhood. The feet on this one are rough and callused—animal foot pads, accustomed to walking the woods or rocks. This man slices into the pool and swims easily. Finding a passage where the rocks are slick with moss he slithers like a sleek otter from pool to pool. The eyes of others follow him: They see a spirit at ease with his animal nature. They do not know, however, that as a boy this one was considered a slow learner because he was dyslexic. He did not easily fit into society's prescribed roles, and so he stayed close to his animal nature. Years ago, perhaps, as boys, some of us might have ridiculed him for his slowness. Today, though, we envy his elemental grace. He teaches through his being, and all of us present respond to the glory of the male form that vibrates with primal grace in this man.

Suddenly, one man splashes another and laughs heartily. Others look on, wondering if the splashing will stay playful or if a more violent energy will erupt as often happens when one man transgresses another's boundaries.

THWACK! A handful of mud slides down my back. I look over my shoulder. There stands Peter. Arms crossed. Shit-eating grin on his face. Challenging my privacy and watching for a reaction. Thus began a playful and enduring friendship that started with two naked men standing in a cool mountain stream.

During a quiet interlude, a number of silent, private ritual cleansings take place. One man releases into the water his self-doubt about whether he has the right to abandon his social obligations to undertake this Quest. Another, declaring his intention, washes away his fears about whether his business will survive without him for ten days. Another stands off to one side, away from the group.

I have been invited to wash away downstream my identity, the name I came with, my professional face, my ideas about my age, the whole constellation of my secure yet limiting personal history. It seemed like a good idea when it was first presented. Yet, here in the deep waters, I hesitate. These identities don't feel merely encrusted on the surface of my skin. They feel like they *are* my skin. I'm not sure I want to let them go quite yet. The best I can do now is to set the intention to let go, and pray for the courage to do so, more and more, with each invitation offered.

With eyes closed, he scoops up handfuls of water and pours them slowly over his head and down his body. He repeats this gesture slowly and methodically three times; his breathing slows down and his body relaxes.

One by one, the river claims us all. . . .

3

THE STORIES WE LIVE BY

When a man possesses his story,
he has all he needs for survival;
but if he loses his story, he's in peril.
　　　　　　　—SIR LAURENS VAN DER POST

I find a quiet spot by the river to sit and reflect on our process thus far. By now, all of our expectations of how this Quest would begin have met with reality; for some it has been a dance, for others, more like a collision. The soaking in the cold waters, though, has brought us from the fragile heights of expectation back down into our bodies; we are more at home here now.

Thus far, our contact and communication with each other has been largely nonspoken. This is done to establish, from the outset, a practice of sustained intimacy with our experience of the present moment. Our practice is to use language in a manner that deepens our intimacy with experience. This is a very difficult task, and we will never achieve its perfection. But in keeping this value before us, we become more mindful of choosing language that is true to the sensual wildness of this forest; speaking words that smell of soil, taste of tears, and radiate the desire of warm blood.

I'm looking forward to our council this evening, our first opportunity to experience the stories and questions that brought each of us here. Slumped comfortably in a moss-cushioned hollow, I set my mind free in search of a theme to open our council.

My attention is drawn to bees busily flying from one wild rose to another. In this late afternoon sun, their legs are burdened with heavy wraps of yellow pollen. Their activity fills the air with a steady hum. I find the frequency and join in with my voice. From a ripe blossom I gather some pollen on the tip of my finger and bring the flower's seed to my tongue. Following the bee's example, I place a touch of pollen on the sticky pistil of a neighboring blossom.

This playful participation gives me entry into fields of perception normally closed to my senses. I can sense the strong currents of attraction that bring flower and bee together. While most of the flowers seem eager to offer their gifts, there are some that have not yet opened. The contained darkness of the bud slowly feeds a ripening inside. Nothing—not the shining color from the petals of their extroverted kin or the warm sun or the beckoning drone of insects—will open them before their time.

I let my imagination travel now inside the bud, inside the pollen, and into the sperm cells developing there. I float within the intracellular universe depicted in my old biology texts, until my fascination leads me to the spiraling strands of DNA. Seated on the strands are not the molecules I was expecting to see, but an endless chain of human figures. At the far bottom of this DNA path, I see the deeply wrinkled faces of old men and women. As the path ascends, the figures gradually become younger and younger until, as the path leads out of sight, there is but a tiny embryo enclosed in its oceanic world. It suddenly dawns on me that these figures are all storytellers. Generation after generation of storytellers—carrying stories from the beginning of time, given from one to the other and slightly changed with each passing. Then I make the connection that these stories are responsible for carrying life forward.

So it is with these flowers: They remain quiet until they have something to say. Within the spiraling DNA of each grain of pollen is the entire story of the rose, from its ancient beginning to its most recent chapter. The open flowers are swapping their stories with each other! And from this generative dialogue come the seeds that will renew their world.

My apprenticeship with the rose suggests to me that the

lifeblood of our Quest community, of any community, flows in the sharing of our stories. Stories of where we find ourselves now, of what we have met along the way, of what we long for, of what we are frightened of, of what we live for, of who we live for. I realize, though, that I should consider my story as only partly "mine." My story is but a chapter that has emerged from the gene-pool alphabet of life—from the fifteen billion years of universal evolution that has come before me. I try to imagine myself as a recent blossoming of a fifteen-billion-year-old universe. The vast dimension of the story that has given birth to my life extends far beyond my mind's reach. But my heart perceives it as a distant oceanic drone on top of which plays the melody of my own life—like a dolphin playing in the surf of some immense ocean.

Such a vision has been lost to the machinelike certainties of the industrial world. The story that calls us to remember ourselves within the community of life has been trivialized by much of both science and religion. Generations of modern men have thus grown alienated from images of manhood connected to the living Earth and to the Great Mystery. "What a catastrophe," cries D. H. Lawrence,

> what a maiming of love when it was made a personal, merely personal feeling, taken away from the rising and setting of the sun, and cut off from the magic connection of the solstice and equinox! This is what is the matter with us, we are bleeding at the roots, because we are cut off from the earth and sun and stars, and love is a grinning mockery, because, poor blossom, we plucked it from its stem on the tree of life, and expected it to keep on blooming in our civilized vase on the table.

A man's animating spirit dies in a life of industrial certainty. The constant challenge of this Quest is in keeping ourselves open to the surprising revelations of our self-nature and to the surprising gestures of remembrance and reunion that touch us from without. It is our task, then, to cast our stories to the wind like pollen grains, setting them free to dance and tumble with the stories of universe, earth, and humanity.

Without such cross-pollination the psychic gene pool dries up; an inbreeding takes place that can disfigure our gifts and faculties. An isolation sets in, the pain of which is often met by further isolation. Keeping one's story to oneself is painful; it exiles a man from the nurturance of community and robs his culture of the gift of his humanness. It keeps him confirmed in a well-worn and static story that no longer responds to a changing world. In this guarded secrecy, our wounds fester rather than heal. And by our example of secrecy, we teach our children to be afraid of their own truth.

Perhaps the greatest gift we can give to each other is our stories—the bare truth of our journey from denial of who we are to acceptance. But let's face it—most of us have learned well to fear such nakedness. To speak these stories, the petals of our hearts must be open; to receive the other's story, the petals of our hearts must be open. We need reminders of the healing force of truth saying and we need ritual forms to support our search for those reminders. The Talking Staff Council is one such form that has arisen in our time from the old rootstock of the heart's longing for truth. It awaits us tonight.

A slowly pulsing drum draws my attention back to camp. It's the dinner call. By the time I return, a rhythm ensemble has formed around the signal drum. The man watching the stew taps the top of the pot with a wooden spoon while others explore the percussive possibilities of their cups and bowls. Once the rhythm sets in there's no stopping it. Men are compelled to join in. Some rush back to unearth drums and rattles from their packs. One man picks up a couple of stones and adds their syncopated voice to the chorus. A couple of the guys lock elbows and dance a jig together, not exactly in time with the rhythm, but with a spirited playfulness that evokes hoots of encouragement from the band.

Grown men acting like a bunch of damn fools. We're off to a good start, I think to myself. On this journey, the sooner each man makes a fool of himself the easier it will be for him. As the Old Ones say, "No foolishness, no growth."

The rhythm reaches a chaotic crescendo as the cook-cum-conductor raises his wooden spoon baton, gathers our attention, then abruptly brings it all crashing to a close. Looks like we're ready to eat.

Our practice of bringing awareness to the simple daily acts of life extends now to our food. The evening meal we share is entered into as an act of beauty; another moment of worship. Our meals invite us to contemplate our participation in that part of the food cycle wherein we are predators. And to hold the predator-prey relationship as part of the sacred wheel of life.

Standing in a circle with our dinner stew placed in the center, we give thanks for those beings that have given their bodies and blood so that we may live. We acknowledge that our bodies will someday find themselves on someone else's dinner table, but for now, it is our time to live. The sunlight trapped within the molecules of the grains and vegetables that go to make our stew will soon find expression in movement and dance, in story and in prayer. We enter into the sacrament of eating and being eaten. In this holy communion is an opportunity to see ourselves, and our Quest, as a conduit through which the spirit of a greater life flows. Our blessing closes with Gary Snyder's remarkable tribute to the rapture of this communion, "Song of the Taste":

Eating the living germs of grasses
Eating the ova of large birds

  the fleshy sweetness packed
  around the sperm of swaying trees

The muscles of the flanks and thighs of
    soft-voiced cows
  the bounce in the lamb's leap
  the swish in the ox's tail

Eating roots grown swoll
    inside the soil

Drawing on life of living
  clustered points of light spun

out of space
hidden in the grape.

Eating each other's seed
eating
ah, each other.

Kissing the lover in the mouth of bread:
lip to lip.

After the meal the drum sounds again, this time calling us to council, the cauldron where our stories serve as food for the spirit.

Within this cauldron we release our stories to the fermentation process of change. To do that we must first know what our story is. We must be willing to tell ourselves the truth about our lives. And then be willing to stand in our truth in the presence of others.

Here we will also leaven our own stories by bearing witness to another's story—by listening, not just with the intellect but with the heart; for the heart has the wisdom to recognize another's story as part of its own. We learn to taste sweet and taste bitter, sitting there just listening. We practice allowing the teller's words and images to inhabit our bodies—and just keep listening. The one revealing his story is our guide into the Mystery. We stalk him, let him take us beyond the borders of comfort and knowing. In the end, though, we will realize that he can't take us anywhere we don't already know how to go.

The council is a great mirror in which we see ourselves projected and reflected. As we listen to the men's stories in council tonight, we will hear the many voices of our own hearts. And, undoubtedly, we will experience many different responses and reactions. Our practice in this council will be neither to deny these reactions nor to give ourselves over to them. Rather, we will simply witness the voices of our inner council, knowing we are fully responsible for each of them.

As we stand before the great mirror of the council we eventually begin to see that the story we have been living is not the only story we could be living. That our destiny is not eternally set in stone but ceases moving only when we stop questioning—stop questing. By witnessing ourselves and each other in silence, we may come to see the larger mythic patterns that govern all our lives. We may come to see that the hero's journey lives within the drama of everyday life. After all, who authored the stories of gods and goddesses? Why should we be surprised, then, to find them living at home?

To encourage this view, we often speak in council of our lives in the third person: "A man feels . . . " rather than "I feel. . . ." This helps us remove ourselves from our crippling sense of self-importance. Instead we look on ourselves from the perspective of the gods. From this distance, insight into what we *believe* we are living for and what we actually *are* living for becomes more visible. It is possible to examine our lives only after we've stepped outside of the context in which we were formerly identified.

We come to council neither to seek advice nor to give advice nor to fix or change anything. Our stories are mirrored in silence, and that silence reflects back *everything*. It has no preferences. It reflects heaven and hell, our glory, and our dismissal of glory. We come simply to sit and bear witness to each other and to do our best at marrying insight with compassion. We trust that any action birthed from that union will be organically meaningful.

>>   <<

By now the night air has wrapped its cool, moist breath around us and gathered us into its fold, as it has the many other beings of this forest. Tall hemlocks are gathered close to our circle. Impossibly rooted and steadfast beings, they arch lacy branches above our heads that touch the sparkling presence of the night sky. A cathedral like none other, containing us and yet open to the universe at the same time.

At the center of our circle is an altar of smooth river rocks adorned with a dozen glowing votive candles. The quiet flames cast a rich, warm light over the faces present here. The intimate solitude of night calls forth nuances of character that daylight washes over. I let my eyes linger, for a moment, on the faces so innocently available now.

A seashell holding a mixture of dried sage and cedar sits before us. I light the end of a small twig on one of the candle flames and touch it to the incense. As the scented smoke curls upward, I offer its fragrance in honor of the Old Ones, the ones who have come before us, the guides to all seekers whose longing for wholeness returns them to the sacred Earth. I invite their presence here to join our council.

I call on us to honor ourselves by speaking our truth here—all colors of our truth. Let us acknowledge that the line between good and evil runs through the center of every human heart. And let us remember, for all who walk a path with heart, truth is our medicine.

I open the pouch that holds our council talking staff and place it on the blanket before me. It is a sacred pipe, a medicine gift I received years ago from a woman who was initiated by pipe carriers of the Lakota people. Lakota tradition says the first pipe was given to the people during a time of turmoil by White Buffalo Woman. Its medicine power lay in its authority to remind the people of their kinship with all life. In the presence of the sacred pipe, one must speak truth or not speak at all. The Old Ones remind us that silence is powerful and sacred. To taint it with lies or half-truths brings harm to the speaker and disharmony to his people. And so, as we hold the pipe in council, we allow its ancient and honored lineage to resonate in our hearts, giving us courage to speak whatever it is we find there.

I pick up the smooth, reddish brown pipestem. Formed from the heartwood of a red cedar tree, it carries a sweet fragrance. I close my eyes and bring the pipe to my nose. The scent releases a memory of my first journey with this pipe.

My wife, Indira, and I are driving north to canoe the Adirondack waterways. My mind wanders, as it often does on long hypnotic drives, until it comes to rest on an image of the pipe, packed away carefully in the back of the car. The rich color of the red cedar wood stands out prominently in my mind's eye. How beautiful it would be, I think, to adorn such a wood with the similarly hued feathers of the red-tailed hawk. I share this image with Indira. Moments later we speed by an object lying by the road that catches the corner of our eyes. "Hawk!" we shout together. I quickly turn onto the shoulder, feeling any wasted time might dispel this mirage. Yes, it is a dead red-tailed hawk, still warm, with no visible signs of injury. The world stops for a moment. And before reason has a chance to reassert itself with an explanation, my heart opens in a shudder of compassion, awe, and gratitude—a trembling that after a number of such "coincidences" I would later come to recognize as the energy released when the two worlds touch.

These are the feathers, a gift from Hawk, that I now attach to this pipestem. Holding the feathered staff in my right hand, I reach toward the heavens above and within us. Like a lightning rod, the staff calls forth the fiery spiritual energies that seek union with matter below and within.

I now grasp the pipe bowl—a crafted piece of red pipestone, the color of dried blood, which was quarried from deep inside the earth. The coolness it has absorbed from the ground feels good in my palm. Holding this vessel in my left hand, I let its weight draw me down to rest with the soil. It is the chalice, the cauldron, the heart, the container that holds the dark, moist, soul mystery of the below. A mystery that seeks union with the above.

Joining stem and bowl at the level of our hearts—the hearth of heaven and earth—I offer this pipe now as our talking staff to all those in the four directions with whom we share life.

My brothers, let us sit in good relation with the community of life that surrounds us here. Feel yourself rooted in a tradition that is far older and wiser than our local particular time and place.

I call on the sacred ancestry of this pipe to encourage us to speak as the authors of our lives. Through our willingness to be who we really are, we discover our oneness with things.

Let us align with the intention to give voice to our heart's truth here tonight. Let us direct this staff to carry us beyond reason into the Great Mystery of our lives. Let us find the wisdom to listen to the other voices present, as an echo of our own voice.

And, given the lateness of this hour, let us also remember the wisdom of simplicity—let us be brief!

Passing the pipe to the man seated to my left, I offer him the three questions that will open the first chapter of our collective story:

Who comes to this Quest?
What does he seek?
What has he met along the way?

After holding the pipe until it rests comfortably in his hands, the first man speaks.

A man comes . . . a man whose heart hungers for actions of meaning and beauty such as this. Whose heart thirsts for the sacred, whose body has grown tired of pacing back and forth within the prison of his own making. He has spent much of his life peering out between the bars of this prison wondering if there were any other men who felt the way he does. He is delighted to find you here. He seeks the support of this community of men and Earth to help him remember what his Earth Walk is really about. He seeks to learn to trust his spiritual life to other men—to let his friends and his world see who he really is. . . .

Having finished speaking, he sits for a moment in the Great Silence that surrounds his words; for it is there, in the Silence, that wholeness is remembered. In the space between thoughts, in the space between words, in the space between breaths, we can best remember who we really are. We come to council not to cultivate words, but silence around words. Silence . . . that which carries the true power of regeneration, that which the world fears and so deeply yearns for.

And so, when he is ready, the one holding the Talking Staff turns to the man next to him, repeats the questions, and passes the pipe along. One by one, we each take a turn at speaking to the questions of this council.

This man comes to this Quest . . . he comes because his wife sent him—a birthday gift. He wishes he had a more noble reason for being here. Everywhere he turns he finds people making decisions for him. What has he met along the way? People pushing him to do this, be that. Always, people pushing him. Yet he finally has to admit to himself that he secretly likes it that way.

All this talk about "being the author of your life" disturbs him. A man is here who is halfway through his life yet is still plagued with the feeling of being a boy wearing an adult mask. He comes to this Quest hoping someone will have the answers for him. Yet he has not even taken the time to find out what his questions are. He feels ashamed. He is not looking forward to waking up tomorrow and looking you guys in the eyes.

He's met nothing but resistance to coming here. He is hoping for a natural disaster that will call this Quest off. He thinks this ritual stuff is weird, and yet he feels he is not worthy to be here. The story of his life is titled "A Man Walks the Earth Who Is Not Worthy." He is sick and tired of his same old story and he's disgusted with how much self-pity he hears in his voice. He feels his words now covering his sadness and anger. He thinks, maybe if he keeps on talking long enough, it'll come out different. He passes this pipe on now because he is tired of hearing himself talk.

The one who just spoke gives me courage to share what's really in my heart. This man comes to you with a new name. He heard our guides speak of the importance of honoring where we are now before rushing headlong into this Quest. Traveling down the rocks in the stream this afternoon he felt his legs shaking. He felt unsure and timid among you. In his head he imagined the guides saying, "Start where you are, trembling fawn."

Trembling Fawn—that is who is here now. He knows that if he rejects this name gift, the rest of his Quest will be a sham. He asks that you call him by this name, allow this part of him a seat in this council.

What has he met along the way? Excitement at the adventure of this Quest, and fear. Fear he won't be as athletic or as physically strong as the rest of you—and will be rejected because of that. Fear of the three days of solitude. Fear of not getting a vision. Fear of getting a vision that will demand too much of him. Fear that this Quest will not really change anything. Fear that this Quest will change him too much, too fast. Fear of not being able, or not wanting, to return to society. . . .

He's beginning to see most of these fears are really one fear—fear of himself. He seeks to claim himself. Trembling Fawn comes to this Quest.

A man comes who has reached many completions in his life. His career has ended, his children have grown, his house is comfortable both physically and spiritually. This man is one who always cried, "I need more time!" Now he has nothing but time. This man is one who said to others, "Why are you in my way—in my space?" Now he has nothing but space. A man comes who seeks to know how to use that time and that space in ways that fulfill him and contribute something of value to his people. . . .

There is a fire burning inside this man—a fire that seeks full recognition—a fire that is too often untended—a fire that proclaims this one's longing to be fully alive. His is the spirit of the eagle. He flies with the longing to be fully alive and yet struggles with turbulent winds of doubt, resistance, and impatience. He comes to this Quest with an inner council that is divided, at war. For each strong yes to the Quest, he feels an equally strong no! This man comes to you weary of fighting the turbulence of conflict. He comes to remember that he is responsible for tending his inner fire. He respects the courage of Trembling Fawn, who came forward, looked us in the eyes, and revealed his fear. This one is used to judging such actions as cowardly, negative back-sliding. He suspects, though, that this Quest will ask him to confront his own trembling—something he does not like doing. He asks that you help him go into the turbulence. . . .

A man comes to the wilderness to learn the names and odors of his passions, to learn to sing the music of his soul, to touch the Earth that has brought him into existence and to know the connections that link him to nature and to this world. He wants to be a human being, not a human doing. He wants to grin so hard and so well that rocks grin back. He wants to laugh from deep in his belly. This man wants to celebrate his manhood instead of always trying to improve on it. . . .

Just before this Quest a drum arrived in the mail. For this man, it was like he received a piece of his masculinity—his balls coming via U.P.S.! He's not the type of guy who can sit around and chant "Om," or make dolphin sounds, or watch his breath go in and out. He's the type of guy who can go down into his cellar and drum his fucking brains out. He drums until his spirit runs out and tumbles around and around—in rage, in tenderness, or sorrow—it doesn't matter, as long as he drums what's in his heart. He wants to come out of the cellar and walk in the world with his heart drumming. . . .

This one comes, sits among you, grateful to be here. He has always complained that his everyday life was meaningless. But tonight he realizes that this experience, right here, has come out of his everyday life. Where else could it have come from? This understanding brings him power. He sees that every experience of his past has brought him to this moment.

He comes as one soon to be married. He will soon make the passage from single man to husband and, he hopes, to father as well. He claims this Quest as his true "stag's night" and asks that his new-found brothers run wild with him through the forest. And at the end of that run to bless him in his passage. He chooses to see his manhood fulfilled in marriage. But he has met fear from so many of his friends who warn him only of the dangers. He is tired of their fear and his own fear. He wants to be met by you as a man in love with his beloved.

The man who sits here has listened to each of your stories. In some way they might all very well be chapters from his own. He honors each of you for your willingness to gift him with glimpses of your soul.

This one's heart is stunned by what is happening in the world these days. He feels moved by the many hopeful movements toward peace and deep sadness at the immensity of suffering that's taking place in the name of "national pride." The grief and pain feels unbearable at times. He questions: Where is the center strong enough to keep the whole world from splitting apart? In the midst of such suffering, how does he live between the extremes of overwhelm and denial?

He quests not only for himself but for his world as well. He's not sure what that really means, but to think otherwise would be meaningless for him now. He quests for that part of his world that asks much of him, and gives much to him—for his parish and the youth with whom he works. One of the most powerful aspects of Native American thought for him is the concept of "living for the good of the people." He enters this Quest to learn in what ways he may serve the good of his people. And, how much of the world he dares consider "his people."

And so, the Talking Staff is passed until it arrives where it started, completing the round. It returns warmer, with more body heat, than before. Holding the pipe before us, I slowly inscribe open circles, stirring the cauldron of Heart we have entered tonight:

I give thanks for our willingness to see and be seen—for the courage, wisdom, and compassion embodied in our giveaways of self.

Let us now gather up all of our offerings, our stories, our medicine and release them. . . .

May the fruits of our labors here tonight be for the benefit of all our people.

I separate the pipestem from the bowl and return them to their deerskin wrapping. The ritual container of this council now opens. There is little talk as we gesture good night and make our ways back through the darkness to our tents. It has been a full day. Our day tomorrow begins at first light.

4

WHERE THE TWO
WORLDS TOUCH

The breeze at dawn has secrets to tell you.
    Don't go back to sleep.
You must ask for what you really want.
    Don't go back to sleep.
People are going back and forth across the doorsill
    where the two worlds touch.
The door is round and open.
    Don't go back to sleep.

—RUMI
TRANSLATION BY JOHN MOYNE AND COLEMAN BARKS

In the light of the stars overhead, the Abenaki people read the story of their origins. The Abenaki, one of the Algonquin-speaking tribes of the U.S. Northeast, call the creator by the name Maheo, the Great Mystery—the Mystery that gives birth to all things and receives all things in the end. I learned this story from Tsonakwa, a medicine teacher. And like all creation stories, this one begins in the beginning . . . when there was nothing.

> Only was there Maheo, who sat in a vast ocean of limitless space and endless time. If Maheo was silent, then all the universe was silent. If Maheo was still, then nothing moved.

And so it was, age upon age, in that endless silent darkness.

In his heart, Maheo felt the stirrings of love, and he thought to himself, "How empty is this place. I have power, but what good is power unless something is done with it?"

And so Maheo moved. With one hand Maheo reached out and grabbed all of Space, both great and small—for the universe is as small as it is large. This space Maheo held in his left hand. Then Maheo reached out and gathered in all of Time—the time passed, the time always now, and all time yet to come. This Maheo held in his right hand. Then Maheo brought his two hands together in a tremendous clap—and a great thundering heartbeat roared across the universe—Sound, the first sound ever to arise from that vast dark ocean. And sparks flew in all directions from Maheo's hands—Light, all of the light that the universe would ever need.

If we look with the eyes of our hearts, we can see in all things, everywhere, the glowing embers from that first fire of creation time. And if we listen with the ears of our hearts, we can still hear the roaring echo of that first heartbeat sound.

Ba-boomm . . . ba-boomm . . . ba-boomm . . . ba-boomm. . . .

By the first dim light of dawn, a gentle yet persistent drumbeat stirs the sleeping men. In giving away our watches the night before, we surrendered ourselves to the rhythms of mythic time. Now this awakening drum, echoing the distant thunder from Maheo's clapping hands, signals the start of the first full day of our journey.

This day begins with a ceremony in which we come together to greet the sunrise. To stand in the presence of the emerging fireball is to remind ourselves of our purpose in being here. To welcome the sun as it breaks the horizon is to honor both the physical and spiritual fire kindling within our hearts. We quest to shed new light on our lives and to align our intent with the desire to shine forth the dawning of our hearts into the world.

The Sunrise Ceremony takes place atop a dome-shaped rocky knoll across the stream from our campsite. Before the other men are awake, I come to this stone altar to lay the wood for a small fire. I fashion a nest of shredded cedar bark to serve as a tinder bundle, receptive to nurturing a tiny spark into flame.

There is an enchanted stillness in this place, suspended now in the moments between night and day. A mist softens the contours of the sleeping landscape below. Above gleams a dark slate blue sky, while low along the horizon a silver sliver of light wedges its way under the darkness, as if peeping through the crack beneath a door. Mounted in the sky is the thin crescent of the waning moon. Beneath this crescent, like jeweled earrings, glisten two bright stars.

The beauty of this moment alone is enough to restore life to a man. I fill my lungs with the invigorating air. A prayer of thanks forms around the sighing outbreath. I place a fragrant wreath of sage and cedar on the wood, giving careful attention to an arrangement that reflects the beauty that surrounds me.

Emerging from their tents a bit groggy and still wrapped in the moist predawn darkness, the men assemble in camp. It has been an uneasy sleep for most. Minds have been restless through the night, as yet on guard against the newness of this environment.

Forgoing the usual routines of breakfast and conversation, the men are led directly across the stream, up the short yet nearly vertical trail, to the top of the knoll. They step onto this rock, breathing in the chill mountain air and take in the view of distant peaks and valleys. We are the only signs of humanity for as far as the eye can see.

We gather around the fire area. Removing flint and steel from my pouch, I prepare to light our ceremonial fire. I recount the Abenaki creation story, where Maheo claps his hands and scatters sparks throughout the universe. These sparks, burning since the beginning, long to be rekindled each day and in each being. We see such a spark in the fireball of the sun. I invite each one of us to be likewise present to our longing to set free the blaze of our heart's desire. I pause to enter into the rich imagery of the origins

of the First Fire. And when this Fire has warmed me, I pick up the
flint rock and faithfully affirm:

> Behold the spark of life,
> Spark from the First Fire of creation,
> Carried in all things!

The flint in my left hand, the steel in my right, like Maheo
standing in that primordial ocean, I bring my hands together in a
dramatic flourish and . . .

And, well, sometimes nothing happens. Now remember, those
sparks have been hiding in the flint for fifteen billion years. They
can be a little shy and hard to coax out. And, like fireflies celebrating their release from a jar, they don't always fly in the direction I
might like.

I strike again. And again. Beneath my ceremonial headband
form beads of ceremonial sweat. At moments like this I try not to
think about the fact that I'm surrounded by a dozen shivering
guys who have traveled hundreds of miles so they could be
dragged out of bed before sunrise to climb this rock and watch a
ritual guide make a ritual jackass of himself. Where are you, Coyote, you Trickster? I hear your lurking laughter!

I persist, though. Soon a spark flickers from the rock. It lands
on a receptive piece of tinder. Instantly I scoop up the nest and
blow on it with gentle breath. A wisp of smoke uncurls from the
dry tinder and the shavings suddenly crackle into flame. I place
them under the arch of twigs and nurture the tiny blaze through
adolescence and into maturity. Fire, offspring of the sun itself!

The warmth and light of the flames draw our circle closer
together. We create, with both our bodies and our intention, the
vessel that will contain us in sacred space. I reach into my pouch
and place a small pinch of tobacco into each man's hands.
Tobacco, sacred herb, the one with power to carry the people's
prayers to the Great Mystery. I remind us that we have come here
to celebrate the awakening of life from the fertile darkness. Before
the sun breaks the horizon, the canvas of the day is still fresh and
unformed, receptive to whatever intentions we may set before it.

We come here to apply the colors of our creative imagination and the desires of our heart.

To this end I ask that we feel ourselves in relationship with life in the Four Directions and with the dimensions of life above and below us. Facing each direction in turn, I send a call:

Great Mystery, we stand before you this morning and give thanks for the fullness of our lives—for those summertime moments when the winds wrap us in warm sweet fragrance that we would hold forever and for those wintertime moments when the winds blow cold and harsh, against which we have felt so lonely and afraid—for all of those experiences that have brought us to this place of beauty. We are here to give voice to the truest intentions of our hearts.

Spirit Keepers of the East, we greet you this morning and call on the spirit of the rising sun, of the new beginnings that are kindled from the ashes of yesterday. We call on the courage to be born anew with each breath we take. And when blessed with the gifts of insight and illumination, help us to take swift and decisive action.

Spirit Keepers of the South, we are men who come to honor our hearts' desire—to burn with generous light and warmth, like the sun as it sits in its full glory, high in the sky. Help us to walk with innocence and trust, a path with heart.

Spirit Keepers of the West, we turn to you this morning and celebrate the special power of the setting sun, poised between the two worlds of day and night. Help us to find the wisdom and strength to walk into our own inner darkness, to say yes to the many deaths that herald rebirth.

Spirit Keepers of the North, we face your realm of fertile silence and stillness that we might learn of the recreative power in accepting our own emptiness. Like this sacred fire before us, help us to burn to completion, till we are ashes scattered by the wind, fully given away. The Old Ones say we are "trees that walk." Let us open our branches to the Great Spirit of Life above us, to Father-Mother Sky who holds billions of stars and lives yet beyond that.

Help us to know ourselves in you.

And to Mother-Father Earth. Brothers, let us sink our roots down into the deep, dark, wet, soulful mysteries of the Below. Let us reclaim the

sacredness of matter and thus stand on True Ground. Beloved Earth,
help us to know ourselves in you.

Placing our hands over our hearts, we invite the powers, the
medicines, of these Six Directions to meet and join here in this
Seventh Place. For the heart alone is able to embrace both longing
and fulfillment, each as gifts of life. From this place we continue
to honor the relationships that magnify our being. We pray for all
our people:

For the ancestors—those who have come before us—
for the courageous men and women whose passion for
living in truth inspires us yet today.
Let us remember ourselves within the red, black, white, and
yellow tapestry of our global family. And let us pray for the leaders
of world governments that they would be at peace
with the rich diversity of the human family.
For our closest friends, family, and loved ones—those who tend the
home fires in support of our being here and who await our return.
For the children, who in turn will receive the torch from our hands,
and for the yet unborn. May our acts here nourish their future.
For all of our relations within the community of life—the Animal
People, the Plant People, the Mineral People—
for all our people. May our acts nourish our future.

We have now prepared the ground for each one of us to honor
his longing in his own way. One by one, each man steps to the
center of the circle and kneels before the fire. Letting his heart
speak in the most genuine voice he is willing to embody in this
moment, he breathes his prayer into the tobacco and releases all
to the spirited flames.

I give thanks for this beautiful morning.
I have been so lost in the conflicts of my life,
I have forgotten to look around me.
Has this beauty been here all this time?
I seek the wisdom to live with the hard questions before me now, the

courage to face them rather than fight them.
Help me to be unafraid of who I am.
Let this man's heart blossom forth into the world—in truth, in
beauty.

Great Mystery, I come before you as a "retired man."
My career work done, my dearest ones dead or dispersed,
and yet my life is far from over.
I am far from "over."
Where am I now to look for fulfillment, where is love to come from?
I ask for vision that will guide this next phase of my life.

This is the anniversary of my father's death.
God, these tears are my prayers . . .
tears for myself, my father, my son.
I ask for forgiveness, for the inner strength to break this chain of
blame, humiliation, and rage that's been passed down generation
after generation by the men in my family.
Dear God, what do I do with the venom I feel in my blood?

This man's heart is heavy—
fucked up with addiction and failure.
Part of me just wants to say, "Fuck God,
And fuck this prayer bullshit."
Another part hopes there is something—something in this universe
that can help him because he can't help himself any longer.
My prayer is: Fuck you God—and Help me God.

Great Spirit, where is my passion?
I want fire in my life.
I want wind and rain and lightning.
I'm tired of being "Okay."
I want to be *alive*.
I want my life back.

I am here to celebrate the full spectrum of myself as a man.
I come to stalk the masculine force in nature and watch how it dances

with the feminine.
I want to feel my nature as wild and integrated and life-sustaining as
the nature around me now.

I want to blow away the foggy images of manhood my culture has
given me and discover what is true for me.
I give tobacco to this fire.
Let the Great Fire burn away whatever is not true with me.
So be it!

Holding his tobacco, one man is inspired to forge a link with oth-ers in our circle. He steps before each one and holds out his palm. He takes a tiny pinch of shredded tobacco and places it in the other man's hand. Wordlessly he seeks, and receives, permission to take a pinch from him and mingle it with his own. By the time he has worked his way around the circle he holds shreds from each of the men present. The image of consigning this mixture to the fire, and having all our prayers merge as one, brings him com-fort. He opens his palm to look at the tangled mass he has har-vested. His joy turns to terror when he sees portrayed within this tangled snarl the hideous face of the Mean Spirit—the nemesis he has come on this Quest to confront. Casting his tobacco into the flame, he prays:

I seek the power to destroy the Mean Spirit as thoroughly as the fire
now destroys this offering. And . . . the courage to enter whatever fire
necessary for me to meet this one.

Time stands still for the moments we are in prayer. Finally the spell is broken by the shrill song of a white-throated sparrow. The faces of the men facing the eastern horizon become flushed with a red-orange light. Sun has risen!

The blazing echo between fire and sun inspires one of us to offer a song. It is traditional, he explains with a twinkle in his eye, for Masai warriors to greet each new sun with a call and response song. He begins with a simple melody. The rest of us easily echo it back. Then he leads us into more intricate warbles and glissades, impossible to remember. Nonetheless we sing with abandon, even as our response bears little resemblance to our leader's call. Masai warriors we are not. We break into a laugh that releases the intense focus of our ceremony.

The flames of the sacred fire have given way to ashes. I scoop up some of them and place them in a special pouch. We will see these ashes again.

Brothers, we stand in Beauty—in the gateway where the Two Worlds touch. We place ourselves now in the hands of the Great Mystery.

>>   <<

At the start of any wilderness journey it is helpful to ask ourselves basic questions: Where am I now? Where do I want to go? What lies in between?

On a spiritual journey these same questions are directed toward our inner landscape:

Where am I now? What does my life center on? What do I live for? Where do I say "Yes, that's me," and where do I judge "No, that is not me?"

Where do I want to go? What parts of self does my heart long to reunite with? What is my sacred dream? If I let myself be born anew in this moment without allegiance to personal history, who might emerge?

What lies in between these two? What tensions, fears, hopes, courage, beliefs, desires, questions, feelings, illusions, intentions, demons, angels—what do I meet as I walk undefended into the space between who I think I am and who I yet may be?

Map and compass are the tools we use for finding our way through the outer landscape. To gain access to the inner world, we need the multifaceted tool of the creative imagination. And one of the primary navigational technologies of the imagination is ritual.

Ritual allows us to travel and communicate between the two worlds. Between the visible and the invisible, between the outer and the inner, between profane and sacred, matter and spirit, conscious and unconscious, history and mystery, civilization and wilderness—between who I think I am now and the dream of myself. When communication between these worlds exist, the potential for whole-ing, or healing, exists.

The language of ritual is a rich amalgam of word, image, and symbolic action. By themselves, words are not capable of guiding us through the wilderness of the soul. They are well-suited to leading us to the edge of our known world and perhaps catapulting us into the unknown, yet they themselves must turn back at the border. Beyond this border lies the realm of the unconscious wherein live constellations of numinous power—what Jung called archetypes, what the Greeks knew as gods and goddesses, what some native peoples call the Old Ones, and what the fairy stories call sleeping beauties, giants, and such. The problem with these inhabitants of the psyche's wilderness is they don't care much for proper syntax or good behavior. Good English isn't enough to get them out of bed. But ... wake before sunrise and speak your heart's desire as if it were the first Word of creation and see *yourself* burning in the sunrise fire until both you and the wood return to ash—now *that* might begin to attract some attention.

Poetry and prayer transcend words in much the same way that a Van Gogh painting transcends pigmented oils or a Mozart concerto transcends the vibrations of plucked strings. "Poetic writing consists of letting the Word resonate behind words," proclaimed Gerhart Hauptmann. Indeed, this is the challenge of our practice of prayer on the Quest: to connect with the Longing, Despair, and Joy that circulate in the deepest wells of life. What would it be like to pray feeling *your* longing as the aperture that reveals *the* Longing to yourself and your community? To pray imagining *your* despair as an upwelling of *the* Despair that pervades the planet? To express *your* joy as the blossoming of *the* Joy that refreshes the world each sunrise? The Word behind the words—*that* is what ritual seeks to awaken, in us and in the world.

There is no static liturgy that we follow in the Sunrise Ceremony, or for that matter in any of the rituals on our Quest. The nature of life is constant change. All forms come and go. Living in the wilderness presents this lesson again and again. A sudden wind or rain may come up demanding spontaneous reform. Or perhaps a dream image comes hurtling through the night that seeks enactment in a sunlit ritual drama. Or a ritual participant may be inspired to elaborate on the essential form, as the man did in his mingling of the tobacco at the Sunrise Ceremony. I encourage each of us to surrender to the essential form of the ritual and then to make it our own by bringing our creative presence to it.

Some of our most effective rituals have emerged from last-minute changes of plans due to inconvenient weather and other surprises. In fact, over the years, I've come to welcome these "inconveniences." They force us to return to the essence of the ritual and ask again: What is our intention here and how can we most simply and elegantly enact that? Our fresh awareness keeps the ritual potent. My rule of thumb here is this: I will use a particular ritual form as long as there is beauty in it and as long as it supports us in staying awake. Our rituals need the moisture of humor, the fertile soil of humility, the heat of desire, and the inspired breath of spirit. They need to be a reflection of the living earth. Placed on such a ground, prayer—a seed of intention—will grow.

This is not just New Age thinking. One of our most esteemed ancestors, that radical mystic from Nazareth, proclaimed this two thousand years ago: "The Sabbath is made for man, and not man the Sabbath" (Mark 2:27). Jesus saw that the soul is a living thing that must be attended to with living ritual forms. That perception did not gain him much popularity with the administrators of the temple, but it woke us up to something. Two thousand years later, and we're still talking about it.

To foster wakefulness, any ritual must continually grow and turn with the people. Raised in a dry and humorless religious environment, I remember trying to force myself to fit into certain religious forms that seemed to deny spirit more than invite it. I obediently followed the rules because that's what I saw the "good Christians" around me doing. And more often than not, my entire focus in those rituals was on whether or not I was performing them correctly. I lost my authority in the fear of making a mistake. We use ritual on a Quest not to foster "good questers" but to foster *presence*. In the place where the two worlds touch, what counts most is relaxed wakefulness, compassionate mindfulness, a sense of humor, and wholehearted surrender to the truth of our own experience.

At the same time, however, it is important to recognize the value of order, discipline, and form. On the surface, this statement seems to contradict the value of spontaneity. Why can't we "just hang out" and "go with the flow"?

If we wanted merely to peek through the door where the two worlds touch, then discipline is probably not all that important. However, if our intention is to *walk* through that door, we'd better be prepared to confront chaos. The transformation of caterpillar to butterfly depends on more than just good intentions. A primary prerequisite is the successful structuring of the threshold state, the chrysalis. Only after the chrysalis is carefully formed can the caterpillar safely enter the darkness of the unknown. There the caterpillar's body literally dissolves into a liquid state. Only within the protective confinement of the chrysalis can this *breakdown* give birth to the *breakthrough* of the butterfly. That is transformation, and—let's not fool ourselves—it requires containment, discipline, and a certain measure of control.

It's a law of the transformational process: Only when you have control where it is needed can you abandon control where it is not needed. Without a healthy respect for control, we may find ourselves hopelessly lost in the wilderness of the psyche, but without respect for abandon, we never really leave home. The art of ritual has to do with balancing these two in any given moment so that we're able to be "at home on the road and on the road at home." This way, we stay responsible to both worlds.

Early in the Quest we make a point of honoring where we are here and now. During the Sunrise Ceremony, we formally give thanks for *all* the circumstances, good and bad, that have brought each of us to this place. I have found such acceptance to be an important foundation for this work. In the words of the vision given to me, "It all starts with forgiveness." It's not likely that every one of us standing on the knoll that first morning will be authentically grateful for all of his past and present condition; *knowing* where we are is not the same as *accepting* where we are. Yet by giving voice to our intention to accept our current condition, we address the issue from the beginning. And often, in so doing, those parts of us that are still holding out, refusing to accept the way things are, make themselves known. Once that happens, we can greet those parts and communicate with them.

Paradoxically, in giving voice to our nonacceptance, we move farther down the path *toward* acceptance. If we pretend to be accepting when we're really not, we turn our Quest into a flight from an imperfect life. Our focus is primarily on what we don't want. But even in fleeing we are held captive by our own desire to be free, because concealed within this desire for freedom is a rejection of reality—of who and where we are now. And any movement from a foundation that is out of touch with reality will only bury us deeper in illusion. So at the very beginning we must take a stand— or in some cases a leap—of faith for the perfection of the wildly imperfect life in which we find ourselves. That does not mean that we deny the pain that can arise from living an imperfect life. No, we feel the pain, but to it we add the wisdom of our experience.

When we live life as a Quest we practice moving *toward* our wounds with forgiveness, because these wounds carry transformational power—the power to wake us up to our sacred dream. Pain is one of the ways the sacred world knocks at our door. If we pathologize our suffering—declare it to be an illness that must be cured—we stay asleep. We find ourselves locked in a state of perpetual pain thinking that its cause lies somewhere outside ourselves. Once we accept suffering as a natural condition of life, the rebirthing process moves forward. We will suffer because we are alive and growing. Whether through our suffering we are diminished or liberated is up to each one of us. The breeze at dawn has secrets to tell. Sometimes it's a gentle sigh and sometimes it's an icy gale. In either case, don't go back to sleep!

Because intention and prayer are central to our Quest, and as each of us often has dramatically different relationships to these acts, it serves to hold a discussion of these matters.

Secular culture tends to emphasize only the most visible aspects of intentionality: "I made up my mind to do such and such." We may boast of our reason's ability to create but, truly, that is only half the story. To give our conscious minds full credit for creation makes as much sense as a giving a farmer full credit for growing tomatoes. The farmer may intelligently align himself with the laws of nature and place a tomato seed on fertile ground, but he could hardly claim responsibility for growing the tomato.

The root meaning of *intentionality* suggests a "stretching, or applying, of the mind toward something"—a preexisting something that lives on a level much deeper than the rational mind can register. This deeper meaning of intentionality suggests that the conscious mind is less the creator than the supporter of something already in motion. Whatever we quest for is already here, now, waiting to be adopted by whoever would stretch toward it and choose it. If we did not already own what we pray for, we would not have the heart to pray for it.

To the extent that we haven't made peace with where we are now, and who we are now, our stated intention for our Quest will be in service of a conflicted and fearful mind. Prayers that arise from allegiance to fear will likely be cries for salvation or perfection—pleas to fix the problem of the heart's suffering. Such prayers are an anesthetic that numbs real feeling—an "anti-aesthetic" that kills beauty. Such prayers define our lives as a problem to be solved, thereby trivializing God as an Oz-like savior who will magically grant our wishes if we promise to be good. It is difficult for us to accept that evolution is not an attempt to fix anything. The human species is not a SWAT team sent by God to clean up a messy universe.

Before we consider what we wish to pray for, it is helpful to first ask, "What is my fundamental intention for this prayer?" To help me escape an unpleasant circumstance (like life itself)? Or to support me in plunging yet deeper into the truth of our circumstance? What would happen if we aligned our Quest with the intention to celebrate, not the tidiness of perfection but the disarray of wholeness—of "whole mess"?

To pray from this place would be a very powerful action,

because then we could say the whole universe is with us. Such prayers do not simply rearrange the furniture in our psychic living rooms; they dissolve the room itself, allowing the potential for rearrangement at a higher level. In dissolving our boundaries, we may find ourselves living in a bigger house, seeing more of ourselves in other people, seeing more of ourselves in the world.

But here's the rub: *We have to be willing to die to get bigger.* Die to our attachment to the relative security of the old living room, as familiar as it may be. Die to the self-identity that carried us this far but that is incapable of taking us farther. Die to our attachment to living in the perfect, unchanging world of our childhood fantasies.

Another important ingredient of a prayerful life is humility. When we choose to live a life of vision we will inevitably make fools of ourselves time and time again. I've entertained the notion of founding what I call the "Flat Face Society." Members would be easily recognized by their uncommonly broad and flat faces— the result of having fallen on them so many times.

Fortunately, perfectionism isn't essential to the Quest. But compassion and forgiveness are—the willingness to learn from our foolishness. Without forgiveness we do not accept our experience and, therefore, cannot learn from it. This is an unnecessarily difficult and lonely path. Here our grandiosity must submit to the powerful realization: "I cannot do this alone. I need to ask for help." Asking for help is an act of surrender. To the uninitiated, surrender equals defeat, pure and simple. But in time, and perhaps also with a good measure of grace, we may come to know surrender as *giving ourselves over to something larger.* To the larger story of ourselves—to the "I" that is "We." Herein lies the power of humility.

However, if our humility lacks clear intention, we may confuse surrender with a refusal to be responsible for our lives. Rather than surrender to the divine imperative toward wholeness that beats in our hearts, we may find ourselves passively waiting for God to step in and save us, fix us, or do unto us in some way. Such passivity is not true surrender. Surrender requires from us our active willingness to die to the small story we've been living so we can be reborn in the larger Story. Hardly a passive act.

So, throughout the Quest we clarify our intention by asking: "What do I need? What do I really want? What is my heart's desire? What do I stand for?" This is an act of will. And to the extent that we discover that will in our hearts, it is God's will as well. Given this perspective, the prayer, "God give me the courage to love," must contain within it the intention to *choose* love. Hidden within "God help me" is the *choice* to be open to receive.

During the Sunrise Ceremony I suggest that we hold the image of ourselves as archers. Imagine yourself on the sunrise knoll. You choose the arrow of intention that you feel best suited to piercing the illusion that separates you from wholeness. You place it in the bow of your heart's desire. Drawing on your bow of desire, you gather the energy required to empower it and set it free. Then, decisively release your will in an act of surrender. Your prayer arrow is in the hands of the Great Mystery now.

What prayers do you seed your day with? What would it be like to begin each day as if you were a co-creator of the world? As if the world awaited your longing to give it direction in its turning?

In the days that follow we will apprentice with the image of the target. For our prayer arrows will now be stalking us, and we must prepare a place in our hearts for their return.

5

THE PATH TO THE INTERIOR

Keep walking, though there's no place to get to.
Don't try to see through the distances.
That's not for human beings. Move within,
but don't move the way fear makes you move.

—RUMI
TRANSLATION BY JOHN MOYNES AND COLEMAN BARKS

Rituals like the Sunrise Ceremony wrap our vulnerability in a supportive and protective container. As the winds of spirit blow through us, smoldering embers of our passion for life may suddenly flare up. We do our best to honor the truth that lives in the heart of each of those embers, even as fear may urge us to recoil from their light and heat.

We each have our own way of making the transition from ritual time and space back to ordinary time and space. Some negotiate the return smoothly and quickly; others need time to find their footing. Those who feel awkward at having exposed their passion for God, love, or truth rush back to the relative security of known role in a known world. When we allow shame in, it attacks our spiritual illumination as ruthlessly as it does our perceived imperfection. Others quietly grieve to feel the permeable boundaries of ritual space give over so soon to the inflexible armor of social posturing. The intimacy shared in sacred space may stand out sharply against the backdrop of secular routine and convention. The door that opened between the worlds

THE PATH TO THE INTERIOR

remains open for some and is forcibly closed by others. Many currents of thought and feeling circulate inside, as we scramble down the knoll and head back to camp.

Talk over breakfast quickly turns toward the journey ahead. Many are eager to pack up and begin the three-mile walk to our interior base camp. Before setting off, however, we will devote careful attention to our bodies. For we will soon be calling on them not only to negotiate unfamiliar wilderness terrain but to do so with more than fifty pounds of food, clothing, and gear on our backs. After cleaning up our breakfast dishes, we gather around the fire pit to explore the attitudes that will enable us to live in this environment with integrity, safety, and passion.

If we injured ourselves on a poorly built city sidewalk, we have the right to sue those we hold responsible for maintaining the walkway. We have structured our world to make it possible to hold others fully responsible for our well-being. Now imagine trying to sue your local park service because you stepped in a hole in the woods and hurt yourself. Or, for that matter, imagine suing the creator for faulty workmanship. Might as well go for the deepest pocket. Civilization often rewards insensibility. But in the wilderness, there are no courts of law that will compensate us for sleepwalking. The wilderness demands we live responsibly. The wilderness gave us our bodies, and its laws and justice live in every cell.

When we walk on a city sidewalk we usually assume the ground will be there to support each foot as it lands. Typically, we modern men locate our center of gravity in our heads. As a result, when walking, we commit our weight to the forward foot before we experientially determine whether the ground is stable enough to support us. Most of the time the ground holds firm. But if the ground surface does not match our assumption, we may trip and fall.

Assumptions are risky in any environment, but in the wilderness even more so. Imagine you're walking along a forest path and you trip across a fallen log. Is your fall caused by the log across your path? Our civilized sensibility may quickly conclude, yes, of course. It might even attempt to solve the injustice by outlawing logs. But there is another part of us—the part that comes from the wilderness—that lives closer to the ground. From its perspective our fall is the result of paying attention to our *ideas* about the way things are rather than the reality at our feet.

The wilderness follows natural law, not human law. Any constitutional right you claim here that is not also a natural right will be matter-of-factly dismissed. The frigid wind would just as soon freeze you solid as it would any other body of water. Fire has as strong an appetite for your flesh as it has for the sinewy limbs of the oak. These laws show no favoritism—nothing personal, mind you—but they cannot be transgressed through arrogant demand or self-pity. Yet, if we learn to meet these laws with humility and acceptance, we may find them more malleable than they otherwise appear.

Our initial twenty-four hours in this camp has confronted each of us with a clear lesson: Whether we accept it or not, the wilderness welcomes us as beginners. And we must learn to walk with beginners' feet, feel with beginners' hearts, and think with beginners' minds. To live at the level of responsibility this forest demands, we must reeducate our body-mind and return to a more primary intelligence than the one we acquired in school. To initiate this return, I remind us of our relationship to what I call our "animal presence."

Inside each of us lives an animal presence that longs to run, fly, swim, leap, wiggle, or squirm in unfenced wild space. It knows the visceral language of creation. It is vividly awake, alert, and responsive. It knows it belongs. We must recover the intelligence we betray each time we distort that tenet of our cultural myth that charges humans with dominion over the earth and all of its creatures. When seen through the lens of fear, the life-affirming responsibility of dominion readily reduces to life-denying domination. At first glance, this misconception promises us a life of privilege and freedom. The problem is, whatever we hope to dominate outside ourselves, we must also subdue within. As a painful consequence most educated modern men live exiled from our native intelligence and our animal nature. Civilization may mask this disability for a time, but in the wilderness it quickly shows its true face. The right-angled thinking and movement that permeates the life of a man imprinted on machine-age ideals shows up as clumsy and accident-prone here. Yet we've lost something far more important than woodsmanship and agility. We've lost our erotic relatedness to the land. We, and all our relations, suffer this loss.

A mature relationship with Eros is fundamental to the recovery of sacred manhood. By Eros I mean the passion for connection that is immanent to the entire universe. By sacred I mean the felt experience, or em-body-ment, of that connection or union. The sacred is not a thing, and therefore, it cannot be found in any particular place. Being no-thing and no-where, it is gained or lost through the aperture of our openness toward life. To experience the enlivening warmth of Eros, a man must come to love the wildness of his physical and emotional body. The body-as-machine relationship that so many of us have adopted is not large enough to hold the charge of this passion. The machine ideal fights against Eros and refuses the sacred. A sacred erotic sensibility has to do with establishing a love relationship with the entire universe *through the body*. As Sam Mackintosh suggests, "Only the man who knows himself as a Son of God would 'have the balls' to do it." On this Quest, this expansive lovemaking is our primary form of worship.

On that note, I ask us to stand and stretch our limbs in preparation for our hike and to stretch our minds by considering this loving attention to our physicality as an act of worship.

That note strikes a dissonant chord in some: "That's not what I came here for. I'm not here to bond with my 'inner lizard' or 'gorilla-self.' I'm here for some higher purpose—initiation into manhood, or something."

I daresay that we cannot live beyond our animal nature by dominating it or by ignoring it; we must learn to marry it. We will not be fully human until we do so. Robert Bly said it well:

> To receive initiation truly means to expand sideways into the glory of oaks, mountains, glaciers, horses, lions, grasses, waterfalls, deer. We need wilderness and extravagance. Whatever shuts a human being away from the waterfall and the tiger will kill him.

It's time now to move into this material. So I call on our animal presence to teach us the ways of moving through the forest as if we had lived here forever. This way of being is exemplified by animals who hunt for prey: They move as if their lives depended on it. A fragment of a poem by Rumi comes to mind. I offer its invitation:

Think that you're gliding out from the face of a cliff
like an eagle. Think you're walking
like a tiger walks by himself in the forest.
You're most handsome when you're after food . . .

And so we move with the invitation to feel the pleasure of our muscles stretching in ways that they haven't for some time. We are invited to feel the sensuality of movement—our claws digging in rich, dark soil; our wings swimming through oceans of limitless sky; our tongues tasting the air; our limbs caressing the ground as the lover, the beloved. We open to our animal presence, to the basic sanity of body and Earth . . . and an old joy returns.

For those who have not befriended their physicality, the route to this joy can be tortuous. Years of repressing the wildness of nature's body have left their marks. Stiff joints rebel against sudden freedom; studied and mechanical movements strain against the primal impulse. One must be willing to die to awkwardness and self-consciousness before being reborn in joy. Our practice here is highly self-revealing. We are challenged to get out from behind the mask of pretending to be an animal and give our bodies over to the animating presence within.

Primal man learns of the world by lending his body to it. The traditional herbalist seeking medicine lends himself to the plant and asks, "Where would you grow inside my body? In the congested, swampy places, in the windy places, in the fiery red blood deltas?" The hunter lends his body to the deer so that when the hunter dances, he looks out through the eyes of the deer, smells the musk that leads him to his mate, the odor that leads to fresh water.

Imagine lending your body to the mountain lion who hunts

inside you. Watch as he bends your knees slightly, lowering your center of gravity closer to the earth. He places each of your paws deliberately on the ground, balanced so that if the ground should give way, the paw is easily drawn back into the center of balance. Only if the ground proves firm does the weight shift slowly forward, the body listening all the time. Expecting nothing, ready for anything, he softens your gaze in a way that brings your environment closer. He melts your mind into every bone, muscle, and tendon in your body—thought gives way to sensation; a hunger brings you into direct and honest contact with the here and now. You are presence incarnated in living flesh. You reclaim your erotic relatedness to the land. And I say again, an old joy returns!

I become the big cat—the Panther. I find the eyes in the soles of my feet. Two hunters stalk me closely on a tiring chase, when I finally leap to a huge fallen tree that bridges the stream. One hunter approaches from the uprooted end, while the other moves to the tree's crown. My instincts come alive, and I instantly know which of these two men carries more fear. With a burst of movement and a bellow of roars, I drive him off. I then turn to find myself face to face with the man at the roots. A large man with hairy chest and powerful muscles, imaginary spear raised to menace me. I move backward step by step on my perilous perch, never taking my eyes off my antagonist. The panther now moves toward the man, challenging his resolve—and my own courage. He retreats and we move with eyes locked until we lock hands and arms as well, testing each other's strength. A snarling dance ensues. I feel a great delight in meeting the strength of this feral other and the joy of being met by him. Suddenly a switch is thrown, and we break into broad grins that rise from the earth through the soles of our feet and out through our faces—respect for each other's prowess. The world stops for a moment as we meet in a robust hug, sweat and odors mixing.

I become the Heron. My long, stalklike legs inherit the patient stance of waiting in still waters. I am the shore bird. The one who wades in the boundary between certainties. I know earth, I know water. With the lightning strike of my snakelike neck, I know fire. The tips of my

*fingers touch the air with fine sensitivity, and an old desire awakens
me into flight. Long wing-feathers caress the air, remembering the
grace that comes from stillness.*

*The Dance is inside the Heron,
but the Heron does not look for it
The Heron Dances.*

After some time of this animated play we do indeed, as Rumi pre-
dicted, become quite handsome. I then direct the group to put on
their backpacks while remaining in their primal bodies. I watch
closely to see how each man relates to this task. One man wrestles
his pack to his shoulders with a resigned expression. His animal
presence has just yielded to civilized compliance. He tells us later
that, yes, all it took was an authority figure giving him a command and he was back in school practicing his good behavior.
There isn't a free animal I know of that would greet such a burden politely. No, the natural first response is likely going to be
rebellion—stomping, snorting, hissing, kicking, bellowing—regis-
tering disapproval in no uncertain terms. Men are taught not to
complain but to grin and bear it: Never cry out in pain, never ask
for help. The most common way to comply with these doctrines is
to stop feeling, go numb, be nice. The sad thing is that much of
the beauty of a man is lost in the process.

>>   <<

The journey we are about to take will lead us into the heart of this
forest wilderness. On another level, each step taken is a step
deeper into our inner landscape. In native cultures, places of great
power, such as Vision Quest sites, are said to lie at the center of
the world. That is our destination.

At the start of the trail that will take us to our base camp, we
assemble for one last moment of orientation. This trailhead is the
place where wilderness and civilization meet. We pause a
moment to be present to these two parts of ourselves. An occasional passing car, the radio music drifting from a campsite across

the road, call one side of us to the familiar: "You could be enjoy-ing a picnic at the beach right now. It's not too late to turn back." The other side is called by unknown woods and distant moun-tains. We pause to stand in the midst of the tension between these two.

I take a moment to inwardly declare my intentions for this journey before setting off. As I do, a squadron of monarch butterflies flits past, dipping their wings in salute to this adventure. The man ahead of me silently points—there, at the very edge of the forest, an immense fat toad squats on a rock. Like a bored ticket taker at an amusement park, he scrutinizes each of us as we walk by. Our guides told us that our expectations for the Quest are our entry tickets. We must surrender those tickets before we can ride. If we cling to them we'll just stay on the known shore and miss the boat. I give the toad my ticket, in the form of a wink and a smile, and he silently witnesses my passing.

I experience an unexpected and deep camaraderie with the other men as we walk in silence. I imagine what it must have been like to be a group of hunters in times past—when the practice of silence was not just a contemplative exercise but a requisite for survival. I am alive in my body in a way I haven't been since I was a kid. As I walk I feel the texture of light and shadow, sounds have smells, smells seem to emit sounds, the whole forest seems intelligent somehow. The old cate-gories are breaking down. Perhaps this awareness is what people refer to as "body-mind." Whatever it is called, I want to live this way.

About a third of the way to our destination our trail crosses the river. Water surges over and around granite boulders, polishing them smooth and shiny. On the physical level, this crossing sim-ply poses a challenge to our rock-hopping abilities. On the spiri-tual level, though, the challenge runs far deeper. For those gifted with stamina and balance, this is not the time or place on the Quest where they will be stretched or challenged. Unless, of course, they see this as a chance to flaunt their prowess, strength, and independence. To be sure, any hubris demonstrated in this crossing is an invitation to Coyote, the Trickster, to bring his slippery medicine to the next one. For others, though, this crossing brings up deep insecurities. Fear swarms to these men like bees drawn to honey. In an instant, the need to ask for help, once a potential source of dread and shame, becomes an appealing alternative. Quite often those who have trouble making the crossing experience a sense of humiliation. They are the lucky ones. I would that we could all be so fortunate as to have the overinflated balloon of the ego popped so soon in the journey.

Ritual humiliation is a common and valuable part of any rite of passage. It strips off the idealized mask that keeps the truth of our totality hidden in shadow. In the respectful light of sacred space, humiliation may be nurtured into humility. Once possessed of humility, we have a chance to step into the shadow and reclaim those exiled aspects of our native humanness that would serve us well on the journey. The Fool is one such aspect. Remember, in the Grail legend it was Parsifal, the "Innocent Fool," not the knights in brilliant armor, who alone could claim the medicine that healed the wounds of the Fisher King. On a Quest for wholeness, there are many ordeals, or crossings, that call for the wisdom of humility. To be honest, if on this hike we didn't come to a natural point of challenge like this crossing, I'd be obliged to create one.

In order to reach the center we have to rock-hop across a stream. Not an easy task even without packs. No problem for me, think I—until in mid-step I tilt slightly. My pack suddenly shifts to one side. And I swear a rock reaches out and pulls me down. I feel a stabbing pain. My shin is bleeding and my pride is fractured. In this moment the river cries out, "Are you sure you want to continue?" I have been chewed up and spit out at the first crossing.

I am nervous and my shoulders are killing me, but I decide that I have to stop this neurotic shit and be a "real" man. If the other guys can ford a stream, so can I! Cautiously, I jump to the first rock. Water splashing at my feet, I hold my tiny bit of ground. I jump to the next rock and I don't slip. One rock to go. I leap in the air, thousands of pounds on my back. In that brief moment I'm a winner—schmuck no more—I can ford a stream! And then I land. Splat! Face down on a large flat rock, pinned down by the weight of my pack. Like a turtle with a smashed shell, I lay totally immobile. But where is the humiliation? I believe this act would fully qualify me for admission into Joseph's Flat Face Society. I feel calm, even dignified, in accepting my predicament. For the first time on the trip, I have surrendered. The mocking voices inside fall silent.

The crossing looks easy until I step up on the first rock and become a bit disoriented looking into the rushing water. My mind is telling me that the trail continues on the far shore. The fact is, the river now is the trail. Unless I can soon master the art of astral projection, this top-heavy pack is depending on me to get it across this stream. I ask myself: What animal would be best suited to negotiate this terrain? "Panther" leaps to mind. I take a slow, deep breath and give over to that fine animal. He brings my center of gravity closer to the earth, and my gaze from the moving water to the still rocks. I'll never forget this feeling of embodied grace that carries me safely to the far shore.

The path continues now away from the river, through open stands of elegant white birch, then through tighter corridors of spruce and fir, past beaver meadows that open the forest canopy to a spacious sky, and through wet ravines touched by only a hint of sunlight. Our walk becomes our spiritual practice, the art of making ourselves available to the very landscape that is availing itself to us.

The path leads us past a thundering waterfall. Here is where most of the casual hikers to this area stop, have their picnic, turn around, and return home. Just beyond the waterfall we come to a large, rough-edged boulder standing resolutely beside the trail. The path narrows at this point, forcing us to turn our bodies slightly to pass. We stop here and wait for the group to gather.

This boulder is a landmark. Like most of the other granite sentinels in this forest, this rock is over a billion years old, placed here by a massive Pleistocene glacier perhaps a million years ago. Imagine being in one place, in one body for that long! Yet this rock won't be found on any of the geological maps of the area. It's too common to be of interest to the geologist. However, it appears prominently on one map—the map that guides our entry into mythological time and space. This boulder we know as Guardian Rock, and it marks the entranceway to the grounds of the temple at the mythological center of our world. When we enter these grounds, we come to the place where Mystery lives magnified. That Mystery, accessed by our willingness to wonder, draws closer to the foreground of our awareness.

The entranceways to many cathedrals and temples are guarded by lions, gargoyles, or other fierce beasts. These custodians serve more than merely a decorative purpose. They wake us from the slumber of habit and certainty, to arouse in us the alert, unassuming perception of both the hunter and the hunted. From this point on, as we pass beyond Guardian Rock, we will remember that we are being watched by all the Tree People, the Rock People, the Animal People, and by those disowned parts of ourselves— angels and demons—that lurk in our shadows waiting to be seen and welcomed home. Each step, every thought, every breath will be noticed. Our presence radiates outward from this place. We will now be known by the relationships we are willing to enter into here.

In the stillness and silence surrounding Guardian Rock, I ask us to recall the intentions we released at sunrise. We feel within our hearts what these intentions have set in motion; slight shifts, turnings, returnings. Then abruptly, out of nowhere, a breeze snakes through the tops of the aspens, shaking their leaves with a sizzling sound that sends eerie sensations up the spine. It remains for just a few seconds before its chilling touch and haunting sound disappear once again into the silence. That breeze, the breath of something far greater than what our hearing could ever follow, calls us to a deeper listening. It calls us beyond our deciphered world to stand, once upon a time, within the Mystery of the greater existence that surrounds us all. The world stops for a moment. Suddenly disarmed, we look up into each other's eyes— the eyes of men momentarily unprotected by the illusion of permanence, men who know they will die. Some of these eyes flicker briefly with the spark of liberation that comes from accepting one's fate. But these sparks find little receptive tinder and soon go out. Not one of us moves during this suspended time, until the breeze gives way to the sound of our own breathing. The path, of course, waits patiently, giving us ground for whatever turnings the mind must make to adjust to such presence.

The trail beyond this threshold guardian belongs more to the labyrinth of the forest than to the marching intent of man. In the shadows lurk Pan and his satyrs; in secret clearings, the dancing nymphs. Wild Man and Wild Woman dwell here, offering boons to those who would embrace them as kin and terrors to those who reject them as Other. The path dips in and out of sight, dropping hints and stringing clues that draw us deeper into its folds. The straight and narrow forest path perceived by the mind begins to yield to the paradoxical contours of the path with heart. The eyes must turn inward as well as outward to remain true to this path. Intuition must partner reason. There are times when the path is known by the faint hollow sound of feet striking packed earth; each step off course is marked by a note out of tune. There are times when the path is known by a felt sense that contradicts reason. Reason alone, we quickly learn, is not comfortably at home in the ebbs and flows of forest life.

Obstacles the path formerly avoided with ease now seem to be more eagerly its intent. With our packs testing the limits of our endurance, we are led to scramble over fallen trees, through the gauntlet of overgrown brush, across mosquito-infested mud holes. And, in turn, through sweet-scented glades of ferns floating like green mist about our feet, past serene vistas that are felt to be both the source and resting place of all sound, all movement. We are led through moments of tenderness, moments of pain, moments of intimacy and rage. We are led to our likes and dislikes, to our clinging and to our aversion, to our yes to life, and to our no to life. And still, the path continues. . . .

As we hike on I get a feeling I'm being watched. The brook notes our presence and rushes to babble the news downstream—"The Two-Leggeds are here!" Leaves on the trees appear to have faces with eyes. I begin to sense the Mean Spirit is here, too, watching me. I thump a tree trunk with my walking stick. Are you hiding in there? Rock,

mushroom, ferns, ground—I prod them all. I'll find you, Mean
Spirit. I become the hunter—sharp, alert, watching the forest as the
forest watches me.

The first half of the journey is surprisingly easy for me. I enjoy helping the other men cross the stream. I even take on part of another's
load at the last rest stop after it becomes clear he isn't going to make
it without help. My mood is like golden sunshine. "I am one hap-
penin' Quester," I think to myself. That is, until we come to a muddy
area by a small stream. One misplaced foot and I am up to my shins
in thick, cold mud. I yank my foot out as fast as I can, hoping no one
sees what just happened. Thuuuuuuck!—out comes my foot, but
there's no longer a boot attached to it. I deftly put my foot down to
regain my balance. This time I'm up to my knee in the stuff. "Fuck
this!" I mutter to myself. Funny how fast golden sunshine can turn
to shit. I thought I'd be able to get through this experience without
getting wet or dirty. If I had been honest at the Sunrise Ceremony, I
would have prayed, "God, get me through this Quest, through life,
without getting dirty or uncomfortable." It's as if some part of my
nature stopped me at the mud hole and said, "This is as far as your
golden-boy image can take you—better get used to this stuff."

I hear drums up ahead. I round the bend and there is Joseph, with a
sixty-pound pack on his back, pounding on stumps of dead trees like a
fucking idiot. Two others have joined his little band. I listen politely
to this concert, sweating and panting and exhausted, hoping we can
press on. But he doesn't stop! I have no alternative but to pick up two
sticks and find a stump of my own. I add my rhythm to the others. As
I play I completely forget about the pain in my back, legs, arms, ass,
sides, and shin (still bleeding from my altercation with the river
rock). Eventually, the rest of our group joins in. Everything suddenly
has meaning—fourteen men with heavy packs all releasing the
rhythms from the stumps and letting out primeval screams. The Wild
Man is loose, and at play.

Resting by the side of the trail, we all fall silent. I am caught up in
the natural beauty of this place. Not the kind of beauty that would

ever find its way to an artist's canvas or photographer's film. It's far too commonplace for that sort of recognition. There's just something soothing about being in a place where everything seems at ease—the rocks, the trees, the wind. How my soul hungers for this simple nourishment! I sit suspended in time, with a peacefulness I remember feeling as a youngster in my secret place in the woods behind our house, in the days before I developed an adversarial relationship to my body and the Earth. As soon as we passed the Guardian Rock I felt the world drop away. As I sit here now, I wonder out loud, "Where are we!?"

The guy next to me says, "Here and now."

A good enough answer; I let it go at that.

Not much farther now. We pass a spot where the river widens. Two small islands rise from the stream like the backs of surfaced whales. In places the water collects in pools, beckoning us to merge with their cool sweet wetness. Through the trees we now glimpse a campsite clearing nestled in a bend of the river.

Our arrival in camp triggers a range of feelings. There's the bittersweet quality of experiencing the completion of the many days of preparation it took to get here. Physical separation from our known world is now clearly gained, setting the stage for our work to free our minds and spirits as well. But speculation on such things is short-lived as our collective animal body, eternally resting in the immediate, takes over. We slough off our pack loads to the ground with grunts, groans, and sighs of relief.

I call us together formally to introduce ourselves to this place. In making a temporary home here we speak our intention to be in right relation with the primary residents of this forest community. Setting up camp becomes an ongoing dialogue with place in which we first listen, then act, and continue to listen to the response to our actions. "Listen, then act"—the primary attitude of the Beauty Way.

Before sending the men off to find their personal tent sites I introduce them to our communal areas. We're standing now in the area we will know as the dance ground: a packed earth clearing about twenty-five feet in diameter. To the east is another small clearing that serves as our council circle. We will shortly cover this area with tarps to provide a sitting space sheltered from wind and rain. Fifteen yards south of the dance ground sits the blackened rock fireplace hearth circled by well-worn sitting logs: our camp kitchen. Just beyond, down a short bank, lies the river. It courses slowly from the west and curves around our site, collecting in a couple of bathing pools in front of us before moving on. Dance ground, council ground, kitchen, river—enough orientation for now. The men are soon off to find sites for their tents.

For me, this moment of solitude comes as a welcome relief from the intensity of our preparations and interactions thus far. I sit, resting my back against a large old hemlock that arches over the dance ground. My gaze rests on the heart of this circle of ground, like the surface of an immense black drum, pounded flat and bare by the feet of many dancers. This resonant ground has witnessed many stories over the years, and it remembers them all. Such is the nature of ground. It holds all events outside of history, outside of past and future, within the time that is always now. I take a long, deep breath and step outside of time. One of these memories then rises, in a slow spiral, to the surface. . . .

We have just arrived at our Quest base camp. Recent rains have washed the area clean. Plant debris, animal and insect tracks, and myriad other signs of forest activity are unusually absent. The smooth earth dance ground looks particularly untouched and available to record the slightest traces of our presence here. This clean-swept ground is an icon of awareness, pure and without the clutter of content—except, that is, for one object resting in the southern quadrant. A man points to it. "Mouse?" he whispers. Sure enough, a dead mouse, its fur untouched by elements or predator, no tracks lead to its resting place, as if it had materialized out of thin air. A few of the men instantly converge on the spot to clear the ground of its presence. But I instinctively raise protective arms: "Wait, not yet."

For me the air crackles with anticipation, the way it does before lightning strikes. I've come to recognize this sign in my psychic atmosphere as a prelude to the two worlds opening to each other.

I am put on notice, as the Yaqui sorcerer Don Juan instructs, to "make every act count."

I cordon off the mouse with a wreath of sticks and ask that we live with the sacrifice of this small one, as is, for a full day. I offer that we *live* whatever questions this event brings up—that we allow this being into our hearts and follow where it leads.

The man who first spotted the mouse responds immediately:

From the moment we first honored the final resting place of Mouse, tender places in my psyche were being nudged into awareness.

When my brother was seven years old, he was crushed by the rear wheel of my grandfather's car while I stood by helpless and screaming. The next time I saw Billy he lay in a casket, wearing a white suit and a maroon bow tie. It all happened too fast; I had never been able to catch up with the feelings stirred by this event. They lay in an impenetrable clump within my chest. Perhaps now, after more than forty years . . . ? And my mother, she had died the year before this Quest. I did not attend her funeral.

I become absorbed by the idea of building a funeral pyre for this creature—in outer world terms an insignificant, often feared, at the very least ignored . . . mouse. I saw in such a ceremony the chance to face the inadequate burials I had given my brother many years before and, more recently, my mother.

The other men accepted my proposal to bury the mouse with blossoms of enthusiasm. Each spoke of a tragic loss that had been left insufficiently mourned. We spoke of father, brother, mother, sister, friend, lover; all lost. And of the feelings we buried, alongside the dead, inside ourselves.

And so, after we had built our Medicine Wheel, we conducted a funeral for the tiny-footed one. Amid lighted candles and simple solemnity the hole was dug at the southern gate of the Wheel. We gingerly cradled the mouse in a birch-bark sarcophagus and lowered this tiny being into the soil. Through a teary mist I saw men place rings, gold chains, and other precious items in the hole. I, too, offered my own tokens of remembrance. The hole was then filled and patted to smoothness by many male hands in gentle and powerful gestures of affection.

As I knelt there, a surge of emotion pumped its way through my mind and into my body. I rose and moved toward the dance ground.

*Standing near the center I felt like an oil rig that shakes and quivers
with the surge of its first gush. Thus my emotions rose and burst out in
a primal proclamation of feelings too long buried, feelings that spoke of
everything I had ever lost, but never mourned.*

*The circle of men formed quickly around me. Within this crucible of
protection I danced, roaring out my pain, beating the ground with my
feet and my fists. Forty-plus years of pent-up anguish, spiced with tears
that now salted Mother Earth's receptive soil.*

Many other men dance and wail in that cradle before the winds of
healing spirit have run their course. The man who spotted the
dying creature emerges with the medicine name Musing Mouse, a
calling he says will lead him from a posture of embittered refusal to
the beginnings of a searching relationship with the mystery of deep
loss. His courage in allowing himself to be defeated by the powerful forces of grief and rage opens the way for others to follow, in
their own way. What he danced for himself, he danced for all of us.

The ground has said so.

>>   <<

Across the stream a woodpecker hammers out a staccato call.
Acrobatic chickadees flit among the hemlock boughs, wresting
seeds from the small cones. High-spirited chipmunks have
already noticed our presence and scurry across the ground picking up stray nuts inadvertently dropped from a lunch bag. Late
afternoon, the forest comes alive with the foraging activity of animals feeding before darkness. Our individual camps established,
we too make our way through the woods gathering fuel for our
cooking fire and water for our pots. We select the grains and vegetables for our evening meal.

After dinner, while our bodies digest our food, we hold council
by candlelight to digest the events of the day. A full day it has
been, from the Sunrise Ceremony to our procession into this place
and the first efforts to establish a home in that place where the
two worlds touch.

6

WHAT THE GROUND KNOWS

When we get out of the glass bottles of our ego,
and when we escape like squirrels turning in the
   cages of our personality
and get into the forests again,
we shall shiver with cold and fright
but things will happen to us
so that we don't know ourselves.

Cool, unlying life will rush in,
and passion will make our bodies taut with power,
we shall stamp our feet with new power
and old things will fall down,
we shall laugh, and institutions will curl up like
   burnt paper.

—D. H. LAWRENCE

The camp is now at rest, each man swaddled in the cocoonlike
containment of his tent and sleeping bag. Beneath the veil of
night, the soul substance stirs in slow, leavening, movement.
Unclaimed events of the day wander about the fluid and ambigu-
ous landscape of the unconscious. Each one will be given night
vision according to ways of wholeness—the ways that bring us
back into relation with that which we have discarded, that which
we fear to celebrate as our own.

Let us enter this dreamtime and pay a visit on some of the
voices and faces we encounter along the night trail. Here we meet

others of those guides and helpers who appear once we accept the call to quest. Whether human or nonhuman, these figures bring gifts of perception uncommon to the daylight world. And if they speak, they do so in the revelatory language of dream: the language of the night council. . . .

> *I'm scurrying around collecting my clothing and equipment for this Quest and I run into an eccentric old man. He looks like a gypsy used-car salesman. He's got a trunkful of all sorts of gadgets. He pulls out a pair of glasses and says "I think these will fit you." I put them on. It's hard to see through them because I'm looking through a filmy image of my own face reflected in the glass. I see my own face mirrored in everything I view. I ask the old man if they do this for everybody. He shrugs and doesn't answer.*

Our guides may call on us to make sacrifices along the way. We may be asked to surrender cherished beliefs, pride, or self-will to hear the call of the heart.

> *Walking alongside a river, I come on a hunter. He has just killed a large hart with a huge set of antlers. I am disturbed as he cuts off the deer's head and throws it into the river. With a mixture of pride and contempt I tell him that his act is not "environmentally appropriate" and prepare myself for either an apology or a fight. Instead, his eyes twinkle with a knowing and a compassion that stops me in my tracks. Putting a hand on my shoulder he says simply, "It's all right." His manner communicates a deep wisdom, compared with which my environmental do-gooding feels superficial and pale. I'm convinced he sees a deeper truth that I cannot. Before we part he gives me two strips of dried venison from the buck and suggests I share it with my people.*

Our guides may lead us to one of the many disciplines of creative play—arts that are essential to the soul's journey.

> *I'm looking for my grandfather's house, riding a bicycle on a road that I vaguely remember from childhood, searching for memories and clues to get me there. I feel deeply homesick and frustrated, as my*

attempts to figure out the route are in vain. I then meet a mysterious woman, quietly attractive, who doesn't say much. I ask her if she knows the way to my grandfather's house. She nods yes, and we ride together. The path leads abruptly to a huge wooden door. She pulls out a key and opens the door. I'm expecting to see the path continue on the other side. Instead I'm surprised to find a recording studio full of musical instruments from all over the world. The woman motions to me to take a seat behind a set of African drums. I hesitate. "Don't think about it," she says, "just play."

Quite often, our guides lead us right into the trouble we try our best to avoid in the daylight world—right into our shadow world. Such trouble, as we have already noted, is cause for celebration on a quest.

I am out walking my dog on a leash. Suddenly, he sees an animal off in the distance and lunges for it. He tugs hard enough to break my grasp and I run after him yelling for him to stop. He pays me no mind and I chase him into a ghettolike area. The streets are lined with despicable-looking characters. I'm terrified as I pass through this gauntlet of dark figures.

In the dreamworld, wholeness is met through the dance of opposites. Wholeness is found in paradox and conflict and sacred doubleness. The very act of following one's bliss, or embodying one's light, calls its opposite into play.

I am flying with more ease and pleasure than ever before. I spread my arms and am able to do impressive-looking flips and turns and somersaults with total control and no fear. I'm thinking to myself, "Wow, I've finally made it." Then I see some of my family members on the ground. There's a demonic look in their eyes and they begin mocking me. They stretch out their arms and pull me to the ground. My mood crashes. I feel heavy, bitter, and confused.

Those jeering family members on the ground may seem like demons, yet might they be the agents of wholeness as well? Without the earthy medicine of humility, the quest for vision may only serve to further inflate our grandiosity and quicken our betrayal. The best medicine may be that which brings us back to the ground as soon as possible.

> *I am in a Red Cross first aid class. On the floor is one of those mannequins used for CPR practice. I put my ear to its chest pretending to check for a heartbeat like you're supposed to, and I freak out—the thing actually has a heartbeat. Just then the mannequin changes into a corpse of a man, but it's alive—an alive corpse! The heartbeat starts to echo louder and louder . . . ba-boom . . . ba-boom . . . ba-boom . . .*
>
> *Next thing I know I'm sitting bolt upright in my sleeping bag. The morning wakeup drum is beating right outside my tent.*

The heartbeat of the wakeup drum calls us through the veil of dreamworld into the dawning day. For these dreamers, wisps of the veil still cling to the senses. We give time to make the transition slowly, to savor the fading scent of the night, even as the fresh morning air beckons us outward.

What a delight it is to body and soul to awaken streamside each morning, to drink and bathe in water that is fresh and wild and singing. One man sits on a water-worn boulder on the edge of a rippling shallows. His thoughts turn to the water that spills from his city tap. How stale and depressed it seems compared with this feisty current. Can water be "depressed," he wonders. Corralled in reservoirs and forced through a huge network of pipes, perhaps it does lose its vitality. Or is he seeing his own depleted life force reflected in his imaginings about his water? His vitality channeled through the flow charts of his corporate-ruled world, his boss's hand on the spigot? Perhaps it is his own heart that grants song to this river; the same heart that dies in submission to the corporate fathers? This morning's visit to the river has quickly turned into an ordeal of self-confrontation.

He moves his fingers lightly along the water's surface, as if stroking the fur of a wild creature. His mind becomes immersed in the hypnotic currents of liquid and light.

"I want my song back," he tells the river.

Reason relaxes its hold on the familiar and a new voice is born from within: the spirit-voice, the voice that leads but never demands, the voice that partners and completes reason.

"Then sing," it echoes off the river's depths. "Let my song carry you into your own."

And so he lends his voice to the river. The river gives it back. Back and forth, their intimate and mournful improvisation builds and recedes and comes again. The song floats downstream where two men tend a smoky fire.

"Sounds like someone's in love," says one.

"Yeah, he's in pretty deep," the other replies.

The piercing cry of a steer-horn trumpet cuts through the forest and echoes off nearby hills. It calls the men to take leave of their private camps and gather on the dance ground for our morning service. We will greet each day together in meditation, poetry, prayer, and movement before setting ourselves to the many tasks before us.

Our liturgy this morning begins with body prayer. We bring a reverent attention to the life force as it moves through that part of the Earth we call "my body." This practice is yet more primal than the movement we discovered in our animal presence work. We're stalking a movement here that follows no image and seeks no goal. We gather to celebrate the basic fact of our aliveness.

To begin, stand still and simply witness the movement inherent in being alive. And once you've contacted that primary movement, let it grow of its own accord. Just say yes to it and let it inhabit your body. Remember, you're a witness, not an actor.

A simple instruction, but nearly impossible for most of us to fulfill. Most of us still suffer from overeducated bodies—bodies that have learned to fear their own nature.

Let the body find its own stretches ... no, not the ones you learned so dutifully in physical education class. Given respect, the body will invent its own out of the erotic longing of the moment. Go to the edges of those places of tension and linger there for a moment. There's no rush; this movement is designed to get you now-here. We were taught to be afraid of those places of conflict and tension. Fear would counsel us to either push through conflict, or back away from it. Try entering the sensation there. Notice how the sensation moves and changes. Just follow it with curiosity. Feel the dance of opposites: pleasure touched with a bit of pain, pain touched with pleasure. Visit whatever places in your body's vast wilderness that long to be renewed with fresh air, with fresh blood, with fresh acceptance. Feel the mind melting deeper and deeper into every cell of the body. You are reeducating your nervous system to be fluent with creation. Go as far in love as you are able now, in love with the life force as it flows through the body, twisting, turning, swimming, prowling, snaking, expanding, contracting, always, always moving. "This is the state of heaven," proclaimed D. H. Lawrence. "And it is the state of a flower, a cobra, a jenny-wren in spring, a man when he knows himself royal and crowned with the sun, with his feet gripping the core of the earth."

Let this movement be our prayer; let our discovery of the sensory currents within this great wilderness body be our blessing. And within the fertile soil of this movement, let us drop the seeds of our intentions for this day.

Having stirred the vitality of the receptive soul substance, with what then will you seed it? To what will you consecrate this day? What matters to you, here and now?

The man, who earlier found renewal in the river's song, steps forth. He asks for a Naming Circle.

This is a simple ritual acknowledgment that we extend to anyone who wishes to explore his identity through a new name. The name may come as a gift of dream vision, from a meaningful encounter in the daylit world, or from a fellow traveler. Or it may come from the quiet whisper of the spirit-voice, as it has for this man. We understand these offerings to be parts of ourselves returning home. Gifts of spirit are generously given, but unless we claim them they are lost on us.

"Early this morning I was called to the river," the man before us announces. "I saw a broken heart. The river sang through the opening. I heard my own voice in the song."

"Who comes to us now," the circle questions.
"Sings Through Broken Heart."
Three times, we reflect what he has claimed:

> "Welcome, Sings Through Broken Heart."
> "Welcome, Sings Through Broken Heart."
> "Welcome, Sings Through Broken Heart."

We now walk with one among us who reminds us of our own brokenness, our own song, each time we call his name.

Our morning service complete, we break the night's fast with a hearty whole-grain cereal, nourishing and simple. Freeze-dried foods would be much easier to carry and store and would be less attractive to the tastes of marauding molds and foraging animals. But if the rest of life is not in competition for our food, what good will it do us?

We devote talk around breakfast to telling our night stories. Our practice here, again, is to enter the mythological truth of these events. For starters, we share them as present-time experiences. Because they are birthed from an area of consciousness that knows nothing of past, or future, we will stay as close to the source as possible. There is an energetic shift in both teller and listener when instead of reporting, "Last night I had a dream that a bear was chasing me ...," the dreamer declares, "I am being chased by a bear now!" Also, we invite the dream to live alongside us with no comment or analysis from the community. If the dreamer wishes some reflection, then he will ask for that, but we refrain from interpreting these untamed reflections of the soul in terms of personal psychological dynamics. We don't want to solve these mysteries, we want to stalk them and let them lead us into an *experience* of their meaning. Dreams are wild; caging them in a cramped belief system drains their vitality. So we set them free and feed them with our attention.

The feeding finished, we break to clean house. The food bags are hung, pots and dishes washed, and leftover food burned in the fire. A man who has taken the name Japa sweeps the dance ground with a broom he has fashioned from the fronds of a fallen hemlock. He then gathers white ash from the fireplace and carefully sprinkles the powder on the ground in delicate patterns. A beautiful and fragile mandala blossoms on the earth. We dub Japa our Commissioner of Free-Hearted Acts of Beauty. Every thriving community needs one.

We secure tents and packs against sudden wind or rain. Latrine sites are visited and cared for. Eating, shitting, cleaning, sweeping: These practical chores help to ground us. Yes, while questing is about opening to vistas beyond our known reality, it is equally important to stay in good relation to the home ground. As a dear teacher of mine, Sun Bear, was fond of saying, "If your philosophy doesn't grow corn, what good is it?"

>>   <<

The trail that has led us to this place soon disappears beyond our camp's edge. We can no longer follow the path of those who have come before us. We have ventured out, well beyond the borders of familiar time and space, to this place on the edge. The spirit that led us here rests now. Or, rather, that spirit is reborn as the desire to find ourselves at home here. Yet how can the questing spirit, which by its nature seeks new ground, keep itself alive and vital at home? What paths will we walk here, in this camp, as we follow our instinct to abide in this place?

The mind serves us well in formulating such questions. However, it is not well designed for living them. Form must mate with energy, with heart's desire, if our questions are to have any potency at all. Our questions must be dropped like seed onto fertile ground, if we expect them to grow into revelation that will truly nourish us. Answers that spring solely from the mind are like food grown in poor soil. They temporarily fill our emptiness, but lack the vitality to truly sustain us. It is not enough to just ask the question. *We must make ourselves the living soil in which the question germinates.* Our bodies must become the breeding ground for new vision.

And so, I call us together, not just to think about these questions, but to follow thinking to the end of its trail . . . and take one more step. As I leap from the edge I remember the dreamtime woman's counsel: "Don't think—just play."

I call us to the dance.

Slowly we walk the perimeter of the dance ground. The boundary of this outer circle is the container that will focus, concentrate, and respectfully hold all that is danced within. It is the container of sacred space.

As we walk, I remind us of the importance of this preparation. Any initiation process dedicated to transformation—to the ongoing experience of death and rebirth—requires a vessel of sacred space. Such a container protects the initiate from outside forces that may not respect the vulnerability of the process occurring within. And it protects the initiate from inner reaction, from those parts of him that become frightened by the healing tremors of rebirth.

For a caterpillar to surrender safely to the dissolving of its known form, it needs a chrysalis strong enough to carry the process through to completion. Our mother's womb served as chrysalis for our physical birth, but for our spiritual rebirthings we must create a second womb ourselves. Whenever a community of people move, breathe, and pray in synchronized fashion toward a common goal, we create empowered space. The individual who steps forward from the group circle to dance in response to the calling of his heart will feel the collective heat of our passion for truth, a heat that quickens the transformational process. But a man must never forget that these community circles are nothing without the sacred intent he holds for himself.

We walk our circle long enough to allow the spirit of these teachings to take up residence in our bodies, to be warmed by blood and scented with sweat. When the moment is right I pick up a small frame drum and add a heartbeat to our movement. The drumbeat livens our step. Our walking shifts, almost imperceptibly, into dance.

Sunwise this circle turns and turns. Through the drum, through synchronized movement we tap into a source of energy that is vital and unpredictable, an energy that unmasks pretense. When we move in this way we unleash the forces of heaven and hell, inviting them to dance on common ground. What will emerge this time, I wonder? We keep on dancing.

The energy rises. The drum now emphasizes the downbeat: *BOOM–bum, BOOM–bum, BOOM–bum, BOOM–bum* . . . and the body responds. One man steps forward and thrusts an imaginary spear into the ground in cadence with each downbeat. "This is to awaken this dance ground to our presence; sometimes yielding, sometimes penetrating," he shouts. Others join in. The thrusting movement grows in intensity. Some faces reveal great delight in this gesture. Others are noticeably in conflict. For them, the urge to withdraw is strong, but the dance keeps them engaged.

I encourage us all to "stalk" the one dancing in the center. That is, find him inside your own body like the native hunter who lends his body-mind to the deer to know the deer. Let your *experience* tell you what is real.

Soon someone else propels himself to the center. Caught in the web of conflict, another man watches the frenzy of this man's dance:

> *Dirt sensuously smeared on his face and bare chest, this gnomelike man fervently slaps the earth with his bare feet and wildly spins round and round. He steps outside the circle briefly, only to reappear in a flash, fully naked. Now he slams his body onto the ground and savagely rolls back and forth. An electric shock from somewhere touches him, and he screams and jerks his body, then continues fiercely rolling in the dry soil, as if fucking the Earth. The men become wilder and wilder, dancing and whooping in full abandon. Cynically, I hold back, criticizing and judging this seemingly manipulated, high-intensity, imitation primitive ritual.*
>
> *But, a part of me whispers, but what if it is real?*
>
> —*TRUE HEART*

I hear that whisper—it runs through my mind as well. But now is not the time for philosophical discussion. We need a more primal way to discover what is true here.

As we continue to circle, I sense other energies present that may be waiting formal invitation:

There's a part of us that says yes to life, and a part of us that says no to life. Let's hear from both sides. First the "No Dance," the dance of refusal, the dance that thrives off of resentment. Are you willing to let that part of yourself be seen by this forest, by these men, and . . .

"Fuck you," a man named Fire-Heart shouts as he leaps from across the circle and thrusts himself fiercely in my face. He calls me into the center. I begin to question if this was such a good idea. This is not exactly what I had in mind. But, he's giving me a lot here, and the group container is holding us well, so we continue our dance.

"Be nice," I offer, stoking the fire a bit.

"No!" he screams. His gestures express a furious power though his eyes reflect a great deal of pain.

Suddenly, there are two other men in my face as well, nostrils flaring, eyes like burning coals. The circle around us now dances in place, chanting "No. No. No." with the drumbeat. The ground shakes with each collective step. It's no longer just the four of us inside that circle. Every unreconciled figure of authority from our histories is there as well: Father, Mother, God. And whomever and whatever else we continue to hold accountable for our lives.

Fire-Heart flings himself to the ground, screaming at the imagined presence of his father. He beats his fists against the Earth, as if to exact justice for the pain and humiliation he suffered by his father's hand. He then turns the sword on himself, soundly beating his thighs and chest. It's not a pretty dance, but there is a powerful raw vitality in it. It is beautiful because it is alive and honest.

We witness, too, the dance of another who draws a clear circle on the ground around himself. He patrols its border with eyes that glare defiantly, and arms tightly folded over his chest. His posture defends him against any truth or vision that threatens to touch his heart. He refuses anything he cannot control.

We move for some time with the energy of *no*. Like a forest fire it flares at times, smokes and nearly goes out, then flares up

THE HOLY LONGING

again. Revealed here is not only the expression of each man's struggle against life but the strength of our ritual container as well. On some level, each one who steps to the center questions: Am I safe here? Will the group container still hold when I rage? Or, out of fear, will it break apart or turn against me? Will it hold when I am in grief? In shame? In ecstasy? How much of life can I safely die to here? Until we vigorously test the container of community, we can only *talk* about transformation.

Eventually, the no current subsides. And when the steady unhurried beat of the drum becomes prominent again, I seed the dance with a whispered "Yes. Yes. Yes."

The invitation to give body to yes floats among us. Strangely, it is slower to evoke a resonating response. At first we are awkward with this dance. Most are not yet ready for the yes. Perhaps it will emerge only after a fuller dying to the no. But glimpses of its true face are seen.

A man with disheveled hair and soaked with sweat steps slowly to the center. He bathes in the soft but incisive yes that is sung around the circle. He cradles his arms around the space in front of his heart, as if holding an infant there. He sings a quiet lullaby offering father's milk to whatever is seeking comfort in his embrace. I stalk his every gesture, mirroring him in the dance ground of the heart. His eyes spill over as he rocks back and forth in time with the drum. I feel a liberation within my own heart as I witness this man standing unashamed in his tears. They flow freely from his eyes, moistening the ground below. He then lifts the one cradled in his arms up to the sun and sky, and then down to the earth and then around to each man in the circle before he folds this one into his own heart. "Yes life," sings Fire-Heart as he returns once again to the outer circle.

A youthful man leaps out with a wild look in his eyes, a twinkling trickster look as if to say, "Yes? . . . You want yes?" Prowling on all fours around the circle, he unfurls a long, wet tongue. Shamelessly he touches it to the dark earth, dragging it along the ground until its sticky surface has acquired a considerable wealth of black soil. He parades his bounty around the circle for each man to witness before that very same tongue returns home to mouth. "Black Tongue!" someone shouts. And by such a name will this one ask to be known.

The dance eventually draws each man into the center, until the ground is familiar with us all. We have danced to climax, but not to completion. The dance is not yet finished with us.

I kneel on the ground; this gesture invites others to do the same. Having merged our rhythms now for quite a long time, we move as one, entrained like a flock of birds. My heart beats strongly in the afterglow of vigorous movement. Sweating and by now fully naked, we lay our bodies down: face to ground, heart to ground, belly to ground, groin to ground. I call on helpers to gather up leaves, bark, and discarded pieces of clothing. We cover our brothers with this debris. The dance ground now a burial ground. The ground supports every instinct.

The spirit-voice leads from here:

Lay your body down. . . . Feel your heart beating on this resonant ground. The ground that gives rise to your body and reclaims your body with equal regard. It loves you both ways. Will you allow this love?

Feel the places where your body rests easily on the ground, and places that will not surrender. Places that say yes to the invitation to union, and places of tension that say no.

The ground supports you whether you say yes or you say no. Will you accept that? If you come to the earth with grief, there will be ground for you and for the grief that moves through you. Come with anger and the ground will be there. Whether you are in confusion or clarity, you are offered a place to stand, a place to rest. Feel what it is like to be held by one who has no designs on you. Will you allow yourself to be held with respect for all of you?

As if someone just declared end to a long war, the pent-up feeling stored in the body during battle spills now onto the soil. The ground touches old wounds with patience and acceptance. Hearts begin to quiver in tenderness, in humility.

Within the warm embrace of this sacred space, let your body mingle with the soil. The body belongs to the Earth and will one day return to soil. It will dissolve, as the caterpillar dissolves inside the sheltered darkness of the chrysalis. Will you let the chrysalis of your loving intent hold you now? Will you let yourself go slowly into the dissolve, cell by cell by cell . . . your flesh so easily received by the soil. . . .

The cells of your body being absorbed by countless bacteria, mold, and fungi . . . your body becoming the humus that feeds life. Cells taken in by tiny root hairs of the trees in this forest, forming bark and leaf and seed. All these, in turn, will be eaten as well. Death, here, the gateway to expanded life. . . .

The entire ground seems to be pulsing with heartbeat—the heartbeat of the Earth, the rhythm that connects all things. Our breathing now carried by the breeze through the trees.

And now, even the one who witnesses the dissolve is being called to die. Let this one go to where there is no separation—mind like a drop of water soaking into an ocean of pure awareness. Awareness without form. Formless, yet waiting with life . . .

> . . . be still, and let the dark come upon you
> Which shall be the darkness of God . . .
> . . . be still, and wait without hope
> For hope would be hope for the wrong thing; wait without love
> For love would be love of the wrong thing; there is yet faith
> But the faith and the love and the hope are all in the waiting.
> Wait without thought, for you are not ready for thought:
> So the darkness shall be the light, and the stillness the dancing.
> —T. S. ELIOT, "EAST COKER"

Even in our dissolving, life remains like a glowing spark. And in time our earth-body, fired by this spark, will once again coalesce and take on form. This return to life is as natural as the lungs filling with breath after a full release. Waiting on the impulse to rise again, we are called by the natural yearning to take on form. Slowly, cell by cell, the body reassembles according to whatever image we hold most dear. The soil says yes and gives itself to form a new human being.

Newborn, arise from the quivering mud to the beating of your own heart. The Great Mystery has created a place for each of you to stand. All of creation attends your awakening. . . .

My helpers and I sing a Beauty Way song to guide our brothers home. Like infants coming into their bodies for the first time, the men gradually emerge from the soil. Slowly they sit up, open their eyes, and move to all fours. And when new blood has filled out their legs, they stand. For those who have accepted the ground, masks have melted away. Eyes blink with soft innocence. The world is new.

> *I can only see myself by looking at my brothers—soil and mud, the traces of afterbirth, anointing our faces, chests, bellies, cocks, knees. Brothers, where did your journey lead you? What have you remembered?*
>
> —BROTHER BLOOD

> *I regress from human, naked and sweaty—to ape—then four-legged—reptile—slithering earthworm, soil all over me, tasting, smelling, feeling, the cool earth of the dance ground—then finally a shapeless life form—part of the earth itself. I sit with the soil, sweat, and smells for a long time, let it all soak in.*
>
> —GEO

> *I taste the earth. It is salty. The coolness feels good to my sweating body. I sink deep beneath the surface. The drum is muffled and I begin to hear the heartbeat of our Mother.*
>
> *I become aware of the pain some of my brothers are enduring. I want to reach out to help, to console—but my hand will not move. I am unborn. Yet something consoles us all.*
>
> *Then faintly I hear the singing—the singing that calls me back. So beautiful—like the voices of angels.*
>
> *I emerge from my cocoon. I look up and see yellow leaves for the very first time. These are leaves spun from gold and splattered across a sky so blue they appear to be floating in water.*
>
> *I look around and see my brothers emerging from the earth womb.*

They look around with the same expression of awe that I must be wearing.
Today I died. Rejoice.

—HEART THAT SOARS

This morning I was born . . .
or did I die?
I am not sure which it was.
I washed my new face in the dermis of my Mother.
It gave me life, for it was the same as mine.
I opened my eyes—slowly—to see a new
heaven and a new Earth.
Together they cried out, "For unto us a child
is born."
I took my first steps . . .
the tentative steps of a child . . . or . . . were they
the stumbling steps of old age?
The walk was mine
and mine alone.
I felt my body. I found my space.
There was a life to be lived.
The birthing ground is always the dying ground . . .
and the dying ground always brings forth new life.

—LIVES HIS VISION

Our work and play this morning has been a sacrament as holy as I have ever experienced in any church. Is this not true religion, this humble offering of ourselves to the soil? And the wholeness remembered, is that not the purpose of all liturgy?

The striking thing about my brothers on this Quest—and they truly feel like brothers now—is their quiet yet powerful presence. These are men of the Earth, standing as Adam stood before the Fall, naked and unashamed.

Clothes will return, as will the knowledge of good and evil. We will fall again from grace, as we have done many times before. Yet as long as this holy soil remains on our bodies, we will remember and abide in the grace that lies in waiting. And perhaps in the next fall we will not be so afraid of hitting the ground.

> For the whole life-effort of man [is] to get his life into direct contact with the elemental life of the cosmos, mountain-life, cloud-life, thunder-life, air-life, earth-life, sun-life. To come into immediate felt contact, and so derive energy, power and a dark sort of joy. This effort into sheer naked contact, without an intermediary or mediator is the root meaning of religion.
> —D. H. LAWRENCE, FROM THE ESSAY "NEW MEXICO"

These words have taken on warm flesh for me today. I stand in this place born again, as a man confirmed by a presence that renews the heart of my identity. I am native to this land, to this Earth. This land matters to me, and I now know that I matter to it.

The light, fragrance, sound, taste, and texture here are born from the same womb as the senses that know them. These rivers rush through my veins, and the rock here feels as kin to me as my bones. The body I slough off at the end of my days will cause no indigestion to this ground. There are times when the tall pine dancing in the wind or the great blue heron waiting in the shallows seem as true a reflection of me as the one that appears in the glass mirror. Every tear I shed comes from the clouds overhead and falls to the ground below. Even the silence of these old mountains is different to these ears than any other.

In this way, I am as Native American as any man can be. It is not by virtue of cultural heritage that I claim this identity, but because the ground recognizes me as such. To deny this not only would diminish me but would also dishonor the very ground that gave its flesh to this spirit and a path for that spirit to walk.

The ground has said so.

7

MAPS OF THE TERRITORY

I live my life in growing orbits
which move out over the things of the world.
Perhaps I can never achieve the last,
but that will be my attempt.

I am circling around God, around the ancient tower,
and I have been circling for a thousand years,
and I still don't know if I am a falcon, or a storm,
or a great song.

—RAINER MARIA RILKE
TRANSLATION BY ROBERT BLY

The story is told that, at the beginning of time, the gods created the Medicine Wheel to help the human beings remember their original purpose, and make of their Earth Walk a pilgrimage of Self-Remembering. In its arrangement of stones, the Wheel would reveal the paths to be taken and the wisdom that might be found along each path. In sacred council, the gods determined that the inner circle of the Wheel would comprise seven stones. Four of these stones held the powers of the Four Directions: East, South, West, and North. The fifth stone embodied the spiritual light of the Above, and the sixth stone was the gateway to the dark soul mysteries of the Below.

The seventh stone was the most precious of all, for it was that place where the four horizontal powers of the material world, and the two vertical powers of the spiritual world, joined. There all opposites united within the embrace of wholeness, revealing the divine radiance within all things. Yet the gods knew that so precious a stone would be eagerly sought by the human beings, who would desire to experience its radiance. Such power would be unwisely given to the power-hungry heart not yet tempered with compassion and insight. Where, then, to place this sacred stone, so that its profound wisdom might be reserved for those whose commitment to wholeness had been tested in the ordeals of life?

"Hear me," said one of the gods. "This stone should live atop the highest mountain on the planet. Only the wisest of the humans would think to look for it there, and only the strongest of them would find it." At first the plan seemed a good one. As they debated, though, the gods realized that the human creatures were clever and adventuresome. One of them would surely soon find the stone and blaze a path to it, making it easier for others to follow.

"Hear me," said another god. "Let us cause the sacred stone to fall to the deepest part of the deepest sea. For there, in the churning waters, paths are erased as soon as they are made. And the humans cannot live within the waters for long before their lungs cry out for air." This plan, too, met with favor—until one of the gods looked down from the sky and saw a human swimming in a lake, using a reed to breathe. The gods realized that it would not be long before these crafty beings would fashion a vessel to carry them to the ocean bottom, where they would too easily find the precious seventh stone. This plan too was scrapped.

Others called for the stone to be placed far to the North, and painted white, that it be hidden within the drifting snows of that place.

"No," cried others. "It would be covered best by the green summer forests of the South. Let us give it the color of summer and hide it there."

"I see a trail that leads to the sun-birth place of the East," said another. "Those who seek it there will be blinded by the beauty of the rising fireball and will seek no further."

"The sun-death place of the West is far better suited for such a prize," argued yet another. "Travelers there would fall into such despair at the coming darkness, that they would surely turn back."

At an impasse, the gods fell to quarreling, shattering the unity of the council. The dark sky rolled with thunder and flashes of angry light. The gods then went before the Great Spirit and spoke their dilemma: "Where," they asked, "should we make the home of this seventh power?"

The Great Spirit replied:

> Surely, the human beings will follow each of the trails you have just created, and it is good that they do so. For the true path to wholeness can only be the one that passes into and through the world of opposites. But your impatience has left you blind to the wisdom of simplicity. Place the stone where the humans would never expect to find it, where they are least likely to look. Place it within the wilderness of each one's innermost heart. For there the stone will be polished like a mirror in the ordeals of life. And those who do reach it will then be able to see the face of the Mystery they had been searching for all along.

Soon after we have attended to our physical needs in establishing our home here, we give our attention to creating an altar that reflects the reality of our spiritual presence. We do this by building a Medicine Wheel of water-smoothed stones that we gather from the river. The Wheel will be placed adjacent to the dance ground in an area large enough to accommodate all of us sitting in a circle. This will serve as a sanctuary were we come to sit in council, to meditate and pray, and to work with the various teaching stories that inform our journey. The story of the quarrelsome gods is one such story, central to our Quest. It introduces us to the teachings of the Medicine Wheel.

We understand Medicine to be the vital power that brings us into right relationship with all life. It is the power that reminds us of our inherent wholeness, our health.

The substances our culture normally calls "medicine" are simply the physical agents that realign us with this healing power.

But Medicine is much larger than these substances. Medicine may be found in a compassionate embrace, or carried in a confrontive, yet loving speaking of truth. Medicine is carried in teaching stories that help us imagine a larger possibility when we're stuck in a nearsighted and repetitive pattern. Medicine helps us remember our story as a reflection of the universe story. Medicine is carried in dreams and visions. Animals carry strong Medicine as they lead us to reclaim lost aspects of our instinctual nature. People carry Medicine too. Our most potent Medicine is the truth of who we are.

The Medicine Wheel is an ancient spiritual symbol that we use to help us navigate the trackless wilderness of the inner world in search of that truth. Unlike road maps that illustrate a limited number of routes to any given destination, the Medicine Wheel reflects as many routes as there are people. The heart does not need a road map, it needs only a mirror—and the permission to follow its longing. The Medicine Wheel is such a mirror.

The symbols and teachings of our Wheel come from many different places—from the teachings of Hyemeyohsts Storm, Sun Bear, and other American Indian sources; from the revelations of early Christian mystics; from transpersonal psychology—all woven into the fabric of our own native human experience. Within the Medicine Wheel, each of our various religious traditions is welcomed and given a place to root within the wisdom tradition of native North America—the place where we live. If we are in accord with the rhythmic order of place, we stand a better chance of being in accord with the spiritual order of the universe.

Legend has it that the Wheel is a gift from the Creator. Before we take up residence in our bodies, we are spirits living beyond the limits of time and space. The evolutionary impulse toward wholeness calls us to undertake an Earth Walk—a life within a body, on a planet where limitation and opposition seem to rule. Our life task is to realize wholeness, to live it fully in all of its beautiful and terrifying complexity, in a place where wholeness seems not possible. The Wheel reminds us that we have not come here to be part of someone else's vision, but to belong to who we are. If you live your own longing, then you know that you belong. If you do not live your longing, then you live with a terrible sense of alienation. And without the gift of your Medicine, the world suffers as well.

The shock of human birth is so great, however, that we forget our origins and the original intent for our Earth Walk. Knowing this, the Creator presents us with the Medicine Wheel as a mirror of who we are and why we're here, and as a reminder that our wholeness and health is inextricably linked with all the other beings of the planet.

Among these beings are the Stone People. In many native traditions stones are honored as the wisest of all the peoples in the universe. Does it seem strange that those who are silent and seem not to move would be held in such high regard? Perhaps, but the greatest teachers are not the ones who stuff our heads with facts and figures; they are ones who help us discover ourselves. The Sanskrit word for sage, *muni,* means "the silent one." When we are lost or confused, fear drives us to look outside ourselves for answers. In their stillness and their silence, the Stone People, among all the expressions of creation, are most adept at returning us back to ourselves.

>>   <<

When we sit with the Stone People, we come into contact with that part of us which is old, wise, eternal, silent, and patient. They teach us that while knowledge might be gained in an hour, wisdom takes time. Stone: ancient one, mirror of truth at each person's level of perception.

The stones are now gathered before us as we prepare the ground to lay our Wheel. We hold these stones with curiosity and wonder. We will use what we know about them, not to imprison them in cold, hard fact but to lead us further into the mystery of our relatedness with them. With that intention, only one question remains. We ask, "Who are you?"

Hands informed with such questioning come alive with a presence and sensitivity that many of us have not felt since childhood. The weight of these beings is not just *measured* but *experienced;* the

MAPS OF THE TERRITORY

colors and texture of their flesh not just *noted* but *reveled in* as well. Of the Stone People we ask, "What is this force, this longing, that compels you to unite with the Earth? And what speak these markings that reveal images, faces, animal shapes—patterns that seem kin to the dreamworld? Our noses want to know you; tongues and ears wonder as well."

Their stillness draws us closer. . . .

We have seen the sparks that leapt from your cold, dark body during our Sunrise Ceremony. Have you a fire inside? Are you offspring of the sun itself?

The stones are becoming warm in our hands. . . .

Birthed over a billion years ago—so many turns of the seasonal round have you witnessed! You, who have been here so long before us and will remain long after our passing, how does time move for you? What stories do you have to tell? Does anyone stop to listen anymore?

They do not interrupt our questioning. . . .

And what of your crystalline nature—facets that blossom with such clarity from opaque mass? You who focus and transmit human voice invisibly through the air, do you not also broadcast the energy of our prayers?

To everything, the stones answer yes.

We aren't ready to learn from the Wheel until that time in our lives when we ask the Sacred Question: Who am I? The world then stops for a moment and all of the descriptions of who we are and how things are no longer seem meaningful. In that uneasy moment we are living that question for the first time. We confront the need, as Don Juan put it, to balance the terror of being a man with the wonder of being a man.

We sit and wonder. And when I feel this wonder has enough body to it, I place a large aqua blue crystal of fluorite at our center. A crystal that reflects the light of the Sacred Question—Who am I?—a light that no two men see the same.

This Sacred Question changes our lives forever. It disturbs the placid idealism of our youth the way a stone dropped in a still pool disrupts its surface. But this disruption creates a dynamic pattern of concentric circles. On the Medicine Wheel we represent the first of these circles with seven stones. Seven men now come forth and place those stones in a close orbit around the centering Question. And seven times, the Question is spoken.

And as we have an inner life and an outer life, the Medicine Wheel also has an inner circle and an outer circle. In the outer circle, we now place a stone at each of the Four Directions. Between each of these are two stones, for a total of twelve, reflecting the number of moons appearing in the cycle of a year.

To symbolize the connection between our inner and outer lives, we now place pathways made of three stones linking each cardinal direction to the inner circle. The circle and the cross—pathways of our Earth Walk now visible before us.

The Wheel has a vertical dimension as well: the invisible, but universally intuited *axis mundi*—the world axis. So we imagine a tree of life growing from the center of the Wheel: its branches reaching up and out toward the heavens, its roots reaching down toward the heart of the earth, its trunk where heaven and earth unite. Each time we come to the Medicine Wheel and sit with these symbols at our center, we honor the heart's perception of reality. And each time we have the courage to ask "Who am I?" we gain an opportunity to see ourselves mirrored within the greater whole.

We bring our attention now to each of the Four Directions stones to seed our imagination with the essential symbols of these pathways. When we sit at the eastern gate, we are in relation to the Medicine of the Rising Sun, to rays of light that awaken new beginnings and spark the creative imagination. We are blessed here with the powers of illumination and intuition. According to native medicine ways, we may cultivate these powers by apprenticing ourselves to Eagle or to other high-flying birds of prey. For Eagle is farseeing and moves with the decisiveness of an arrow shot from the sun. No internal debate, just quick initiatory action.

Eagle, your flight inspires us toward greater vision. Be here with us, help us to soar on the winds of turbulence and guide us to the courage to act from the truth of what we see.

There are times when we need this Medicine of daybreak. Yet Eagle Medicine must live in good relation to the others.

The South is the place of the Full-Hearted Sun, generously warming the world from its zenith at high noon. The Medicine here is the power of innocence and trusting. If we sit with Mouse we may learn of its ways. Eagle can see a rabbit in a field from two miles up but rarely visits the ground. Mouse can barely see beyond his whiskers but gets very close to things. Mouse acts in ways that are true to its gifts of perception. *Innocence* literally means "nonharming." An innocent heart does no harm to itself. It trusts all that is held within its care. Follow Mouse, the Old Ones say, to learn of these things.

Mouse, your humility brings us close to what matters most in our lives. Be here with us, help us to touch, with love and respect, our heart's desire.

Coyote also lives in the South and carries these teachings in his inimitable way. Coyote brings us into relationship with the folly of life. Coyote makes sure we don't take things too seriously or rigidly—especially this Quest of ours. He shakes up our world, giving us the opportunity to fall flat on our face, so that we see the self-harm that comes with holding on to rigid beliefs. And in his mournful cry, we can perhaps recognize our own voice.

Coyote, your song returns us unashamedly to our holy longing. Be here with us and help us to sing the deepest chords of our soul.

In turning to the West, we stand in relation to Setting Sun Medicine. The power of perception here is that of introspection, or looking within. Bear presides over these teachings. We learn from Bear that there is a time when we can benefit from turning our eyes inward. When we enter into darkness we learn to navigate not with our physical eyes, but with our inner eye. Here we learn to be at home in the deep wilderness of the dreamworld.

Bear, your nurturing strength encourages our willingness to face both light and darkness. Be here with us, help us to surrender to the truth of what we cannot see or touch, the truth that lives inside our bones.

As we move to the North, we complete the fourfold cycle of the Wheel. We face the Medicine of midwinter darkness, the power of wisdom and renewal. Our guide here is Buffalo. Buffalo is willing to give away all of his flesh, bones, and sinew to feed the people. Buffalo reflects the quality of total surrender, of giving away to the point of emptiness. Wisdom comes from knowing that in giving everything away, we can know who we are, not in temporal and material terms but on the deepest spiritual level.

Buffalo, your generosity returns us to our gratitude for all life. Be here with us and keep us connected in prayer with all our relations.

East and West, North and South meet in a dance of polarity. Sunset and sunrise reflect two sides of one truth, just as death and birth are intimately linked as expressions of life. Where Eagle acts with unflinching precision, Bear questions and ponders. High noon and midnight are likewise equal but very different expressions of the life force. Where Mouse scurries about collecting things, Buffalo gives all away.

The Medicine Wheel shows that if we want to be whole we must be willing to hold in balance the different qualities reflected in the Four Directions, to respect them equally. It's our human tendency to focus our energies in one or perhaps two of the gates. Because we spend less time in these other places, we tend to regard them with fear and suspicion. In our culture, for example, we tend to prize Eagle's qualities of ascent, daring, and swift action. We give much less weight and importance to Bear's gifts of introspection and questioning and to Buffalo's example of the giveaway. In emphasizing perpetual youth we fall out of balance in our relationship to decay and death. This is especially true for men who have learned to fear the descent, the waning erection, the empty space between events of our days and our lives.

The beauty of the Medicine Wheel is in its ability to help us perceive the divine spirit in all things. Nature is not foe to our spiritual life, it is the revelation of the divine. On the Medicine Wheel, we learn of the many faces of spirit through the turning of sun, moon, and stars; the steady presence of the trees; the movements and disciplines of animals. We apprentice ourselves to Heron, Oak, or Turtle to enter into the particular grace that each embodies. We pay close attention to what moves inside of us when a falcon, or a storm, or a song, engages our interest. As we give ourselves over to these beings and forces, they extend our imagination and sense of identity beyond the confines of our human-centered world. Deep calls to deep; alienation subsides, and we become rooted once again in the basic sanity of Earth.

There is much more to be said about the Medicine Wheel, but better it be said through our interaction with it, over time. The wheel of the day has turned considerably since we first sat to create our sanctuary. By now it is twilight. The fine-edged boundaries of mid-afternoon have given way to the softer contours of diffuse, low-angled light. Clouds of swarming insects drift above the pool in the river. An occasional trout breaks the surface to feed. The sun sitting in its western gate casts low shadows across all the events of the day.

We bring our council to a close by moving in unison around the Wheel.

It feels good to be moving after sitting for so long. I add a soft drumbeat to our steps. As we pass through each of the four gates we call on its elemental forces and animal powers. We ask them to visit us in our time of need. In return we offer to greet whatever comes as part of ourselves. We dance around this Wheel now, calling out to the Four Directions, the Above, the Below—calling in a manner that touches on a supreme loneliness in my heart. We sing to Eagle and to Mouse, to Bear and to Buffalo. We sing to Pine, and Heron, and Snake and send our voices to the Cloud-Life, Thunder-Life, Soil-Life. I know it is not you who have abandoned me, but I who have turned away from you. Will you not see that my heart now carries the longing to know you and be known by you?

>>   <<

I've always been drawn to twilight. There's a certain peace that descends on the world as the day sighs its last long outbreath. I need its soothing Medicine now. It's been another full day, and there's a restless voice inside that I can't quite hear amid all the activity and conversation taking place in camp. I take my leave, and after a ten-minute walk, I arrive at my favorite sitting place by the river.

The river here is broad, slow, and shallow and runs over a pebbled bottom before spilling into a quiet, reflective pool. Endless varieties of forest green are mirrored and blended on its surface in patterns that call to the playful imagination. There is movement here, but the movement is not far separated from its source in stillness. And the faint sound of the water—it too is kin to silence. Wind and water have smoothed over the footprints from my last meandering here, but have left undisturbed the well-worn contours of the place where I sit. I feel strongly welcomed this time.

The unrelenting presence of this place invites me to join it with more passion. In the waning light, I pull a flute from my knapsack. For a moment I hold the flute as I would hold my Medicine Pipe. I offer its music to all my relations and to the spirit of this place. "This is for you," I whisper, as I touch my lips to the mouthpiece. I draw breath from a passing breeze. And the flute begins to sing like I've never heard it sing before. A mournful melody takes to the wind. Effortlessly, it swirls among the treetops and drifts up to the sky. I do not compose this song. I simply step out of its way.

The breeze dies down and finds its way out through one last sustained note that I give away as if it were my last breath. I give it all away and slowly release my lips from the flute's mouth . . . but the note remains! From the ridges above me it rings on and on until it cracks into its next higher octave!

Coyote!

Coyote, singing with longing and abandon from the ridgetop. Shape-shifter, prankster, soul brother—you've snatched my song from the breeze! You've met my heart's desire with your own. I stand revealed!

8

THE ROAD OF TRIALS

Ask and it shall be answered.
Being answered, you shall be troubled.
Knowing trouble, you shall come to see God.

—JOHANINE GOSPELS
GREEK TRANSLATION

Once we've established our Medicine Wheel, it usually isn't long before its claims for revealing and harmonizing conflict are tested.

Jim calls Robert out to the dance ground to confront the tension that's been building between them for the last couple of days. At first they try to resolve the conflict through peaceful dialogue, but the effort soon breaks down. They quickly don their defensive armor and square off. The love bond here is clearly uneasy, but it's just as clear that only those with lovers' hearts glare at each other with the same passion I see in these men's eyes. For the opposite of love is not hate, but indifference. There is no indifference here. Jim reaches his hand toward Robert's shoulder.

"Don't touch me, motherfucker!" Robert shouts.

Instinctively, the rest of us draw together in a circle around them, forming a vessel to contain this energy. I ask that we see more than just two men at odds. The struggle between these two is the local staging of a much larger play. The essential conflict of all duality is being enacted before us, and this conflict demands ritual containment. I draw an encircled cross on the ground between them. That they stand on opposite sides of the same truth is now better illuminated.

"You're throwing daggers at me all the time," says Jim, his voice trembling. "And I'm sick of it. You cut me off every time I speak . . . "

Robert throws the exact words back to Jim in a falsely therapeutic manner: "*You* throw daggers at *yourself. You're* sick of *yourself. You* cut *yourself* off . . . "

Though the tone of contempt is obvious, he will not speak it openly. His armor is up stronger than ever. Confusion and longing hide behind painted masks of fierceness.

For some minutes they argue and glower at each other, struggling to tap into some vein of feeling that will release them from the suffering. However, it seems that these two gladiators are not only protected by but imprisoned within their armor.

A shift finally comes when Jim volunteers that he has been invaded his whole life. He is sad that the pattern still carries forth into this Quest. Robert can no longer mirror these words with mockery. They are truly his words as well. "I'm not going to give you anything, asshole. If I have to fight to keep you from sucking my energy dry, I will." As he shares more of his rage, more of his vulnerability is revealed as well.

"If I'm doing that, I'm not aware of it. I'm sorry," says Jim hesitantly.

Robert shrugs off Jim's apology then offers a noncommitted hand toward his nemesis. Jim moves in quickly to take advantage of the fragile opening he feels between them. The two men embrace uneasily, as if this were how such clashes are supposed to end. But the spirit of wholeness will have nothing to do with such niceties. It rushes in, as if to say "What's true here?" The men quickly pull themselves apart. It is not merging these guys need to practice; the pretense of unity can be more dangerous than honest warfare. Instead, they agree first to practice respecting each other in their differences. Resolution will come in its own time, and we agree to wait—wait until these two are willing to draw a circle between them with their own hands.

When we next sit around the Medicine Wheel, we are all called to explore our relationship to conflict. I place a forked stick in the middle of the Wheel. The inspiration for this comes from a Medicine Wheel teaching offered by Hyemeyohsts Storm. It is the teaching of the Forked Tree.

Essentially, the Forked Tree reminds us of the twinness of our nature. Like the Forked Tree, we humans have two branches. Unlike the rest of creation, we call one of the branches "good" and the other "bad." The branch of ourselves that we like, we show to the world. That branch receives sunlight and thus it grows. The branch of self that we dislike, we keep hidden from the world and from ourselves. That branch receives no light and thus it withers. In fear we think that all will be set to order if we could only cut off the evil branch. But fear blinds us to the fact that by cutting into the one branch, we weaken the integrity of the whole tree. Our challenge, then, is to bring the side of ourselves that lives in shadow into the light. We often see that part of our self mirrored in others first. That is a healthy step beyond denial. The next step, though, is to recognize the other as self. Yet it's amazing how much fear, self-will, and pride we have to wade through at times to see clearly. The Medicine Wheel serves up a story to illuminate this struggle:

> In the time before time, Sunrise and Sunset were at war. Though they had never met, each thought itself to be the crowning glory of life.
>
> "I am the bringer of light," said Sunrise. "My Medicine is strong, as it awakens all creation. I should rightfully rule the entire day."
>
> "My Medicine is far superior," countered Sunset, "for I bring recreative darkness and renewal to all things. It is I who should prevail for all time."
>
> All of this bickering was driving the animals crazy, so they gathered together to try to get this foolishness settled. They came up with a plan. Half of the animals traveled to the highest point of land in the eastern end of the world and called to Sunrise. "How radiantly beautiful the day has become," they sang. This caught Sunrise's attention, for he loved the music of dawn.

While this was going on, the other half of the animals journeyed to the highest point of land far to the west. There, they called to Sunset. "What sweet peace descends on us now," they sang. This caught Sunset's attention, for he loved the music of the evening song.

Then, all of a sudden, Eagle sent out a shrill cry and all of the animals quickly disappeared into the forest.

It was then that Sunrise and Sunset first set eyes on each other, and the world was made right again. Whoever sees the other half of Self, sees truth.

As we continue our exploration of conflict we uncover many differences of experience and opinion, but there is one condition on which we all agree: We will not tolerate physical violence in any of our interactions. But neither will we close our hearts to violence. Our intention here is to stalk power, and a closed heart is the furthest thing from power. Both the wimp and the bully live in fear and live inside every man. The wimp, having little positive aggression, flees from invitations of power. The bully, possessed by violent aggression, attempts to destroy the invitation. Part of the responsibility of mature manhood is to find these two and bring them home.

We gain true power by entering into the fiery midst of conflict with our hearts open on all sides. Our mettle is tempered by standing in such a fire. As we develop a capacity to suffer the uneasy defeat by the sword of truth, we may learn to wield our own sword to cut through pretense and stand revealed.

Or we may be called by power into the furious winds and flood waters of the storm. And in surrendering shield and armor, we may learn to trust the watery midst of what Chögyam Trungpa called the "sad and tender heart of the warrior." Fear dissolves in such a water.

This is a troubling notion for many of us—the possibility that we do not gain a warrior's heart through our victories, but through our defeats. It is troubling because we've defined so much of our manhood in agreement with the cultural ideal of victory. But, "Life *is* trouble," cries Zorba in the face of compliance to outer authority, "only death is not. To be alive is to undo your belt and *look* for trouble."

To avoid trouble is to avoid life—look at any caterpillar who refused to be defeated by the chrysalis. Or, for that matter, look at any man who refuses to be defeated by the calling of his destiny.

One of the major threshold crossings in the maturing of a man occurs when he accepts the fact that to be fully alive means to be troubled. We mature as we bring our demand for perfection— "unconditional" love, "total" happiness, "unending" pleasure, and "permanent" relief from pain—face to face with the terrible inconsistencies of life. To celebrate trouble is to go *into it* with compassion and imagination. To celebrate trouble means to let go of the hand of fear, which promises to lead us on an easy path around difficulty. We are not given the choice whether to be troubled or not. Every man who is truly alive is troubled. Our only real choice is whether or not we will responsibly meet the trouble entrusted to us.

Rilke's poem "The Man Watching" is an extraordinary tribute to the glory of being defeated by a greater loving. In it he said:

What we choose to fight is so tiny!
What fights with us is so great!
If only we would let ourselves be dominated
as things do by some immense storm,
we would become strong too, and not need names.
When we win it's with small things,
and the triumph itself makes us small.
What is extraordinary and eternal
does not *want* to be bent by us.

And later in the poem, he concluded:

Winning does not tempt that man.
This is how he grows: by being defeated, decisively,
by constantly greater beings.

The willingness to accept defeat is a primary condition of the spiritual life. "When God begins to infuse his light of knowledge and understanding into the spirit of a man drawn to contempla-tion," wrote the Christian monk Thomas Merton, "the experience is often not so much one of fulfillment as of defeat."

This is perhaps why holy men and warriors, from Crazy Horse to Gandhi, from Martin Luther King Jr. to the Dalai Lama have proclaimed, "Our enemies are sacred because they make us stronger." It is not physical strength that is celebrated here but a soul force far superior to any physical weapon.

Trouble! Defeat! Nothing holy comes without it!

Day three. We sit on logs around the stones of our Medicine Wheel. I've been here long enough to begin to feel relaxed. Suddenly, a big, big man rises up from the North part of the Wheel, steps toward me and says, "What's with your T-shirt? I find it offensive, it's violent, and it's a distraction from this place."

I had cut the sleeves off this T-shirt with my knife. It is black, with a skull and feathers on front. Some say that symbol is the sole property of the Hell's Angels, but it matched my studded gloves, and I loved wearing it as me and thirty or forty other Harleys tore up the road at night. And I love wearing it here. What's he saying? There's no place for me at this Wheel?

I eyeball his T-shirt. It is light blue, it has the Earth on the front, and it still has sleeves, and it is loose. Oh, how nice.

Everyone looks at us as if we are two gunfighters out on the street.

Some spirit brings me to my feet, probably the spirit of this Medicine Wheel. I tear off my T-shirt, throw it at him, and say, "Wear it."

He immediately rips his T-shirt off, throws it at me . . . "Put it on."

More than T-shirts are exchanged—it is skin. I am wearing his chest, back, bones, and blood. Our personalities, identity, and expe-rience are transferred in an instant. I think of two warriors, braves, meeting on the plain, searching each other's shield or feathers for power and knowledge, telling the story of his Earth Walk. "You will know me as you walk in my moccasins, as you wear my skin . . . "

He and I hug and laugh. The people around us feel safe again. Everyone, including the Earth, feels safe whenever men act in such a manner.

I still have that T-shirt. When I wear it I feel warm and calm. I've got this man's hide around me and I feel my strength as a man doubled.

—PANTHER BEAR

There are times when traversing a trackless wilderness is made easier by following an animal herd path. It is common, though, for a herd path to lead initially in the direction you wish to go, but over a distance begin to veer off your intended mark. The well-seasoned traveler develops an instinct for knowing when to stay on the hopeful trail and when to abandon it.

The spiritual journey eventually forces the same decision on those who travel its wild terrain. There are many paths, and they all lead somewhere fruitful. Yet, as Don Juan suggests, if we are not traveling a path with heart, our warrior's spirit will never be truly free. If such is the case, we are well advised to follow our heart for a time where there are no trails.

Not all of the men who are with us at the beginning of the Quest stay to the end. Eric is clearly struggling with his decision to stay or to leave. He suspects he has made a rash decision in coming. His life at home has been very stressful recently. Captivated by the exciting images of adventure, risk, and challenge, his mind is what brought him to Quest. Now that he is here his body is pleading to be heard. In council, Eric clearly speaks his need for rest.

I awake one morning to someone scratching at my tent door. "Joseph," a voice says, "I've decided to leave." It is Eric, with his pack on, ready to head back down the trail. None of the others are up yet. I encourage him to reconsider—not his decision, but the way he is acting on his decision. His movements are quick and panicked. His eyes clearly reveal that fear is his counsel now. I invite him to consider the consequences of leaving in fear. He takes a deep breath and discovers that it would be important to speak with the other men before he departs.

We call a special council and Eric speaks his truth. And, as is often the case when undefended truth stands before us, all heaven and hell break loose. Parts of us, inspired by Eric's willingness to follow his heart, bless his passage. Other parts feel betrayed and enraged.

Through fear's eyes Eric becomes the friend who never answers our calls, the lover who abandoned us, the child who no longer writes home. He is the god who has forsaken us in our time of deepest suffering and the parent who does not love us perfectly. It's a long council and Eric bears up pretty well as we alternately bless him and damn him. In time we recognize and withdraw more and more of our projections. What is revealed, then, is simply a man who has taken a stand in following his heart.

In the end we form a gauntlet for Eric to pass through on his way out of camp. He hoists his pack and stands before two lines of men who face each other. We each bid him farewell by placing a hand on his heart as he walks through the passage and disappears down the trail.

By standing in his truth before us, this man has unknowingly given us a great gift. His leaving throws us all back on ourselves. He has raised a question that tests our commitment in real terms: "Does my heart say yes to this Quest in this moment?" One by one we all agree to continue. Eric's leaving confirms our staying. This Quest may now be seen for what it truly is: an empty form that becomes alive and meaningful only as we bring our heart-illuminated authority to it.

Now that we're present and accounted for, we will walk closer to the edge of the abyss that awaits us.

PART TWO

~~~~~~

INTO THE ABYSS

Mankind owns four things
that are no good at sea:
rudder, anchor, oars
and the fear of going down.

—ANTONIO MACHADO
TRANSLATION BY ROBERT BLY

9

FIRES OF PURIFICATION

And so long as you haven't experienced
this: to die and so to grow,
you are only a troubled guest
on the dark earth.

—GOETHE
TRANSLATION BY ROBERT BLY

"It is a good day to die." For the Lakota warrior, this is not a lament, but a song of power. The song affirms the expansion of life that comes from dying to a cause or to an identity that is larger than oneself. It is also the song of initiation, one that the caterpillar sings as it enters the chrysalis. And, too, it is the song a man must sing when he faces a task that demands more of himself than he presently knows.

"Acts have power," said Don Juan, "especially when the person acting knows that those acts are his last battle. There is a strange consuming happiness in acting with the full knowledge that whatever one is doing may very well be one's last act on earth."

With this song and teaching, we greet this day—our last day together before our time of solitude. The spiritual practice that overlights all we do today is letting go of the assumption that we will live to see another sunrise. Living with this uncertainty brings a startling clarity to our morning council.

As we sit around the Medicine Wheel, I ask us to bring our

attention to our breath: each breath, our first; each breath, our last. With each inbreath we come into life. With each outbreath we leave that life behind. One lifetime after another. We experience the rising breath of spring, the full breath of summer, the give-away breath of autumn, the empty breath of winter. The sunrise breath of rebirth, the high-noon breath of passionate fullness, the sunset breath of surrender, the midnight breath of stillness.

We follow each outbreath down and linger in that moment of emptiness that exists as we let go of the assumption of anything to follow. If a new breath comes, we will celebrate another life-time. But for now we wait at the very bottom of the breath; wait there without hope, without love, without faith, without thought. And we simply listen there, listen with the ears of our last breath—look out through the eyes of our last breath—let the breeze touch skin that has breathed its last breath.

Breathe from the heart, and back into the heart, the "sad and tender heart of the warrior." The warrior's heart opens out into the world and feels everything—the world's joy, the world's sorrow—as its own. All of the laughter in the world is given space to be, and all of the tears that have ever been shed are held there. It is a heart that softens when touched by life, with a tenderness that only a man of great love and courage is able to bear. Will you open your warrior's heart to yourself as you are now? To the world as it is now? Will you allow your heart to be the transformative vessel wherein your pain dissolves and unites with the vastness of world pain; where your pleasure touches and becomes one with God's pleasure; where your self returns home to the Self? Breathe into that possibility and go as far as you will. The warrior who is not afraid of dying, dies into greater intimacy with all life. And both he, and the world, are changed forever by his love.

Will you give yourself permission to act today with the full knowl-edge that whatever you are doing may very well be your last act on Earth? It is a good day to die.

For us, this day is set apart from all others. It marks the formal beginning of our passage from the separation phase of our work through the threshold into the initiation time of solitude. This

threshold will be marked this evening by the offering of the Sweat Lodge purification rite. We will emerge from the lodge in conversational silence. This silence will carry through the three days and nights of solitude, through our return from solitude, and through the Vision Dance ceremony that will complete the cycle of initiation. We attend now to all the details that will see us through these next four days. We choose solo questing sites, review emergency systems, and make final decisions on what food and equipment each man will take.

The area within a mile or so of our base camp offers many choices: rocky ridges, deep forest clearings, streamside sites, caves. Each environment has qualities that reflect different parts of ourselves back to ourselves. Those wanting to stalk their desire for open space and far vision will naturally be drawn to the sites along the ridge, while those who want to explore the darker zones might choose the cave. The river often attracts those thirsting for nurturance.

Approaching this threshold time, there are parts of us that feel both fear and elation. The thought of being plunked down in the middle of the forest, with nothing in particular to build, create, accomplish, or save, can make us nervous. Some fear the emptiness of the three days, while others relish the opportunity to just be. Whatever our inner condition, it will be mirrored back to us perfectly.

To keep the mirror as clear as possible, I offer only the slightest suggestion of form for the three days of solitude. The first day may be devoted to making contact with the spirit of place: establishing camp with utmost care, paying attention to beauty while defining your ceremonial space, greeting the beings with whom you'll be living, and announcing your intentions. As they say in parts of Africa, you can't hunt in the tribal lands until the territory knows you. The first acts are to create a container that will support you in remembering your purpose. Then introduce yourself and your purpose to those around you.

The second day may focus on a ritual discipline. This discipline must come from your own desire and imagination, from contact with the ritual elder that lives inside you. It may involve extended periods of sitting in meditation or prayer. Or perhaps a commitment to give kinesthetic expression to everything that moves through you at sunrise and sunset. Or the choice to stay awake through the night. Perhaps you will choose to use no words, but communicate through dance, or through drumming, for an entire day. Because nature speaks the language of sensation, we are well advised to stop thinking and enter into as much sensation as we can bear. Enter into the nuances of color, movement, patterns, smells; open your erotic sensibilities toward the wind, rain, and stars; invite the shrill cry of Hawk to enter your body-mind and stir your soul substance into movement that the universe has never before seen. Let the beauty you love be what you do, as Kabir suggests. When you drop your Sacred Question into the creative chaos of such a movement, you have placed a seed into fertile soil. You can then follow your discipline to stay attentive to what emerges.

We are essentially looking for a practice that will support us in stopping the world long enough to be present with all of our self. A practice that will take us to the border where, as is said in the Indian Upanishads, "words turn back, together with the mind, not having attained." This place where words turn back is the place where language surrenders to the more intimate movement of direct experience. This is the between-worlds state of the threshold of initiation. Our ritual discipline becomes a vehicle to communicate our purpose, focus our attention, and ultimately carry us beyond our mind's comprehension into the abyss of not-knowing—and back again. In fact, we will each go as far into the unknown as we have developed the soul strength to endure radical change.

The last day may be one of surrender, of stillness, allowing the inchoate images stirring within our hearts to rise to the surface. A day of pregnant listening, a day when all trying and all seeking stops, a day devoted to trusting whatever is given. For vision comes when we stop looking.

Our essential practice today, though, is to loosen the lines that keep us moored to the known shores, not only of the world we left behind but of this Quest community as well.

A time of solitude is a key element in the archetypal hero's journey. Jesus, Buddha, and Muhammad all went by themselves into the wilderness to confront their destiny. King Arthur's knights left the community of the Round Table to search on their own for the Grail. Solitude is a primary initiatory ordeal of the hero's journey practiced in virtually all traditional societies. In solitude, in the wilderness, nature becomes the mirror of our native self. It's likely that never in our entire lives have we spent so much time—three days and nights—completely alone. Even if we have managed to avoid human contact for a time, we probably remained connected through television, radio, and newspapers. In the threshold of solitude, though, there are none of these support systems, none of these diversions. Each man faces the Mystery without intermediaries.

The mythology of the hero's journey is clear: We access this threshold, not by overpowering the unknown, but by surrendering to the unknown. The hero is required to jump into the abyss of not knowing and disappear, as it were, to reemerge in greater accord with greater life. This act is symbolized in the image, familiar to cultures the world over, of the journey into and out of the belly of the whale.

On some level we are all familiar with that journey, for our spirits have all surrendered to a nine-month gestation in such a "belly." Within the containment of the womb, we slowly grow a body, cell by cell, around a vision that we call our Self. At birth, we leave the ocean of the womb to walk on two legs as an air-breathing mammal. As Otto Rank suggested, we are all heroes in our birth.

This act of surrender to the physicality of the womb gives us our physical birth. To grow beyond that, in accord with the destiny of our Earth Walk, we will have to die and be born many times.

On our Quest, we must strengthen ourselves to endure the experience of being defeated by vision, defeated by God. In our spiritual immaturity, we commonly expect vision to come as a supremely blissful experience. We somehow think vision will clear up all our problems. The ego, looking for pleasure all of the time, is going to experience quite a shock when vision does come. Because, more often than not, vision wounds us deeply. It leads us deeper *into* trouble rather than away from it. Deep down we may suspect that life would be much safer if we didn't look beyond what we already know. We may secretly fear any change in the direction of our lives or a change that will require restructuring the persona we have so carefully created. We must each become aware of what we have invested in *not* receiving new vision, in keeping our circle of self enclosed within the imagined security of certainty. For it is a fundamental law: New energy added to a closed system will only reinforce that system *against* change.

These themes of death and rebirth, defeat and victory are with us on the Quest from the beginning and are returned to throughout. But the consummate ritual expression of empowerment through defeat comes with the offering of our Sweat Lodge rite.

Although the sweat lodge is found in varied forms among people the world over, its ritual use is perhaps most highly refined among American Indian tribes of North America. And this was the source of my introduction to the ritual practice. Yet, as with all other ritual forms I use, my current offering of the Sweat Lodge rite is aligned more with the spirit of the practice, than with the exact form of another culture's practice.

I learned to accept this assignment the hard way. When I first began working with the lodge I attempted to replicate an "official Native American" ritual, complete with songs and prayers that I learned from various teachers. All went well in the beginning. But after a year or so I started getting severe headaches after emerging from the lodge. Assuming I wasn't doing the form well enough, I attempted to solve the problem by trying harder to get the ritual exact. This did, indeed, change the nature of the headaches—they got much worse.

One day, I finally allowed the pain and confusion to drop me to my knees, and I submitted to inner guidance. "Why," I asked, "am I doing everything right and still getting sick?"

The response was immediate and clear: "It is not appropriate for you to be speaking another man's prayers. You have been given a voice; use *it*."

I guided the next lodge without a script and managed to exit without a headache for the first time in a while. Slowly, I gained confidence in my own prayerfulness as I respectfully and gratefully let go of the form that guided me to it.

The sweat lodge is typically a dome-shaped structure, about four feet high at the center, covered with tarps and blankets. The tarps are well secured to the ground with stones except for a single low doorway at one end. In the center of the lodge is a circular hole in the ground. This medicine hole acts as an altar that receives hot rocks from a fire burning outside the lodge. The door flap opens toward the outer fire pit, but when the flap is closed, the lodge is in total darkness.

The ritual is essentially a guided invitation to jump into the heart of this darkness—into the abyss of not knowing—and have this crisis held in sacred containment. Water added to the glowing rocks in the center of the lodge releases intense steam and heat. The purification process that ensues sends the blood roaring through every capillary, cleansing the physical body of toxins. With the addition of clear intent, prayer and song, the emotional body and mental body are likewise invited to let go of obstacles that impede the flow of spiritual vitality.

In the Sweat Lodge rite, we remember our relationship to creation as a *present time occurrence*. Creation is not just something that happened fifteen billion years ago, it is an ongoing event—an expression of the fiery passion of this universe. We will be invited to relinquish the encrustations of fear that separate us from that passion. We go to the sweat lodge to strengthen our ability to surrender, for once we have declared our intention to *seek* vision, we must then be prepared to *receive* whatever arises. For many men, the latter is often more difficult.

We devote a good part of this day to preparing the site and constructing our lodge. We work more slowly than normal because we are concerned with what we are building within us as much as what we build outside of us. If we work in disharmony, we create disorder, but if we work in beauty, we create beauty. There can be no other way.

Traditionally, a sweat lodge is made with saplings that are cut, stuck into the ground, bent over, and tied together to form a dome. Because our Quest site is on public land where it is environmentally unsound to cut so many live trees year after year, we construct our lodge using a grid work of rope that we then cover with tarps. Some men work on the lodge, while another group collects wood for the pyre that will heat the rocks.

The sun is low on the western horizon by the time our preparations are complete. The fire lies waiting for the spark to ignite it; the lodge waits to receive the hot rocks and our willingness to surrender.

The sun's descent below the horizon signals the moment to light the fire. We gather around the pyre and give thanks to the trees and rocks in the form of words and tobacco offerings. We hold in our mind's eye the solar fire that is captured within the molecules of wood. We imagine the rocks' great receptivity to take this fire into their flesh. We remember the mutuality between us and the Tree People, between us and the Rock People, and between us and the Mystery that gives birth to all things. We dare to trust the resonance we feel between the unknown depths in ourselves and the unknown depths in the nature of things. The ritual of the Sweat Lodge is built on this foundation of mutuality, and each step we take must be balanced within this perception.

The fire is struck and flames leap from the dry wood, hungry and passionate. An explosion of sparks shoot skyward as if to seed the night sky with new configurations of stars. Some of the men are called to sing and drum as the fire dances. Others find refuge in quiet inner reflection. Looking into the faces of the men standing near me, I see the flames reflected off the still waters of their eyes, and the beauty of this image brings tears to my own. I am reminded that this may very well be our last act on Earth. In such remembrance, the fire in my brothers' eyes is alone enough to restore a life.

With the onset of evening, as the funeral pyre blazes away in the distance, the camp takes on a beautiful and somber air. Each man privately turns toward his approaching death, facing it in a personal way. Conversation is minimal. Some men write letters to the ones who wait at home. Others sit by the river in quiet contemplation. From deep inside a tent comes sobs that are felt and understood by everyone in this camp. Some write poems, celebrations of faces seen in the mirror of death.

> The night is dark
> My soul is empty.
> I have drunk deep at the well of tears.
> I cry over the years lost . . .
> the relationships that will be no more
> the dreams that will never come true
> the manhood that will never be realized.
> The flame is out!
> Death be not proud
> Take all of me.
> —LIVES HIS VISION

> One day I must die
> like the leaves that fall from the trees
> and are carried to their burials
> on the running water's back
> I must die
> falling back to Father-Mother Earth
> like the raindrops
> breaking into countless pieces
> each one containing the whole
> and dissolving
> into numberless other bodies
> to become large once more
> I must die
> like the sparks that leap
> from the fire
> to blaze and fade
> my heat passing out
> in one last gift

to the universe
No man knows the hour of his death
no leaf knows the breeze
that will cut it loose
no raindrop the cloud
that will shake it free
no spark the twig
that will dissolve in flame
and send its light to the sky
Today is a good day to die
Today is a good day to live
—RUNNING WATER

Listen!
Listen!
Softly, it comes—
the Silence within
the Breath of the wind.
It calls out my name
one last time
Listen!
—TALL STANDING PINE

We move now to our final council before we give ourselves over to the Sweat Lodge. Here we review the form of the ceremony and listen to last-minute questions.

We designate our fire keepers, those who will carry the heated rocks, on shovels, into the lodge. During the ritual there will be four segments, sometimes called "doors" or "endurances." Each man must choose for himself to enter the lodge and must, at every moment, choose for himself whether to stay or leave. There is no coercion; participation in this rite must be voluntary or else it is meaningless. There is one suggestion, though, given to those who might choose to leave out of fear: If it gets too hot, pray harder but, more important, give yourself permission to receive help. Soften around the edges of the heat. Pray for the courage and strength to be defeated decisively. Find the true endurance that comes from surrender—surrender, the warrior's act of giving himself over to something larger.

The Sweat Lodge is a great teacher of the power of humility. When the heat's on, the lower you get to the ground, the cooler it is. You can get lower by physically bending over, and lower still by asking for help. Sometimes grasping the hand of the man next to us is all it takes to get us through the crisis. Or we can ask for help by calling out to the unseen world, to God, to the Mystery. Most of the help we get comes from the simple act of asking for it, for this puts us in truer relationship with the larger whole.

The sky has now turned its dark face toward us. The Medicine Wheel, aglow with the flickering lights of votive candles, is laid out before us like a fine banquet table. Among the stones are various offerings and tokens. Next to the northern stone rests a small sandstone carving of a Buddha. A clear quartz crystal sits at the Buddha's feet, radiating the candlelight in all directions. Across the Wheel at the southern stone a crucifix, displaying the sacred heart of Jesus, stands beside a candle. The fiery heart of Jesus and the crystal mind of Buddha—in good relation on this Wheel.

The eastern stone has attracted an Alcoholics Anonymous first-anniversary medallion, commemorating a full year of sobriety. It was placed by a man who now speaks of the medal as a symbol of his new dawn. The western stone is home to yet another medal, a Purple Heart, gained in service in Vietnam. With tears in his eyes, the vet explains that this is the first public showing of his medal. Until now he had been too ashamed of his participation in the war to reveal this part of his heart to a spiritual brotherhood. He asks us to look at him. He asks to be forgiven for all of the damage he inflicted on other human beings. He does not listen to our words; he will see in our eyes whether or not there is a home for him in our hearts. He is looking for help in making a home for himself.

A wedding band, which over the past few days has traveled around the circumference of the Wheel, now rests between two stones in the northwest quadrant. Placed by a man who describes his marriage as "stuck between sundown and midnight," he declares that the ring will stay until he learns either to accept this part of love's cycle or to express his fury about it.

Feathers, knives, pendants, prayers—each offering carrying a story, placed in relationship with the whole, surrounded in beauty. A monument to the growing level of trust we place in this community of men.

The tender silence of our contemplation is broken by sudden movement—something swiftly but silently approaches above the trees across the river. A chill runs up my spine as unearthly shrieks pierce the air like knives.

Owls.

Six or seven night warriors—close enough for us to see their big yellow eyes. They glare at our circle, bearing down on us with a fierce presence. Conversation stops, thought stops, and for some, breathing nearly stops as well.

"Welcome," a man whispers, his voice betraying more ambivalence than courtesy.

The owls shriek intently; civilized niceties are useless in situations like this.

"Oh, shit," the man adds. That response feels a bit more honest.

Welcome, you say? We are not here to be welcomed; we are here to hunt. You guys have been courting death all day. Now it is night . . . which one of you will be first?

The romance of the hero's journey now meets the reality of this path. The sudden appearance of the owls has caught us all off guard. Like sorcerer's apprentices, we fumble for belief systems or incantations that will buy us time to put this all in perspective.

Perspective, hell—there's a force here meeting you face to face with a sword ready to run you through. It's your move now, what do you do?

Within a split second each one of us confronts the sober truth of our relationship with death. The warmup is over; this is the test. And not one of us emerges without seeing clearly his ambivalence toward the great unknown. The heat's on already. The power of our collective intent has brought to us what we asked for—not in the way we expected it to come but in a way that honors the depth of our desire to confront ourselves honestly within the Great Mystery.

Owls, soul watchers, harbingers of night wisdom—you who see truth hidden in darkness. We have called on the Medicine of purification, and you have come. Are you not a reflection of that part of us that is willing to inhabit our own darkness? Your shrill cry has awakened us tonight to more of our truth. As we stand on the precipice of change we take heed of your wisdom:
Be careful what you pray for—you may get it.

Predetermined plans would have had us all in the sweat lodge some time ago. However, this journey requires that we respond to the ever-changing reality of the moment. The owls have given us a gift, and we will not turn it down in favor of a tidy plan.

I unwrap the Talking Staff Pipe and place it before us with the admonition we received from the owls: Be careful what you pray for.

Throughout this separation phase, we have slowly, inexorably loosened our grip on our various attachments to the world. Now, in this council, we will reduce all our questions to just one. What question will we hold in our hearts as we cross the threshold into an unknown realm?

Condensing our longings into one image is a challenge for most. To ask just one question forces us to go deeper. At the ego level of questing, answers are nothing more than superficial solutions: I want a better job, a better relationship, more money, a clearer sense of purpose, a bigger house, a stronger identity. Usually these answers are fast-fading blossoms of desire whose roots lie deep in fear. The heart, however, does not trade questions for answers like commodities. Instead it greets the challenge of the One Question as an invitation to jump into experience. The answer arrived at by the heart is not a single thing but a *process*. Sacred questions produce not solutions but offspring that grow in unpredictable ways. Only the heart can honestly come up with just one question and feel fulfilled in that quest. The One Question, connected to every other question in your life, places your Quest in service of the heart. What will it be?

Our Talking Staff round concludes. We pass into ritual silence and make our way to the lodge, its hulking shape outlined in the glow of the burning pyre.

At the door to the lodge we undress. I enter first through the low opening, crawling sunwise around the center to take a seat by the doorway. The rest follow in like manner, sitting in the order of arrival. We sit around the empty medicine hole and wait.

Outside the lodge, the fire keepers break apart the fire and dig out the rocks from a massive bed of coals. Inside, it is our responsibility to stay present and welcome each rock as it is placed before us. Let our attention rest in the immediate.

I call for the rocks.

Each rock lands in the stone-lined pit with a sharp clack. They glow red-hot and are seemingly translucent. The heat from even a single rock presses against the skin. One by one the rocks are carried in, the first seven bringing us into relation with the Seven Directions of the Medicine Wheel. I call for seven more, and then seven more again, before calling in the fire keepers. The door flap is lowered. The light from the outer fire is gone.

The glow of the rocks illumines the torsos and faces of the men—each body like an ember about to be claimed by the surrounding darkness. As the embers gradually fade, we ease our awareness into the time beyond time, where the physical eyes give way to the eyes of spirit, where light sets on the outer landscape and rises to illuminate the inner world, where the eye turned inward sees images that dance before the soul, leading it onward.

In the dim red-orange light these men look old, more than old—ancient. I see myself, in what mirror I do not know, but I see myself as clear as day. I too am ancient. My skin is wrinkled and indistinguishable from the bark of some tree I lean against. My hair is white and wispy, like spider silk. I am a native man. I belong.
—SEES THROUGH THE MOON

I offer cedar to the rocks. It crackles and dances across their fiery surfaces before filling the lodge with its cleansing fragrance. A ladleful of water is then offered. As soon as the liquid touches the rocks it explodes into steam with a loud crack. We begin our opening round of prayer. Prayer that brings our local acts here into accord with a larger sphere of relationship. Prayer that opens the door between the two worlds and reveals our true intent.

We remember those who have come before us, those spirits once embodied in the flesh of this world who now walk the spirit road. We honor our ancestors.

We remember that we sit in relationship with the community of all life. We embrace the present.

We remember that there are those who will come after us. We dedicate the fruits of our labors here to the generations that follow. May our acts nourish the future.

We remember all of our teachers, especially the first peoples of this land and give thanks for the guidance and ways that have been passed on to us here in our moment of need.

May each man here be given the spirit power to clear the way to see with new eyes, hear with new ears, speak with new tongues. May each one be strengthened so that his heart may live without armor, undefended before the source of his spiritual vitality. Ho—so be it!

A splash of water is offered with each prayer. The lodge quickly fills with thick clouds of hissing steam. Men groan in alternating spasms of fright and pleasure as their pores begin to open and sweat begins to flow. I take up the drum and call for these sighs to find their way into song. Our wordless chant calls in the spiritual presence of the guides, medicines, and deities we wish to have present with us. We sing our thankfulness for our lives, for the opportunity to sit here in brotherhood, on the Earth, in a sacred manner.

The fierce heat at our center melts my mind into past epochs held in stone, earth, and water. While holding the hands of men on either side and chanting-moaning with one voice, anointed with sweat, my

world stops. Within the community of men, in the tomb of the lodge, in the womb of the earth, I re-member my greater self.
                                        —LISTENING IN STILLNESS

The steam now circulates with the breath of our song. When our prayer is finished I call for our first door. The man sitting by the entrance opens the flap. Light from the fire outside illuminates the billowing clouds that exit the lodge. Our song leaves on these clouds, fertilizing the soul substance of our universe.

The fresh air that pours into the lodge renews our flesh and strengthens our resolve. How precious this air feels now, filling the lungs, cooling the skin, renewing the spirit. Each breath experienced here, truly a gift.

I call for the second round. The flap closes. Darkness once again. I pour water and once again the air is filled with stinging vapor. The rocks carry but a faint glow now, their fire retreating deeper inside. More water, some sage, and the air is charged with pungent intensity. Some men cry out in fear, their lungs gasping for air. The nostrils seem not to be able to open wide enough. We must find another way to breathe.

Many lessons line up, one after another: arrogance, fear, anger, resentment, letting go, and getting what you asked for. The water hits this time and I nearly go through the walls. My shoulders feel scalded, I'm shocked, hurt, angry. What the FUCK is he doing? Thank God I have my towel. I get as low as I can and cover my back. I've already spent too much time dealing with this ordeal my old way, toughing it out, figuring in my head how much time is left and hanging on until I make it. I'm working with a new way: letting go. That's not coming easy, but it is coming. Better now.
                                        —DEFENDER OF CHILDREN

Soften around each breath. Slowly and steadily, each breath a careful and conscious act. Feel the effect of hardening against the heat or of forcing the breath. Do these strategies bring you what you look for? Try breathing through the skin. Let the skin soften, slowly and gently; give yourself over to the heat.

Now feel the breath at the heart. Breathe the steam into the heart. And send the breath out through the heart. Let the heart soften around whatever it experiences. You are so much bigger than the fear in this lodge, there is no need to resist it. Practice breathing in the fear, negativity, and chaos. Breathe these into your heart, not into your mind. Fear will fester in the mind. In the heart, fear dissolves into sadness and tenderness. Keep dropping your awareness down into the heart—into the sadness and tenderness of your warrior's heart. And let the breath leave the heart. Let your spirit touch each man who sits in darkness here. Let it touch his desire for life, his suffering, his imperfection, his struggle. Send him your breath. Send him courage through your breath.

I offer four more splashes of water, water for all our relations— human and nonhuman—in the Four Directions. A geyser of steam hits the ceiling of the lodge and crawls down the sides, digging its claws in our backs. Time to pray.

Soften around the intensity and struggle of the planet now. Let us send our breath to those relations across the planet who touch our hearts with their suffering. Breathe through the frigid numbness of denial, breathe through the raging fire of anger, breathe through the helplessness. Simply be present, with your man's heart, to the pain of the world. Breathe in as much as you can bear. Soften around each breath. Breathe out as much compassion as you can bear. Send the world courage.

With the drum maintaining a steady heartbeat, we name the world suffering that we find in our hearts. That is where we send our prayers, for in our own hearts is where world healing takes place. And after what feels like a lifetime of heartbeats, we open the door to this fiery cauldron and send a wailing howl out into the night sky.

The light from the fire reveals many men doubled over in exhaustion from this last round. Sweat pours from our flesh. The great salty ocean soaking into the receptive earth.

Someone calls out for water. It's about time, I sigh. I thank him for his willingness to voice his needs. He speaks for many of us here. A ladleful of water is passed around the circle. Precious water of life. Each drink here, truly life renewing.

I call for our third round. The flap encloses us once again, now in complete darkness.

This round is dedicated to those places inside our own body-mind that suffer from lack of loving presence. I bless this next water to the purpose of self-loving.

Let us enter the dissolve once again and let the steam generated from this sacred intent penetrate to those places inside that are in pain. All the world of help and healing waits for your permission. Place a hand on those places that may not have been touched by love in a long time and send your breath there. Let the contact and warmth be felt deeply. Hold yourself in your own loving arms as you are held within the respectful containment of this lodge. The acceptance of the Lover, the action of the Warrior: true comrades in this lodge.

It's hot, too hot. I'm suffocating in this pitch black grave. I can't get out. Panic comes and goes like waves of fire. The hiss of more heat, and I scream "Open the gate, open the gate!"

I've got to go down, remember my intention, the root of my heart's desire. My belly on the Earth now, my face in the soil, I dive deeper. There's a cold running river down here. I drink, and I breathe cool air. Just moments before, my body was crumpled in a death panic. Now I sit up! I raise my head, sniffing at the hot air like a curious animal, my eyes open—searching the glowing rocks for a glimpse of the Great Mystery.

Into my consciousness comes a horse and night rider. The rider, with great tapered wings and a full headdress with feathers like spears. He raises an arrow to his bow, points it straight at me. I raise a wall of protection and the rider vanishes across the threshold of consciousness. While my physical body continues to burn, my soul body sits by the underground river, reminds me that this is a good day to die. I say yes. The rider returns. I open my heart toward the point of his arrow. The arrow flies from the bow passing through my chest without pain. I don't feel fear, I feel like the beloved! What this arrow loves most is the open heart of a man.

—BROKEN WALK

*It's hot as hell in here. I can't breathe. My body's in a knot. I want to
surrender. I want to do it. I want to be in charge as I go. I want to do
it. I don't want to be done to. I'll surrender on my terms.*

*My terms? I'm suffocating in my terms. I finally see it—the
prayer that's been leading my life: "Great Spirit, give me vision—
here are the specs . . . "*

—*Frozen River*

*Mother . . . she is here, beckoning me to open my legs so she could
again fondle my genitals. Out of habit, my legs open, I continue to
cry—but then a new sound comes out of my throat: "No! No! No!
NOOO!" I kick with my legs and push her away—and she is gone.
My back relaxes for the first time in ages. I fall crumpled and free into
a heap on the earthen floor of the lodge. I say yes to that child's no, for
the first time.*

—*Trumpeter Swan*

A soft chant rises out of the darkness of the lodge and weaves its
way between lingering cries and moans. It carries the feeling of a
lullaby, a sweet offering to places that hurt. I pass the ladle
around at the close of this door, water for drinking, water for
those who have just come out of exile, water to soothe and nourish. I call for the open door. We wait for our vessel to empty once
again.

The fire keepers bring in four fresh stones to see us through
our last round. The glow returns to the lodge. We move slowly
and peacefully through our completion round. We give thanks
and release the spirits who have attended our defeat. This purg-
ing process has stripped away defensive armor—not all of it but
enough to clear the way to hear the spirit voice more clearly. In
our birth from this womb-lodge we may remember how it feels to
live in the world naked and unashamed. The door to the Grail
Castle will be momentarily glimpsed, momentarily opened. Each
one here will know whether he has the power and humility to
walk undefended through that opening.

I offer rhythmic splashes of water—a small amount for each
man present. It has been an honor to pour water for these men

who have revealed so much of themselves in the short time we have been together. I remember the arrows of intention we loosed during our Sunrise Ceremony days ago. These arrows are looking to return to us, looking for receptive targets now. Will we allow ourselves to be penetrated by life? We shall see. For now, we start with small steps.

We crawl out of this lodge like infants into the arms of this cool night.

Our wet, slippery, fragile, newborn bodies will be shaped according to whatever vision we will hold. Let us not be too quick to put ourselves back together, too quick to reach for a recognizable identity. The newborn butterfly waits for his wings to fill with blood before he will fly. Let us rest in the safety we have created here and linger in between thoughts, in between worlds, as long as it takes for our true wings to unfold.

One by one we are birthed through the small doorway of the lodge. The waning firelight illuminates a primordial procession to the river, a migration of soft, steaming bodies back to the waters. Some then find their way to stand before the radiant embers of the pyre, others bathe in the cool light cascading from the moon. Each one in relationship with a reflection of his soul.

I emerge from the lodge in a state of shock. Every nerve has been fried—or boiled. My pores gape open, and when the wind blows I am a flute with a hundred thousand holes. Blind, overpowered, I stagger toward the river.

I totter on the rocks, stoop down, look into the water, and surrender to it. For a moment I float halfway between heaven and Earth, naked yet clothed in the waters of the stream, hot, cold, dead, alive— simply being.

I emerge with a cry—of pain, relief, shock, joy. I stumble out of the river and take hold of a tree for support. The touch of the bark startles me—as if I had never touched a tree before. I gaze around. Without my glasses things are a strange blur but still clear. I can see stars. I can see the dying fire across the river where those stones had been made to glow. There is water, sky, cold air, my steaming body, and what seems to be a thousand naked newborn men.

I make my way back to my tent site. I lie on the ground watching the sky.

—RUNNING WATER

Eventually, we each move off into the night. We have made the first of many threshold crossings.

10

THE MIRROR OF SOLITUDE

In this high place
it is as simple as this,
leave everything you know behind.

Step toward the cold surface,
say the old prayer of rough love
and open both arms.

Those who come with empty hands
will stare into the lake astonished,
there in the cold light
reflecting pure snow
the true shape of your own face.

—DAVID WHYTE

The wakeup drum finds most men already up this morning, making final preparations. Some will be taking nearly everything with them. Others will leave behind food, tent, and sleeping bags, traveling only with the clothes on their backs and a few essential emergency items.

All our preparations for the Quest, all the rituals and meditations and dances up to this point lead us now to the edge of the threshold world of solitude. Whether to step across that threshold, however, is a decision each man must make for himself. The spiritual warrior is one who chooses to enter the wilderness battleground of his own heart. Guiding him through this realm is the fundamental question: Who am I? But if he is to penetrate the innermost chamber of his heart of hearts, he must leave even this one question behind. Only in inner silence will he be able to hear the whisper of his true voice; only in communion with the "council of all beings" will he discover the vision that reflects the true breadth of his being.

Eventually, all are gathered and waiting on the dance ground. Those who will be questing atop the ridges fasten the three-gallon water bags to their packs. The weight of such cargo, no matter how essential, brings worried looks to some faces. Finally, all equipment, questions, fears, and expectations are packed, secured, and ready to go.

The drum calls us to stand around the Medicine Wheel for a ritual of farewell. Here, bathed in the sweet scent of cedar incense, and still fresh-born from the sweat the night before, we peer into each other's eyes. The feeling of brotherhood that fills our hearts at this moment spills out as tears, hugs, and whispered words of parting. Many have never touched such intimacy, such depth of feeling with other men. As one man bid me good-bye, tears wet the cheeks of his face, a face that had been dry of feeling since childhood. He whispered that he felt ashamed because he wanted to be strong. "Brother," I reminded him, "those tears are all the strength you'll need."

Here, at the hub of our community wheel, the men formally declare their choice to leave behind the trail that led to this place and to this community. Here they declare their intention to enter the trackless wilderness of solitude. Flanked by two medicine helpers, I stand at the northern gate of the Wheel, the gate of emptiness that all must pass through before new vision is possible. From this point on, we will view these men as spirits, invisible and intangible. It is a gesture of releasing the last vestiges of personal history we have shared in our time together, so that when they return we can greet them with eyes less clouded by expectation.

In my hands is a cup of ashes, reminders of the First Fire of creation time. Mingled among these are ashes from the fire that ignited our Sunrise Ceremony on a morning now long ago, atop a rocky knoll now far away. One by one each man moves to the northern gate. I hold the ashes before each one: "Ashes from creation's fire: what remains when the fire of the body goes out." I dip my finger in the cup and smudge his right cheek: "You are leaving our time now." I smudge the left cheek: "Leaving our place now." Ashing his forehead: "Becoming invisible to this world and more available to the next. I place you now in the hands of the Great Mystery."

Once all have passed around the Wheel, we take a moment to witness the ashed faces—some stoic, some streaked with muddy tears. It is time to leave.

I feel the ashes erase the surface features of my face. I pray that each moment of solitude impress on this face its signature, and in its dying be released. May these ashes wash my face until no trace of a former life is left that I may offer my devotion to this present moment. And, as echoes from the past emerge, let them dissolve on the surface of this ashed face. Let my next expression arise out of the nothingness that is ever faithful to truth—let nothing stand between me and the ever-changing face of creation.

—STANDS BY HIS HEART

One last look as we move delicately away from each other, in silence, toward the solitary time. God could kick us around like a football out there alone on the ridge or up the river. The loneliness might never cease, and fear could drive us mad. Whatever I've been denying all these years could fall out of my ribs and stand before me like Eve!

Brother, I'll never see you, never see myself, know myself quite the same again. Man, I'm just a ghost out there! All I got is a patch of earth to cling to.

Brothers, I have your eyes, your tears, and this soft man-grace. As I turn and walk away something in my heart feels so loose, and I can't remember much about myself. Oh God. . . . This is a good day to die! I go.

—FROG PRINCE

My helpers and I escort each man to his solo site. And there we leave him with reminders of the essential practice:

Remember yourselves as seekers of truth, certainly, but also as carriers of truth—as both arrow and target. May you see yourself reflected in many worlds.

Remember your purpose.

Be attentive.

Trust whatever comes.

Each one crosses into the threshold world and disappears.

In the unformed openness of solitude, the heart will do what it came here to do. For each man, that will be something different. No man here will presume to know, and certainly will not prescribe for another, what it is he must do to honor his destiny. Each will move according to the currents within himself: at times following his true voice, at times hiding from it; at times following this heart, at times taking the hand of fear. We will bear witness to each one as he discovers his own way to truth.

I follow Blue Heron's long loping stride . . . through the ferns, down the trail, along the stream. Silence between us, concentration, speed, effort, and effortlessness—walk all day or not another step. His winged arm lifts, pointing to the boundary rock of my territory. One beaked nose to another, he blesses the depth of my questioning. I loose the arrow from the bow. He turns and goes.

Through the deep-leaf-mold-fern incline I pick my way along. Up through the split in the rock wall. Am I going to find the right place? Can I let whatever I find be the right place? This idea of "right"— trouble already!

Right enough for what?

To make me worthy. To make my father finally say that he's proud of his third son. To make me sufficient to love. Right enough to hide from the two-faced contempt/inferiority demon. Keep trudging up the hill, Jack.

I come on a little rock ledge, all coated in moss, half a foot deep. Small white pines taking root. A yellow birch sapling grows out of a crack. There are tiny gray feathers, half a dozen with bright orange tips, a small hollow bird bone, and another pile of scattered feathers— these with bright yellow tips. I follow the path, it leads into a crevice beneath the rock wall. Scat. I imagine the predator—alert, patient, crouching. The bird—bright, restless, perching, singing. Then the quick-darting bite, before the note is finished, before the seed is swallowed—before your next step is taken, walking man. Pay attention, Jack.

I want to stay here, but this is the fox's camp, or dinner table. I follow up the ledge around the cliff, hoping for a trail or passage up through to the mountain above. Around the bend there are, of course, two clefts in the stone wall. Undoubtedly, poisonous snakes lie above in the right cleft and a bear with an attitude is waiting on the left. God I love options. What did Joseph say about sacred choice? I go left. The bear will get it over with quicker. Keep stumbling uphill, with this fucking Winnebago of a backpack getting tangled in the brush. I climb into a clearing; it's a nice spot, but up ahead I'm sure I'll find something spectacular. Always looking for a special place just beyond my orbit. I go on and on—so like me. I tire of my hungry eyes and head back down to the place that I liked. Not too pretentious, a minor quest site, no nesting eagles. I call it home.

—BLACK TONGUE

After the experience of the Sweat Lodge—which for me was far more searing emotionally than it was physically—I was glad for the monastic silence that followed. My mind was still ajitter from my disorientation after the sweat, but even with no words, various brothers managed to convey their sympathy and support. Concerned glances, smiles, hugs, and the gift of a peacock feather "for protection" helped ground me and filled me with deep emotion I couldn't put a name on.

As a group of us struck out downriver hunting for our solo sites, I thought of the stories I'd read about Indians being placed in harsh, unprotected spots for their solitary quests to allow their bodies to be battered by the elements. A hillock, which overcropped the river, caught my eye. I wondered if this might be such a place.

When I reached the crest, I found a beautiful campsite that had obviously been used before. In a circle of stones were the carefully built makings of a fire. Under the shelter of some trees was a perfectly flat surface, cleared of brush and stones—it would be as easy to pitch

a tent here as in my own backyard. A few steps away was another sheltered clearing that would be perfect for a Medicine Wheel.

My first reaction was "No! I can't stay here! This would be too easy." But then I caught myself. Nowhere is it written, except perhaps in the annals of my personal history, that my time of solitude has to be a grueling ordeal. Must I always look for suffering to prove myself worthy? The more I let it, the more this hilltop clearing beckoned me to enjoy its hospitality. I accepted.

—MENDING HEART

Awareness of choice is the precious gift awarded to the seeker who is willing to endure the struggle through the maze of outer directives. The day dawns fresh and clear when a man wakes up and realizes that the road taken by his father is but one of many roads. A man's task, as Don Juan has said, is to walk the path that has heart. This is the only path that can possibly lead us home—and no one can walk it for us.

>>   <<

Back in base camp, my fellow guides and I sit in the vacuum created by the men's leaving. A mixture of relief and sadness quickly fills the space—the past few days have been a rich banquet of intense interaction. The Quest demands more presence than we usually bring to bear on life and we are, frankly, exhausted by the effort and glad for the quiet of this incubation time. Yet the bonds we have made with these men have run deep, and our hearts feel their absence.

We are careful to take good care of ourselves during these days, even as we go about the preparations required to receive the men on their return from solitude.

Our primary practice, though, is to continue to hold the container for this journey. We practice the art of soul watching: the art of spiritual attunement to each man's journey and well-being. There are no magical forms to this practice. What is essential is love—a willingness to extend ourselves toward each man and bless him in his uniqueness and imperfection.

Our love guides us periodically to sit around the Medicine Wheel. We light candles in honor of each one now offering himself in solitude to the Mystery. The calling to travel alongside these men as guides gives us a precious opportunity to be privy to deep turnings of their souls. We set aside time here to open ourselves to the soul essence of each man.

One by one we will call out each man's name. We pray for him in the manner taught by the Oglala holy man Black Elk: "Great Mystery, send our brothers vision, so that all of our people may live." Even as these men are alone, they are alone together. And even as they now celebrate their separation from the known world, we keep before us the awareness of our people. Without a context larger than ourselves, there is no room for new vision.

We are careful not to presume to know what is best for these guys. We pray that they each receive whatever experience best serves their awakening. We must practice the faithfulness that we so fervently prescribe for them.

So we sit in the silence with each of them. We invite them to come to us in images, feelings, and symbols. We may give our imaginations wings or legs that prowl silently and invisibly through the forest. In the silence, we may feel hearts beating through the ground.

The heart-ground stirs as we call out the name of the man we once knew as Will. . . .

I come to this ridge certain that an eagle will be messenger of my vision. If not eagle, then some other high-flying bird of prey. For hours I look up into the sky, my eyes riveted and ready to catch hold of any movement whatsoever. For hours I sit in the blazing sun, a steadfast warrior practicing my faithfulness. All the while, however, an endless column of ants makes its way across the hot bedrock and across my bare legs. For a while the ants are interesting, but I soon tire of them and get really irritated. I start flicking them off my legs and screaming at them as if to say, "Can't you see I'm doing something very important?" All the while, they diligently continue to pull at my attention.

Finally, I give in, look down, and just watch them. Searching the sky has rewarded me with little more than a strained neck and a bad sunburn. But as I watch the ants, I shift from annoyance to admiration for their resolute devotion to whatever they are doing. "What are you doing? What's the message?" I finally ask.

They whisper in my inner ear: "It's time to pick up the pieces. Some important details in your life need attention. The God you seek is in these details. And by the way, like us, you won't be able to do this work alone."

—Ant Warrior

How will vision come to us? Where will it lead us? No one can know in advance, but the ego, of course, wants to call the shots on this one. It creates categories of "meaningful" and "meaningless" and continually upholds this split by judging what is important and what is not.

For the soul, however, *all* experience is meaningful. All experience at a deep level is epiphany, for all experience holds a key that may help us manifest our divinity. This lesson comes very slowly for most of us. We may need to be repeatedly disappointed, repeatedly annoyed, repeatedly let down before we allow the heart to celebrate what is right in front of us. Coyote, the Trickster, is the master teacher of this:

One day Coyote was walking along the riverbank and saw some plums floating on the water. Now, Coyote loves to eat, so he reached out over the bank for those plums but they disappeared. He kept doing this, and they kept disappearing. So he really reached out the next time, but he lost his balance and fell to the bottom of the river. He nearly drowned trying to get at those plums.

Three days later his wife came by and found him still splashing around in that river.

"Woman," he said, "during the day juicy ripe plums float in this magical spot—but at night they go away."

"Stupid dog-of-a-dog," she said, "those plums are still on the tree. You worthless fool of a husband—chasing shadows when the truth hangs on a tree right above your head."

She hit him over the head with a stick and brought him home. Coyote never did get those plums.

Sitting at the base camp Medicine Wheel, we continue to sound the names of our questing brothers, visiting each one through our silent vigil. Each one, opening eyes long closed. . . .

I came on an old tree that had fallen over a long time ago. The massive root crown was exposed and was bleached nearly white by the sun. I had seen this tree when I first arrived, and I was immediately intrigued by it. But I was moving too fast inside to pay any attention to it or anything else for very long.

At sunset I finally sat down in front of that tree and let go of everything else that was pulling at my mind. The moon rose and its light revealed the weathered face of an old man in the trunk. It was a broad face with a long, sharp nose, evenly set eyes, and strong cheeks. A curl of wood formed the lower lip of an open mouth, and two angled cones poked below, forming a neatly bearded chin. From his forehead sprang two root-antlers, one reaching up to the sky, the other curving down, its tip resting on the ground.

I sat there for a long time captivated by this figure. I wanted something of him. But I began to doubt myself because I had come here with the intention of making contact with some of the wonder and joyfulness I had had as a boy, before I had learned to be my father's idea of courageous. So, now it was odd to be not with the young one but with the old one.

I felt myself doing again what I did with older men I wanted to know: I pretended to act older and more responsible, hoping that mask would make up the distance between us, make up for my lack. I have tried to get older men to take me among them and bless me. So it is, too, with my old man here on the ridge. But the more I pretend, the more I feel absent from his vastness and knowledge.

After I sat with the old man for the next whole day, I saw something I had not noticed before. Where his long curving horn met the ground, a tiny spruce grew, a foot high and brilliantly green. The old face was actually tilted toward the young spruce. They were together, one full of experience and one full of hope and desire. And the old figure was most generous, not distant at all, his mouth open but quiet as he passed his sap and his life to the young one through the broad swirling grain of his horn.

For most of my life I've felt like a boy, a pretender. In the spruce I saw a boy, and at his shoulder was a man, and both are mine.

—NATE

Wilderness is home to wildness. The animated winds that sing through these mountains invites awareness to take wing; the wild waters of river and storm cleanse the dust over perception's eyes; lightning and fire lead awareness to secrets held in darkness; and the glacier-scarred rock gives perception ancient eyes, at ease with the slow movement of earth time.

Yes, awareness is a wild thing. Its natural predilection is to leap and bound across categories of thought. We don't need a lot of schooling to reclaim the vitality of awareness. We need only to give ourselves over to whatever it is we find fascinating. And then allow that alluring other to return us back to ourselves with eyes more open.

I step from the tree cover out onto the ridge. The sudden beauty of the surrounding peaks and valleys overwhelms me. At the sight of it all, I burst into tears.

Having been so violated as a child, I'm now always vigilant about boundaries. I trust Joseph Blue Heron as a careful man, who rarely makes "you" statements. But, looking out at the valley, he turned to me and said, "I'm glad you will shed your tears in this place, my brother. Trust."

I hear, "You Trust," and am amazed. Trust!—the Medicine of the South, of its green color. Not in this lifetime!

After erecting my tent, I carefully select stones for a power circle to sit in. I live "safely," always "covered." So I know I want to spend my alone time naked. I shed my clothes and enter my circle, believing nothing and ready for whatever—maybe.

But I haven't arrived. I'm not fully here. To do that, I slowly sur-

mise I must masturbate. My sexuality is where I was most deeply shamed and where I continue to shame myself. "I'm no longer seventeen, I should be past this." As a married man, "What am I, some sort of a wimp who doesn't get enough with his wife?" It's certainly the sign of how defective and unblessed I am as a man.

So, it feels daring to jerk off in this sacred place. But somehow I know it's okay—what better way for me to arrive here, shame and all? I try to get off fast—maybe do it, but not do it. But that doesn't work. The trees tell me to work on myself slowly, sensuously, with full attention. I do this, and my final release is enormous.

I feel great. I then start to think about the ceremonial garment I'd spent so much time on preparing for the Quest. I'd carefully included strips of red, green, black, and white for the Four Directions and their medicines. But now, I hesitantly regret I'd included no blue—the color for spirituality. This Quest is moving me at very deep levels— but hey, none of this spiritual stuff for me. If it isn't solid and real, I don't want to hear it.

Then, it begins.

From my left, a butterfly flies into my circle. It hovers for a moment, flies all around me in one direction, then in the other, three times in all. I sit utterly still. I've never experienced a butterfly that came toward me. They always fly away.

This one now lands on my right foot!—which I call my wound foot, and which I'd actually wounded skipping over the rocks on the first day of the Quest! From there, it hops up to my raised right knee. As it lingers silently, its two large, dark eyes stare directly into mine.

But do you expect me to believe this?!

It dives to flutter wildly between my legs, threatening my dick, making me fear I'd be struck—a blow to my penis, like in the initiation stories I read about. No way! No. No. No.

Bad enough, but now, the really unimaginable. The butterfly flies to the pool of my seed and begins to drink. It's drinking my cum like nectar! Like food for its life! I literally slap my face. Goddamn—this is actually happening.

It continues to drink. This messenger from the earth accepts the product from my erect cock and balls—of my sin. It accepts me, the essence of me. What I am gives life. I'm too shaken even to cry.

I gaze at it closely. I see the butterfly's body and the first third of its raised wings are black. My color, the color of my birth medicine, the dark West. Then I notice the middle third of its wings is a band of white, for the North. And the outer third is a band of red, for the East. Up to that moment, the butterfly had kept its wings erect, but now it lowers them to a flat display. And on the upper side of each wing, the upper side is blue! The earth has sent me the spirit color I had neglected to give myself!

Though my head is literally reeling, the rationalist in me dies hard. I think critically, "What a pity there's no green on this butterfly. Then all the Medicines would be represented."

At that second, in my head I hear a deep, reverberating boom. And for the first time I see. I look out at a whole world around me, of hills and valleys vested in green, a world dressed in the color of trust. I cannot stop crying—the tears of a butterfly soul maybe coming home to itself at last.

In the end, I'm afraid. This'd be fucking incredible if it were happening in a dream. What does the earth want of me if it hits this unblessed unbeliever over the head with such a sign for real?

—Medicine Butterfly

Those beings who look kindly on the parts of us we have learned to distrust shine a ray of light into our darkest places. They open a way to self-remembering. We go to the wilderness because it helps us to love ourselves as we are. It teaches by example. If nothing else, nature is totally and shamelessly self-accepting.

The sky that surrounds Mark on top of the ridge is fuming with a boiling energy. The day's heat drives the clouds into massive thunderhead columns. The air is also filled with a celebration and vitality he has not felt for years.

The storm tugs at me. It asks me to leave the sleepy secrecy of my tent to stand with my face to the wind. I leave the tent, leaving behind a part of me that says no—the part that doesn't want trouble.

I stomp around and around a ten-foot circle, so many times I lose count. I dance until there is a grooved path in the earth below my feet. There is a rage that moves through me, screaming until I lose my voice.

Something moves me to pick up a huge boulder and throw it at a dead tree nearly fifteen feet away. To my surprise the boulder hits dead center. I pick up one rock after another and hurl them with great accuracy until the tree collapses. I start moving my body in ways I'm not accustomed to—like some instinctive animal. I feel deeply connected to the world around me. Who is this primitive, raw man that lives in me?

After a long time of this, I collapse on the ground and begin to shake. Tears flow from my eyes, but I can't even name the feeling. Who is this man who could kill a deer with his bare hands one minute and praise the beauty of a wildflower the next? I cry myself to sleep lying there on the earth.

When I awake, I hear the sound of one of the men singing from deep within the valley below me. Fallen into sleep on the earth, stirred awake by a song from a man's heart—this is not the same world as before.

I watch the mountains across the valley to the south until the sun sets below the horizon. I speak no words, but again I feel that deep connection to the world.

When darkness settles in, I slowly move toward my tent to be with the one I left behind there. I have a story he needs to hear.

—BLACK CROW

Chuck has established his threshold camp on an open rise just above the river. He comes with a clear sense of purpose. Just six months ago he had resolved to tell his parents about his gay sexuality. He especially wanted to ask his father to bear witness to his truth. But before he could act on his resolve, both his parents were suddenly taken to the hospital for entirely different illnesses. Less than two weeks later both were dead. This sudden overturning of life had left him in a state of shock. His unfinished bereavement has brought him to this place to find completion. A ritual of forgiveness between him and his father begins to unfold.

I sit in front of a small twig fire. A brilliant full moon hangs overhead. The watery blue moonlight and the yellow radiance of the fire are so different, yet their blending cast my surroundings in a myste-rious and harmonious light.

I was terribly disappointed I didn't get a chance to clear with my father when he was alive. But I finally understand that what I must do does not require that he be here to respond to me—I just need to speak my truth clearly and fully. His presence in my psyche is just as real to me as his presence in body.

In front of the fire I place a mirror, a smudge stick, a photo of my father as a young man, his written biography, and an object that had touched his body—a paisley tie.

"I want to tell you everything I have stored in my heart but never told you . . . everything." I tell him all I can remember about his life, reviewing all of the details he had left behind in his autobiography. I tell him what I see between the lines that he did not come out and say. I speak freely of how much I love to express myself through dance—of how much Eros and joy I experience. Dancing is my favorite form of prayer. I speak of my love of men and of my sexual attraction. I let him know how I feel knowing that he had been physically abused by his father. And I finally bring up the one incident that has estranged me from him since I was eleven—held in place all these years by my unwillingness to forgive him or myself. I look at his eyes in the photo and at my own eyes in the mirror, and speak to him about the time he fondled my genitals when I was a boy. It happened only once, that I can recall, but it was never spoken of. I speak of it now. And I reveal everything else I ever felt and thought in all the years we talked, fished, and rattled sabers.

I close this ritual by burying his tie under a large rock. And then the wolf in me encircles that burial stone with my scent and with water to speed the decay. Knowing that few people would understand this—or even worse, knowing that they would attempt to explain it away with some Freudian theorizing—I nonetheless follow my instincts and urinate on this spot. If there's nothing else this Quest has taught me, it is to remain faithful to my instincts. I step away from that spot, at peace with myself and with my father.

And my vision comes in a dream:

The sale of my parents' house in Florida had closed, and I went there as the new owners were settling in. . . . There were lots of people and my father appeared looking healthy and fit. I realized that I was the only one who could see or hear him. I asked him, "What's it like for you on the other side?"

He said, "It's wonderful. By the way, I always loved your dancing—and thanks for taking me camping in the Adirondacks."

—BLUE STAR

Another man has placed himself by a quiet bend in the river. The water's soothing song has called him to this place to seek nourishment. He is a capable man, a leader and a caretaker in the outer world. Yet he repeatedly uses Thoreau's phrase "quiet desperation" to describe the condition of his inner life. He is here because his soul has been calling out for the healing balm of flowing water since he arrived.

In base camp all I could think about was how badly I wanted to be alone. Now that I'm here, I'd give anything to be back in community. My attention is jumping all over the place in its typical monkey-mind fashion. At one point, I start innocently humming the "Here and Now" chant that we sang at our first welcome dance circle. I discover that is just what I needed. I continue to use it to help me stay focused in this place. I sing it over and over again as I lie by the river. I start to get drowsy and sing it as if it were a lullaby, until I drift off to sleep.

During my nap I roam into the dreamworld:

I am sitting in a pool of water—the pool we went to on the first day of this Quest for our river cleansing. Suddenly, it is winter, and I'm now with a group of old men sitting in a pool surrounded by ice—like members of the Polar Bear Club. I look downstream and see a young boy and a woman walking across the river ice. The boy falls through the ice but the woman just stands there, with a shovel in her hand, pointing to him but doing nothing. I rush to the scene, grab the shovel from her and begin breaking away the ice. The boy is lying motionless on the river bottom. I reach down and grab him and lift him out. He is frozen solid, pale, and without a heartbeat. I open my jacket and hold him close to my body heat. It looks like he is a goner, but I continue to hold him until he revives. He opens his eyes and looks at me with pleading eyes. I hold him tight to my body, because my body is teaching his body how to keep the fire going inside. It's a direct body-to-body transmission.

I wake from my nap as the sun is beginning to set. I make a doll-like replica of that boy and sit by the fire cradling him. I keep him warm and tell him stories under the stars. I feed him "father's milk." For all three nights, this is all I do. And some part of my life, that I never realized was missing, is gradually restored.

—STANDS BY HIS HEART

There are parts of ourselves that only come out at night. Those parts that we have cast out of our daylit world. Many have been wandering through the wilderness of darkness for so long that they act in unpredictable ways. Our fear of them keeps them in exile.

But every so often we are called out to meet these dark faces. They will be met, but only on their turf. To know the dark, we must go there without artificial light—that is, without prejudice and presumption. This skill is learned only through experience. The wilderness gives us ample opportunities to practice.

I've always been afraid of being alone at night—especially alone at night in the woods. I remember the Quest guides saying we should expect demons—that demons feed off of fear. If that's the case, then I'm a McDonald's for some pretty fat spooks. For the first two days of my solitude, I have been expecting a major attack, something along the lines of a scene from Star Wars. *But nothing happened. The fact that I made sure I was in my tent asleep an hour before sundown might have something to do with the scarcity of demon sightings. Or maybe they've just been making their way up the ridge visiting the others first—saving me for dessert?*

By the third night I gave up on the idea that demons would come and finally relaxed a bit. Even so, I continued to sleep with a stout stick by my side, just in case.

The last night I dreamt:

I am standing next to this strange, dark guy who is putting off weird vibes. His back is to me, so I can't see his face. I want to leave, but I'm stuck in place as if there's a magnetic field of attraction flowing between us. Suddenly, he turns around and looks at me. He's ugly, with a huge hooked nose and bloodshot eyes. He just stares at me and yells "Arrrrgggghhhh!"

And oddly enough, I'm not afraid. And I say, "I got it!"

And I wake right up.

Somehow I understood that he was challenging me to be in the night. So I got up out of my tent and went out and stood in the night. I didn't take my flashlight . . . but I did take my stick—just in case. (Demons hate sticks.) Someday, I might be able to face this thing without the stick, but for now, this is a good thing. The world is dark half the time. I'm finally willing to walk into that.

—Earth Drum Dancer

One night I had a vision. I don't mean a dream or a hallucination, but a mental image that was as powerful to me as any dream I've had:

I'm in a heavy wood cabin in the English wilderness during the Middle Ages. The interior is very simple and all the pots, pans, utensils, shelves, and furniture are coarse and rough. It is clear that I am a man of simple means. There's a knock at the door. I open it, and there on the other side of the doorway is myself. With one exception: The me that has knocked is terrified, shaking, and grimacing, unable to speak. Here is my fear. I motion for him to come in and bid him sit at my table. As he takes a seat, he continues to shake, and his face is a mask of muscular tension. I offer him food. He will not eat. I hold him tenderly. It does not comfort him. I ask him what he wants, and he does not reply. And then I realize he wanted to be invited in, that is all. I can go about my business, now that I have acknowledged his presence and have turned toward him.

This has changed my relationship to fear.

—Seth Weaver

Bud dedicates his solitude to exploring what he calls the Dark Council—the shadow sides of his being. He is inspired in this by Robert Bly, who wrote, "How many years pass before a man finds the dark parts of himself that he threw away? When he retrieves those parts, other people will begin to trust him." Gradually, in his meditations over the three days, Bud discovers the names of those who sit on this council: Judgment, Misplaced Anger, Perfectionism, Praise Craving, Fear of Ridicule, and Guilt. He discovers their faces, too—gruesome, twisted masks, which he paints in his sketchbook. He goes into his inner darkness to find them but then takes them out of hiding, into the light of awareness. He speaks to each of them—some he holds with compassion, others with fierce contempt. And this dialogue is the beginning of true relationship, the foundation of trust.

Ron enters into solitude with the intention to track down the Mean Spirit that lives within him and destroy it. In the threshold time he glimpses the face of the Mean Spirit in many places: the twisted bole of a tree trunk, the ripples of the stream, and the embers of a fire.

> *Then it dawns on me: This Mean Spirit is part of all things. It is part of me, too. I can't purge it—completely. I can only learn to accept that it exists and live with it some, before I determine what needs to be done with it. To honor this insight, I create a ceremony service involving the Four Elements. A rock is Earth, a leaf that had floated on the breeze is Air, a burned match is Fire, and droplets from the stream are Water. I bury only part of each thing, signifying that the Mean Spirit still remains in all things. I say a prayer of gratitude for this new way of seeing.*

When we explore unknown territory, there's always a risk we will get lost. That, after all, is the point of the initial phase of any passage rite. It's not always easy, though, to welcome being lost, let alone intend it. But thankfully, the part of our nature that is continually seeking wholeness is not afraid of loss. And it faithfully leads us into that part of the inner/outer wilderness that we have not yet learned to love.

> *I was quite tired and weak due to fasting. On the third day, still having had no vision, I went for a hike to shout at the universe and vent my anger at this "bullshitting game of Vision Questing." Given my state of mind, it's not surprising that I quickly got totally lost. In my*

confusion I made things worse by roaming about aimlessly trying to find the way back. Suddenly, I heard the sound of a large animal moving. Frightened, I froze in place. For the first time on this journey I stood still and was fully aware. Only then did I see a large doe looking right at me. I watched her, and she watched me for what seemed like forever. Finally, she moved away slowly. I stood there wondering if this was supposed to be "my vision." It was quite an ordinary sighting and not an unusual exchange, I thought. Except—except that after the deer left I somehow had the clarity of mind to discern my direction home.

Although I resisted at first, I am grateful for this initiation into aware stillness. Knowing that this is a path that will lead me home, I look forward to growing into it more fully in the journey ahead.

—LISTENING IN STILLNESS

One man finds himself lost not once but twice—and on the same day. After conducting a Sunrise Ceremony some distance from his camp, Don tries to return to his tent, but becomes disoriented.

Quickly, I lose the peacefulness I had started the day with. My breath quickens, and my heart begins to pound. I panic and have trouble thinking clearly. I twist my ankle and lose my footing several times, scraping my hands across coarse black rocks. Twice I call out in pain, made worse by the knowledge that no one can hear. Then it starts to rain. As my fear grows and takes hold, I slide down a six-foot rock ramp and land flat on my back with a painless but humiliating thud. My mind alternates between working at finding my way back and giving myself shit for getting lost. I recognize my critical, never-satisfied, how-will-I-ever-taste-greatness, thank-you-dad self. Cold, bruised, wet, and hungry, I am lost on a mountain in the middle of the Adirondacks.

After a while I finally pause to re-collect myself. I move slower, with more attention and intention. Almost immediately, I recognize the landscape—it's the view I have from my solo site. Turning, I spot my blue tent and howl with joy. I realize now that the view I used to orient myself had been part of me throughout this whole ordeal. Fear had kept me from seeing it. Returning, I collapse, sweaty and exhausted, and weep with relief.

His adventure, however, is not over. Along toward sunset Don, who has taken the medicine name Burning Heart, imagines that he hears a distress signal—three short blasts on the horn.

I am instantly in the same dry-mouthed, adrenaline-charged state I was in this morning. I imagine a fellow quester—his femur broken, an artery open, lying stiff and paralyzed by an awful fall. I reread the instructions for emergencies printed on the map. I am on my feet, my senses alive. I listen and pray for someone else to answer the call, but no one does. Cursing and trembling, I commit myself and answer the distress signals, which are now coming in rapid, panicked succession. I am certain someone is dying.

In the dwindling daylight Burning Heart again thrashes through the wilderness in the direction of the signals.

I picture myself beside a dying man, helping him stay warm as the life ebbs from him. I wonder what I could possibly offer him besides my jacket or some Hollywood deathbed chatter like "Hang on, Tex, you'll be all right." I begin calling out, "Hello!" Finally I hear an answer. "Who is it?" I scream.
"It's me—Lynx—I'm lost."
I find him, dazed and disoriented, in a small valley.
He tells me he's been lost for most of the day. I am worried about the approaching darkness and the likelihood of being lost again, this time at night.
I am really pissed—first at this man who called me away from my peaceful camp and who turns out not to be lying bleeding to death on a rock after all. Then at myself, this solo time, and the whole idea of questing. Cold, tired, hungry, angry, and lost for the second time today, the darkness of dusk fills my heart.

On their return trip they encounter another quester who is able to point them both in the direction of their sites.

Back at camp I collapse, knees shaking, drenched with cold sweat. I begin to sob—first with tremendous relief that the fear and exertion is over, and then with shame because of my anger toward a fellow man. I know this experience carries great significance for me, but I'm too confused and humiliated by my own selfish reaction to know what it means just now.

In a single day, this man has lived as one who is lost and as one who comes to the aid of others who are lost. He has been gifted with trouble; the pain of this trouble takes him beyond categories of what *should be* to what *is*. Through another, he has experienced how he relates to that part of himself that wanders through the forest lost. He has also seen the current of resentment that moves like an undertow beneath compassionate action.

His destiny calls him toward world service. This experience has mirrored both his gift of service and his distortion of service. He has been put on notice that service to others is healing, as long as it is in balance with equal regard for himself.

For Lynx, the man Burning Heart rescued, the frustration of being lost also brought much introspection and the activation of his will to face himself more truthfully.

I thought I knew the area well and have often turned to walking alone to clarify my direction. This time, I became hopelessly lost. To use my signal horn meant I would call attention to myself. I was reluctant to advertise myself as a loser. Better I somehow find my camp on my own and pretend this didn't happen. But after hours of wandering in circles, I finally had to face myself.

I remembered that in my letter of application to this Quest, I had written that I felt I was "muddling through life—lost without direction." And that I was afraid of being just "a voice crying alone in the wilderness." And that one of my greatest fears was that this Quest would "exacerbate the separateness I feel." But I also remembered asking in that letter for "a radical departure from the quiescence I've lived in for the last decade." A Quest for a "radical spin-off" as I called it. And I thought, my God!, it's coming true—everything I wrote about is coming true here! I became aware of the "Four L's" that form the theme of my life: Late, Lost, Losing, and Lonely. Suddenly, I was ripping the past decade of my life apart, yelling out loud.

I decided then and there that I needed to do something to balance these Four L's. Four fundamental choices became clear to me— choices I would need to take a stand for and renew each day:

I choose to accept both the light and the darkness of life.
I choose to be present and to accept the limitation of time.
I choose to claim and to give the gift of myself to others—before I perfect the gift—starting now.
I choose to ask for help.

I knew these woods would not let me get away with just a promise to act on these choices sometime later. I was lost now, the sun was setting, I was in need, and there was no way I could get out of this predicament alone. So I signaled for help. And I discovered that there is help out there. But it comes only if I am willing to reach out to others when I find myself late, lost, losing, and lonely. It reminds me of that old hymn, "I was lost but now am found." I would put that into the present: "I am finding and am being found."

Our devotion of solitude brings us face to face with the beauty of all things. And in its presence, we are moved. For living in beauty is one of the deepest longings of the human heart. Great emotion wells up inside. We may find ourselves crying in the presence of an old-growth forest or an unbroken vista of mountain peaks. We may feel the grief of our absence from beauty alongside tears of joy at our return. Or we may shut down the full charge of our aesthetic response for fear it will overwhelm us. We may get angry to gain a measure of control or seek refuge in boredom and lethargy. There are countless ways we defend against the great beauty of creation, which includes the beauty of ourselves. For beauty confronts us with disturbing questions, like: Who are you, and what do you live for, and how have you cultivated your life? Or, as the poet Antonio Machado so courageously asked of himself, "What have you done with the garden that was entrusted to you?"

And an inherent part of the beauty of this wilderness is the deep silence that presides here. Silence is such a rare presence in the civilized world because we fear it so. We've lost sight of its beauty. Yet, as the Oglala holy man Black Elk once remarked, the greatest of all of the teachings of nature is the Great Silence. For the beauty of silence undoes us. The surface din of our lives dissolves in its spacious presence, and we may then hear the voice of our heart's desire. It is here that the voice of God, the voice of the Great Mystery, speaks in us.

Many of us have been raised to value the voice of someone outside ourselves who speaks with loud conviction over that "still, small voice within." So for many, it is a long road we travel before we wake up to the wisdom of the Baghavad Gita: Better to live out one's own life poorly, than someone else's well.

One man enters the Great Silence having been recently discharged from his job of fifteen years. The hectic din of his corporate lifestyle had been suddenly silenced. And it is the meeting of these two silences that draws from him an uncommon willingness to surrender.

For someone as directed and purposeful and aggressive as I am, this waiting in silence is not easy. It is all I can do to hold back from trying to force an immediate answer to the "right" question.

There is a rock that I have fallen in love with here. It is a big rock and it is my major solace in this place. My mind knows it's "just a rock," but my heart feels it as a beloved master—centered, grounded, wise, and still. My mind leads me to a dead end; my heart leads into the unknown. Having nothing to lose, I take the road less traveled.

It's not easy to sit with the fact of my being fired. I come to the rock with all the confusing feelings of excitement, shame, fear, and freedom. I put my arms around it, and let my mind go blank. I feel tears welling up in my eyes. I will be open to whatever comes. The rock is pretty big so my arms really have to stretch out to take in the rock. And as I take deep breaths, and stretch out further on the exhalation, a startling thought blazes into my awareness: I have to expand until I am larger than the corporation.

By firing me they had made me feel small and insignificant. I had let go of creation's definition of who I was in favor of the corporation's definition. Yet, here I am now, in the midst of great beauty, with the

*sun in my face and the wind in my hair and the river singing nearby.
I imagine my old office. I keep breathing until I am larger than the
office and expand to include the whole thirty-third floor, and then the
entire building, and the offices in California, London, Rome—and all
of the people involved. I imagine them there in the circle of my arms.
Whenever I feel tense as an old image comes—a board member who
voted to fire me or the final notice—I breathe and expand further. My
arms encircle a large pile of images and I breathe space around them
all. Finally I allow the image of this entire constellation to float away.
I come back to my body and feel my arms still outstretched around
the rock.*

*I spent many bitter hours, even after this experience, but I could
move through those hours using that image—knowing that there is a
place inside me that is much bigger than any corporation, job, or
identity. That part of myself I know to be a healthy and nurturing
aspect of my soul that I call on in times of trouble.*

*I am grateful for the steadfast witness of this rock. My trust in the
journey is restored.*

—MAN WITH TEARS

Sam enters the threshold world truly prepared to die to what he
left behind. His instincts lead him first to the expansive surround
of a mountain summit and, later, to the solitary confinement and
darkness of a small cave. A spirit being comes in response to his
prayers. This spirit gives him a new name, imposes on him certain restrictions, and charges him with a lifelong obligation.

*During the first watch of the night, the moon came to me and healed
me of the pains of the first half of my life. As I relinquished my hold
on those old scripts, I felt my sacrum bone somehow realigned, and I
was able to sit on the ground as if I belonged there.*

*During the second watch, my attention was drawn to the planet
Jupiter, hanging brilliantly in the sky. I experienced the light as the
Father (of the Gods) shining benevolently on me. I had spent the day
praying explicitly for all the world, naming categories and individuals for many, many hours. At the very end I thought I was done and
then remembered that I had left myself out. So I said the prayers for*

me. As I finished and was about to say an amen, the Father-God said it for me. He became a shooting star and dropped down through my mouth directly into my heart.

I felt confirmed and validated in all the works of my life—all the struggles, the often lonely efforts to follow the paths I felt called to follow. I find it difficult to say precisely what was confirmed because it was "me"—the whole of my life.

On the third night I was called to seek out the darkness of a small rock cavern hidden below the summit of this ridge. What called me was something that runs very deep. Scientists might see it as a "psychological drive" and theologians would certainly call it God, yet I experience it most immediately as the force of evolution itself—the power and mystery of the universe calling me to the conditions best suited to the ongoing empowerment of life. Whatever the genius behind the scenes, it brought the darkness of the cave and my faith in the Mystery together.

My practice was simple: I divided my time between praying and lying naked in the cave in a fetal position, awaiting rebirth. I prayed to the Council of Animals for a messenger to show me the meaning of the second half of my life.

In response, Coyote was sent to me. He took me out west; it was probably Wyoming, maybe Yellowstone. There, in a parking lot in the back of a tourist restaurant, a black bear was scrounging in the trash cans for food. Pointing to him, Coyote said, "That's you. You are to live off of the Mystery that the 'tourists' have overlooked, discarded, or damaged." He added that I was not to mourn the Mystery's loss or hate those who damage it. That I was to be "Scavenger of the Sacred Mysteries." And that the exact details of this calling would be revealed in time.

—SCAVENGER

Much of the story that has delivered Marcus to this time and place has centered on his journey as a Roman Catholic priest. He has found a particular niche ministering to those who, like himself, are willing to ask real questions and suffer the growth-producing consequences of refusing easy, absolute answers. Yet for nearly two-thirds of his forty-nine years, he has lived within a

religious hierarchy that defines his manhood and selfhood as "intrinsically disordered." He is a gay priest.

The official church sees his sexuality as "ordered toward an intrinsic moral evil." The church is absolutely certain about this. There is precious little wilderness left within the boundaries of the official church. Much of the Mystery has been clear cut and replanted with neat rows of absolute doctrine. And, therefore, there is no home in the church for his Quest.

Marcus comes to his time of solitude with potent questions and, perhaps more important, the willingness to live into the answers.

Each day of the Quest I feel the tension building. The guides remind us to clarify our intention and keep it pure. They push us to go deep. I resist bringing my intention to consciousness. I try to find another intention but cannot escape the one that is deep inside: Should I leave the priesthood and the ordered religious life or should I stay? For some years, I have been afraid to leave. Now, enveloped by the power of spirits in the wilderness all around me and removed from my usual surroundings, I become aware that I am also afraid to stay.

In a ritual dance with the other men one morning, I claim my power to say no! I touch old feelings about being the good little boy in the family and the seminary. I verbalize a family script: "What will the neighbors say?" I enter the circle as a pouting three-year-old, hands on my hips, face clenched, totally defiant. Climbing Buffalo physically challenges my no. I challenge his. Nude, we wrestle on the soft, moist dance floor. Neither of us breaks away. I sense the deep eroticism of claiming my own power and he claiming his. I rise healed and powerful. I sense he does too.

One afternoon some of the brothers begin drumming. I try to accompany them on some African rattles, fearful I might throw off the rhythm. Family scripts surface again: "Our family cannot play music or sing." But I am beginning to dance. I decide to go deep. I enter the circle of drummers, gaining confidence as I dance. It's time to challenge the family scripts. I go deeper. I remove my clothes to dance in the nude. I feel the eroticism of being free.

During the evening Talking Staff Council before the Sweat Lodge

I touch my fear of the lodge, aware of claustrophobia the last time I tried to participate in one. The power of the staff draws brave words from some, but from me, loud sobs and protests: "I don't wanna go! I don't wanna go!" I am afraid of what deaths the lodge might demand. I am still resisting naming my intention. Everyone urges me to face the fears and pledges to support me.

The next afternoon I twice enter the lodge alone to confront the claustrophobia. It helps, but when we finally enter for the ritual, I panic. I call on the man named Spirit Bear, next to me, for help. He commands, "Stay in your gut. Get out of your head." It works. I stay. I have looked at fear and death again. That appears to be the doorway I am being called to pass through continually on this journey.

Now, into the realm of solitude . . .

Marcus shoulders his pack up a steep incline to an open ledge just beneath a mountain summit. He is seeking the far-seeing Medicine of Eagle and finds an appropriate place to nest—close to the sun.

The climb is arduous but I am rewarded with a large space and a 270-degree view. By noon I discover that it's also close to 270 degrees hot with the sun beating on black granite. I have a minimal amount of water for the three days. I will need to ration it.

I spend the first day preparing my tent, my Medicine Wheel on the hot rock, and two shady contemplation spots. I drink a cup of water and gauge how close I am to my ration for the day. I fight the black ants. I fight my intention. I vaguely tell myself that tomorrow I will look at the positive aspects of my vocation and on the third day the negative ones. At sunset on the third day I will decide whether to leave the priesthood or stay. Sounds reasonable to me. I drink another cup of water. I sleep outside my tent under the full moon.

On the second day I think about the positive aspects of my life and ministry. But I am restless. My review seems unfocused. The heat builds. So does my thirst. I fight the black ants and worry about the water supply. I feel a sudden urge to have the conversation with my parents that I have long wanted: about my life, my achievements, my doubts, my homosexuality. I have not spoken to my father since before

his death thirty years ago nor to my mother since her death nineteen years ago. I make effigies of my parents to help me touch their spirits and I put the effigies in the northeast quadrant of my Medicine Wheel.

At sunset I begin my conversation. I breeze through the list of topics I had outlined. Even telling them I am gay arouses no emotion. But then an unexpected cry erupts. "I don't want to be spanked anymore!" My words, my sobs echo back from the mountains. Soon I am touching contradictory feelings: I want to be noticed for my uniqueness yet want to be the same as everyone else. I am both the good little boy and the rebel. Surprised and exhausted, I drink my last cup of water for the day and crawl into my tent. I never do finish my list.

Day three dawns hotter than the first two. Time to look at the negative aspects of my life. I wander around the rock, sit near the Medicine Wheel, sit in the two shaded contemplation sites. I fight the black ants. The sun is too hot and I sweat too much. I drink another cup of water, resisting a sudden urge to drink it all. I feel confined. I wish the long afternoon would end. I am frustrated over my lack of progress with my lists. I am very thirsty and the urge to drink all the water gets stronger.

I find a new position on my stone chair. I hear the voice of one of the guides whisper, "Go deep." And I remember Spirit Bear's command, "Get out of your head and stay in your gut." I go into the urge to drink all the water. Without resistance and to my great surprise, I cry out, "I want to drink all the fucking water!" My words and my sobs echo off the mountains. "I want to drink all the fucking water!" I collapse as the next words come softer, yet no less painfully: "I don't wanna go! I don't wanna go!" The same words I used about the Sweat Lodge! Instantly I know I am voicing the pain over leaving the priesthood and facing the unknown. I don't know when the decision was made or where, but I feel it coming out. I let it out from deep within. It is a moment, not of decision, but of awareness.

There is nothing left to decide at sunset. There is only second-guessing and fear to deal with. I know I am not suffering from a sunstroke hallucination. I am simply suffering from a great thirst. And I will drink. And immediately I sense again the power of the medicine name that has come to me: Soaring Eagle. I know I am no longer a

priest, yet I am still circling around God—on some invisible cur-
rents. I will go! I will go!

— *Soaring Eagle*

Whatever each of us needs to know, nature will sooner or later reveal to us. Perhaps it will be on this time of solitude, perhaps at some other time. Perhaps on our return past Guardian Rock to the world we left behind. We make no demands on spirit here, for demands come from fear and fear only leads to more of itself. That is why all of our practices to this point have been in some fashion exercises in trust. If the life force that moves through all things cannot be trusted, then what hope is there, why choose to live another day?

The soul has come here to move in ways that the rational mind may be slow to understand, if in fact it ever does. Some have come to offer themselves in rituals of self-purification. Some have come to celebrate completions. Some have come to open to new understandings of themselves, new chapters in their unfolding destinies. Some come not knowing what it is they are really here for and must trust in the openness of solitude to call this forth. Some clearly see that their fear of "not getting a vision" was merely a cover for a much greater fear of receiving new vision, a fear of claiming the full power and beauty of their lives. Some come to take small steps, some to leap wildly. Whoever would judge one as success or another as failure, we recognize as a thinly veiled conceit of fear. It bears repeating: Fear only leads to more fear.

Solitude mirrors back a different image for each of us. Yet there is one thing that is perhaps universal in our experience. As a man named Flying Bear observed, "It may be the biggest lesson in all of this is just to sit still and listen to your heart. No other miracle, no marvelous revelation can match the value of this light along the path."

11

THE VISION DANCE

I think I have told you, but if I have not, you must have understood, that a man who has a vision is not able to use the power of it until after he has performed the vision on Earth for the people to see.

—BLACK ELK

Vision is a spark born from an eternal fire. We may call that fire Truth, Love, God—by whatever name, the spark is the fire's means of spreading. Yet, no matter how potent the spark, if it does not touch receptive tinder, it quickly fades.

The spark of vision finds its first home within the individual willing to bear its fiery potential. That spark becomes fire when it finds a home within the hearth of the community. Vision must be performed—that is, brought into form and witnessed before others—before it will be of any value to the individual or the community. And this is why each man who quests must leave the virgin surrounds of his solitary haven to reenter the body of the community.

On the fourth morning of solitude time, a big drum sounds its call urging the men to return. Those whose tolerance for the ordeals of solitude have been severely tested celebrate this call with great relief. In other hearts, the call to leave the pristine silence stirs currents of grief and resistance.

"Here is but another death I must confront," cries one man as he prepares to leave his solitude camp. An atrophied part of his manhood—his relation to the sacredness of creation—has been revived in this place. "This Quest offers up one transition after another, asking me to reinvent myself again and again and again." He offers one last prayer to be "less afraid of the river of life." And he ritualizes this intent by taking a final plunge into the cold stream by his solo site. He allows himself to float on the current, embodying his prayerfulness. He sees that his plunge back into community, after the initial shock, may be similarly renewing.

A man named Geo makes his way back with bare feet, his two-legged footpads leaving the trail with unaccustomed markings. He has awakened within himself an appreciation for the importance of staying present to times of transition. He chooses to feel the nuances of his return and so he moves slowly, taking time to stop if he should find his thoughts rushing ahead of him on the trail. He begins walking again only after his awareness returns home to flesh. This one floats into camp on a nearly seamless trail.

And there are those who return as fragile as newborn sparrows. Some men meet in eager physical embrace, others in the recognition that their rhythm of reunion moves more slowly. Each makes the transition in his own time, in his own way. We pay attention to what we meet in this transition, for what we learn now will be of great service to our return home from this place.

The entire story of the time of solitude is written across the faces here. There are faces who return radically changed—faces that reflect fertile possibilities, like freshly plowed earth. They are an open mystery that has not yet crystallized around a static image. These are faces of men who have allowed themselves to be defeated decisively by greater forces. Faces that have said no; faces that have said yes. Ravaged as they are, these are not the ones I grieve for, because in their defeat and renewal lies hope for us all. Rather, tears come for those who have withstood the ravages of life unchanged. Faces that remain unmovable against the fury of storm and fire. Faces that dare not reflect the hopeful wonder of the rainbow or the aching despair of hunger. For these men, the world is not yet safe enough to assent to their being plowed under and penetrated by life. But the Medicine Wheel has taught us to look on each face as our own. In so doing we may welcome those parts of us that have passionately surrendered to life, those that have stood in passionate defiance, and those caught in the lifeless middle of dispassionate indifference.

All return in silence, honoring the commitment made before leaving, to refrain from speaking until we might improve on the silence. The spark of vision is easily extinguished by a lot of hot air. So at this point, my helpers and I simply welcome the men back, give thanks for a safe return, and ask them to allow their threshold experiences to simmer a while longer.

The men find a camp transformed by their willingness to return from the threshold world and share their vision with their people. This spiritual brotherhood is the first of many circles of community to which they will return. The dance ground is decorated with banners that depict the symbols and teachings of the Four Directions. On the heart of the dance ground, our Commissioner of Beauty has carefully laid another mandala made of ashes; it radiates a welcoming presence. And a big ceremonial drum has been set in place at the far edge of the ground. Behind the drum hangs a large blue Earth flag, a backdrop that gives us a big view of who our people are. Other simple adornments made of water-sculpted driftwood, stones, and candles grace the ground, defining this area as the site of a formal performance scheduled for this evening. It is a performance that invites us both as actor—and as acted on. It is a performance that will honor the stories conceived in solitude as well as the men who are willing to bear them. It is our Vision Dance.

The Vision Dance is the ritual doorway that marks our passage from the threshold world of initiation to the work of reincorporation. It is the mythopoetic theater of the sacred in which we enact a liturgy created by the mystics and prophets of our community here. We imagine this dance as a breeding ground for the new story. We will pour all the dreams, visions, struggles, and graces of our journey into this big cauldron. We stir it with our dance and heat it with our passion for life-affirming myth. We will watch it simmer for many hours. And from this soulful stew may come an image or a story that will restore us to a life of vision and beauty.

What is required of the vision dancer is that he simply trust what was given to him in the threshold world. He must trust the power of his own experience and claim his life as meaningful. Not so easy a task for the progeny of a culture that defines mature citizenship as the ability to live in perpetual agreement with the experts. But no one can claim our lives for us; no one but ourselves can give birth to the images that live inside us. Parents, teachers, gurus, priests, therapists, and medicine men may offer support and guidance. In the end, though, it is only we who can *claim* our own truth. As we do so our truth seeks to be *proclaimed*—given away in a form that expresses its vital essence.

This is the most difficult and primary challenge of the reincor- poration process—communicating that which is experienced in the world-beyond-words in terms that the world-held-together- by-words can share. For vision cannot live in its full power if we insist that it live entirely within the vocabulary of the world. The task, claimed Joseph Campbell, is "to communicate directly from one inward world to another, in such a way that an actual shock of experience will have been rendered: not a mere statement for the information or persuasion of a brain, but an effective commu- nication across the void of space and time from one center of con- sciousness to another."

Vision must enter the world with a boldness that causes the world to reinvent itself around a larger perspective, yet also with a humility that allows for both the vision and the world to be changed by the engagement. Vision pierces the world as the sperm cell pierces the egg. If vision tries to overpower the world—no new creation. If the world remains hardened against vision—no new creation. Re-creation comes from responsive dia- logue, not from overpowering domination. New words, syntax, images, gestures, rhythms, songs are both the language and the fruits of vision. Rabindranath Tagore put it to us simply:

Clothed in facts
truth feels oppressed;

in the garb of poetry
it moves easy and free.

We need to don the garb of poetic expression if we are to stand a chance at communicating anything beyond the surface foam of our encounters with the Mystery. For, in art, Mystery lives in the cracks between certainties. Art is the only language wild enough to articulate vision. What is required, then, is that each of these men returning claim himself as artist.

Here again, many of us find ourselves moving against the grain of our culture. Ask a group of kindergarten children if they can sing, and you'll likely be answered with a song. Ask the same question of college students, and you may get a chorus of "not on your life." We have accepted the idea that art must have a sophisticated complexity and artists must be trained. Compare this with the culture of Bali where no word exists for the concept of "art" or "artist." Everyone is considered an artist of one sort or another, because to the Balinese, being an artist is inherent in being human. In the Vision Dance, we are invited to return to the simple and elegant relationship we had with art before we were educated.

If your heart is beating, then you are a drum. Stay interested in your heartbeat, and you will find yourself a drummer. If you are breathing, then you are a song. Stay interested in your breathing, and you will find yourself singing. If you are alive, then you are a dance. Stay interested in your life and you can't help but find yourself dancing.

So, two things lie before us in preparing for the Vision Dance. The first is that we claim our experience as meaningful. To that end, I encourage the men:

Hold your threshold time lightly, as if it were a dream. Then let yourself wander among these questions as if they were mirrors—some you may see reflections in; others perhaps not:

What is your relationship to power, to claiming your truth as Medicine? Where and how do you say yes and where and how do you say no to the power of your experience?

What dragons did you meet in solitude? How were you tested? In what form did your trials come?

What allies within and without came to offer aid? What animals, symbols, spirits, dreams spoke to you, and where did they lead you?

What was the power of your place, and how is that a reflection of yourself? What was confirmed or remembered in you? What was birthed in you? What was laid to rest?

Is there something you met in solitude that seeks blessing and confirmation? Are there ways this community of men might be of service in this?

Such introspection sheds some light for some; for others it is yet too soon for active questioning. We must exercise great discernment in using these questions not as a way to analyze the experience but rather as curing agents.

Our second task is to proclaim our experience by bringing it into form. An array of materials is laid out: colored cloths, ribbons, markers, and other art supplies. Some men will use these to create banners or shields. Body paints are also available. The world of cosmetics is foreign to most men in our culture. But that's not because of lack of interest. It is a marvel to witness the enthusiasm with which men in this environment bedeck themselves with face and body paints, feathers, and ribbons. This is a native human response of those who live in a world alive with sacred mystery. It is a symptom of an animated virility, a participatory engagement with the beauty of creation. The word *cosmetic* is related to the word *cosmos*, which means "the order of the universe." The cosmetics we apply here, then, reveal the patterns that connect our personal universe to the universe at large.

The ground rules for the Vision Dance are few, but important: no chatter, stay connected, if you choose to begin the dance you must stay through to completion, have as much fun as you possibly can. Once the dance begins, and a man feels moved to enact his story, he will take up the Witness Wand—a decorated stick— to call for our attention. Between each man's enactments, the activity is playfully focused on making music and dance together. This final turn of our threshold round will be made with festivity.

* * *

Our final preparation is to enter into a relationship with the big drum and its ceremonial ways. Ours is actually an old Salvation Army marching band bass drum. We have recommissioned it to our use by wrapping it in a skirt of deerhide. Though a full three feet across, it is light enough to pack in and out of our camp. The drum is suspended on wooden stakes so it sits horizontally to the ground. Log chairs are provided for the four men who will sit together to play.

This powerful instrument is the heartbeat of our Vision Dance. The drum has been central to the religious life of human beings for at least thirty thousand years, with the notable exception of modern Western civilization. So, before bringing the drum into our ceremony, we need to reacquaint ourselves with our roots.

The first drum was likely the Earth itself. Stomping the ground with dancing feet, clapping the hands together, the emotional body wailing to the spirit of the moment—our ancestors expressed everything from hatred to bliss. Dancing, singing, and drumming arose as a simultaneous event. Only recently have we imagined them as separate activities. War shields struck with hand or stick ignited and fueled the fires that led to contest—to competitive games or to war. Sometime later it was discovered that hollow logs, or small holes in the ground struck with the flat of the hand, gave a fuller sound. With that was born the discovery that hollowness, or emptiness, was a primary condition of both resonance and rhythm. All of the drums since then have been variations on these themes.

From the beginning, the universe was primed to produce drums—that is to say that it was full of emptiness. Worldwide cosmologies posit a still and silent void as the first condition of the waiting universe. And then, the percussive impulse to life set itself on the void, setting it into motion, which grew into the patterned expression that we call creation. Genesis has the spirit of God moving on the face of still waters, Hindu scripture shows us Shiva drumming and dancing the waiting world into form, Abenaki people speak of the creator bringing his hands together in one great clap that resonated the universe into being, and our science tells of the Big Bang. And so it goes: emptiness, creative desire, percussive proclamation giving rise to the terrifying and beautiful blossoming of life.

The human heartbeat is that first song of creation time, echoing within the undersea canyons of the womb. Our mother's heartbeat provided the bass line while our tiny heart-drums played in double time. We are all ensemble players. We have been from the beginning.

The thundering heartbeat of the drum reminds us of this—no wonder its call is so entrancing! And it's no wonder that the drum's call has been greeted by Industrial Age culture with such ambivalence! The drum calls up the deep, the ancient, the primal, the erotic impulse to life. It reminds us of the wildness that many of us gave up very early to our mothers, fathers, religions, and educations. It returns us to a time before mechanistic, rationalistic rhythm overpowered nature's groove—to a time of thinking in cycles, before Industrial Age thinking straightened us out. It returns us to the heart, with all its longings, fears, passions, and mystery. It returns us into resonant community with each other, with creation. It is the voice of that deep soulful part within us that wishes to find expression in language more faithful to the invisible life than words can ever be.

There is something about drumming that is not nice. Christianity knows this—that is, the mainstream of Christianity, as there is a wellspring of faith within the tradition where Eros is well celebrated. This source, recently rediscovered by theologian Matthew Fox, offers a wholesome alternative to theologies that split the universe into warring factions of "good" and "evil."

The doctrine of good and evil, applied to our bodies, deeded all territory below the heart to the Devil, leaving only the higher regions to God. Whatever moved the lower parts was suspect. All that was wild—meaning all that was not easily controlled—was systematically hunted down, weeded out, or otherwise rendered impotent. As Christianity cut itself off from its primal source, drumming and dancing were among the first celebrations of life to go. The church declared that there were no seats in heaven for drummers. And sure enough, anyone caught drumming also caught hell. Drumming has the potential for calling forth the Wild Man—the one whose animal presence is yet strong, who is at home in erotically charged landscapes. He is that part of our being connected to the rising and the setting of the sun, to the pulsing of blood and sap in our veins, to living not by design, but through passion. Reflected in the mirror of fear, the Wild Man's image was distorted into the Devil. So the church fathers agreed: If you want to tame a man, to keep him "nice," you must take away his drum, his dance, and his song. Without a way to call on the Wild Man, a man becomes fearful, and then you've got him—by the "lower parts!"

Nice boys and overly civilized men do not make terribly good drummers. Oh, we can keep a beat and our technique may be impeccable, but something is missing. Machines keep beats, rhythms you can count on and trust to produce no surprises. But good drumming is at once something you can count on and an expression of continuous surprise. For fifteen billion years, the universe has been pulsing itself into life, and it's been one surprise after another. *That* is good drumming.

The drum is the heartbeat of the dance. It must not falter or the dance will fall apart. The beat must be simple and repetitive, yet alive from start to finish of the dance.

In some native traditions, a place at the big drum is a seat of honor reserved only for the elders—those who have journeyed around the sun at least fifty times. The feeling is that only through the experience of many seasons can we develop the level of presence needed to maintain the repetitive rhythm required for a dance that may last all night. When we're young, what holds our attention is syncopation and novelty. After about seven minutes, repetition lulls a young soul into sleep or trance—precisely what you do not want to see in those responsible for keeping the heartbeat. If a young drummer begins to get bored, the space between the beats becomes very wide and deep. He might fall into that space and become lost.

The elders are likely to know more of death. Therefore, they have a greater capacity for living with silence, space, the emptiness between beats. They have less need to keep themselves awake with novel syncopations. So, those of us younger than fifty will have to reach down deep inside if we choose to take a seat at the heart drum.

The remainder of the day is given to creating the images, costumes, and poetry we will bring to the dance. Currents of creative energy ebb and flow, though the camp is still quiet. We channel the urge for communication through whatever art forms we each are drawn to. When night has fallen, and all preparations for the dance are complete, the men are called to the dance ground.

I marvel at the transfiguration that has occurred over these past days. An eager large fire casts its flickering light from one end of the dance ground. Across the way, the big drum sits in the silence before the storm. The faces assembled here wait too—not the faces that we wear in the daylight, but faces that have lived in exile, in the shadow cast by the sunlit personality. The night welcomes those in exile. And we have certainly answered its invitation to be known.

Among us are gentle, green forest beings—skin mottled in leaves and bark, and the dark detritus of forest soil. In this thin light, these men easily go unnoticed until they move, or until a breeze comes to rustle their garb. And there are those who have released some beaten spirit of their underworld lives—their skin now canvas for horrific images that will be noticed, no matter how quiet the light. A man across the way stands painted head to toe, half his naked body white, half black. He has come to dance his struggle with his—and the world's—dual nature. Another stands with the word *coward* written in black across his back. The word is crossed out by lines that lead the eye to the word *lover* inscribed in red, suggesting that during his time in solitude some authority was returned to him. Next to him is a two-legged psychedelic dream: a garishly painted bird in a dye-streaked sheet with wings of neon orange. This bird-man, by far the youngest of our group, stands in stark contrast next to a middle-aged man, covered simply with pieces of tape, his ego attachments illustrated on each piece—pride, lust, greed, fear, and so on.

As I look on the diversity here I take great pleasure in this incredible sight. These are the same men who, in the world beyond Guardian Rock, argue cases before judges and juries, who minister to congregations, who sit behind desks in corporate offices, who design computer systems, who coach Little League baseball. Therapists, university professors, carpenters, surgeons, bakers, nurses, musicians—every guy you meet on the street has a face such as these living inside, every one of them.

I laugh out loud as I witness my reasoning mind searching madly for a reference that will make sense of this gathering. To say that my personal history comes up blank is a glaring under-statement. The reference is felt, more than it is understood. For I sense that our celebration tonight is somehow encoded in our DNA.

The religious worldview that engenders this dance has been the experience of everyone everywhere, as Mircea Eliade said, for about 98 percent of human history. We could take this dance to the Kalahari of southern Africa, and our brothers and sisters there would understand the stories we are about to tell. We could dance our stories before the island peoples of Indonesia, the mountain peoples of the Andes, the citizens of the Brazilian rain forests—and they too would understand. Not in precise terms, perhaps, but in terms that the heart knows well. The language we use tonight is the native human tongue of ritual festivity.

And by virtue of this bizarre gathering, I am once again reminded of the value of spiritual community. For I see some part of myself in each and every one of the mirrors standing before me. And as I cannot do all of these dances at once, I look forward to stalking these others-myself tonight. I wonder, to what conti-nents of my own inner world will they lead me?

I call to mind the names assembled here, and others who have danced this ground over the years: Broken Walk, Heart Father, Garnet Heart, Soul Watcher, Owl Hunting His Passion Heart, Wounded Wolf, Crystal Phoenix, Flying Bear, Scavenger, Stands By His Heart, Running Water, Defender of Children, Yisrael, Looks Beneath the Surface, Donkey-Eagle, Blue Star, Humming-bird Monk, Turtle, Slug, Between Two Worlds, Blue Light, Roar-ing Mouse, Sings Through Broken Heart, Earth-Sky, Dragon Son,

Piercing Heart's Arrow, Mending Heart, Thunder Song. . . .

And what of these names? Foolish regressions to boyhood cowboy-and-Indian games? Perhaps in part, for some. Yet what new ground has ever been claimed without a good measure of foolishness? How can a man expect to grow if he does not allow himself to step outside of certainty? How else can spirit speak to us except through images and symbols as these—callings that extend our being as we inhabit them? We will be called to the dance tonight by these names, names that have caught our attention and lure us deeper into the forest of self-discovery.

The sky is cool and clear. The forest canopy opens high above the dance ground to reveal stars shimmering in an ocean of inky blackness. It is a good night to dance.

We begin this ceremony as we begin all ceremonies, declaring our intention and attuning to our relations in the Six Directions. I take hold of the Witness Wand, pausing to reacquaint myself with its story, before recommending it to the dance. The Wand is fashioned out of a forked stick about a foot and a half long. From one of its two branches hangs a white feather; from the other branch, a black feather. They remind us of the teachings of the Medicine Wheel of the Forked Tree—to bring both sides of ourselves to this dance and so create this dance in beauty.

Brothers, we stand between heaven and earth, infused with the breath of the Great Mystery. We come here to this place to offer ourselves once again to life. We carry gifts of ourselves—our yes, our no, the stories that live through us—gifts that need to be given to be received, given lest they be taken away. We come to dance, for after all we've been through, what else is there left to do?!

It is said that in the day, we can practice our differences, but at night, we all return to the same house. . . . In the day, we remember our names, and at night, we remember who we really are. . . . In the day, we speak the language of *our* people, but at night, we speak the language of *all* people. . . . In the day, we can gather up all our possessions, but at night—at night, we give them all away.

Dear brothers, have faith in your dance. The Earth is our drum
tonight. May we dance in beauty!

"After we are all censed with sage," remembers Owl Heart,
"the elders of our group—Redwood, SummerWind, and I—are
led by Blue Heron to the heart drum to begin the dance. The four
of us begin the steady pounding. Other drums, instruments, and
chants come and go, but the steady throb of heart drum continues
uninterrupted for many hours."

The dance unwinds, slowly at first, yet with the enthusiasm
that stirs most beginnings. The outer circle of dancers begins a
unified chant as they move with simple, short steps around the
perimeter of the ground. After some initial wavering, the drum
picks up a determined cadence that sounds like thunder rolling
down from the mountains. Men who have come eager to move
begin spilling out into the center ground—stretching their wings,
prowling the circle to find their range boundaries. We are but a
small circle in such a big forest, circling around some passion, as
the Earth turns tonight around its burning star.

Then comes the moment when the initiatory impulse moves one
of us to take up the Witness Wand.

Steven, an ordained Catholic priest, seizes the Wand, and
dances it into our midst. He calls on us to witness his vows of initiation into an expanded order of ministry in which he takes the
name—and the responsibility—of Earth Healer. He asks the drum
to support him with slow, soft heartbeats. Then he chooses one of
us to perform the rite of calling forth his vows:

Who is it that comes?
—I, one known as Earth Healer.
What is it that you seek?
—To have the Earth Healer called forth from me. To expand my
ordained priesthood to include care and healing of the Earth and the
plants and animals, rocks and waters that live within her.
Will you preach and teach oneness with each other, the Earth, and
all Creation?

—I will, God being my teacher.
Will you tell your people of their connectedness to the Earth, and
remind them that they are stewards of God's great gift?
—I will.

At this point we lay hands on him. Around his neck two men
place a stole made of ribbon, with a feather attached to one end
and a hemlock branch on the other. Now, we commend him: "Go
and heal!"
"That was a very powerful moment for me," Steven later
wrote. "I felt that my priesthood had been expanded during that
holy time. As I returned to my place within the circle, I felt as
elated as when I was first ordained a priest."

The drum picks up after Earth Healer returns the Witness Wand
to its resting place on the Medicine Wheel. A man who has been
somewhat withdrawn of late makes a decisive move to the center
of the circle. As the dancers move in to surround him in unified
rhythmic movement, he digs a deep hole in the ground with his
hands. He then produces a large stone that he holds as if it were
embedded in his heart. His gestures reveal the stone to be a heavy
burden of some sort. He then lets out a sustained cry of anger and
rips the stone from his chest. The circle continues to pulse in a
steady supportive cadence around him. The stone, now invested
with his anguished cry, is laid to rest in the hole. As he begins to
replace the soil, a voice from the circle asks, "Will you talk to the
stone?" The man nods. He acknowledges the ways this thing—his
hardness, his unwillingness to yield— has served him in the past.
He then carefully fills in the hole. As he stands, the container
expands, the way the chest does when taking in new breath. And
the dance continues.
The one called Running Water enters with a mask of sticks and
leaves representing the Mean Spirit he had been pursuing in the
threshold world. With a hatchet he chops the mask in two. He
buries half of it, and sticks the other half inside his shirt. By such
a gesture he reveals his understanding that the Mean Spirit lives
inside of him and cannot be destroyed. The line that separates

good and evil is less likely to separate him from the rest of the world, now that he sees this line drawn through the center of his own heart.

"No way to do justice to this event with mere words," reflects Peter. "Too much energy, feeling, drumming feet, hands, gongs, and the dances of our vision. The great heart—the circle of men and trees—the resonance of the dance ground under our feet. Working the log drums, the music and beat take over, driving in, through, and around the other rhythms, teasing out the stories that are being born before our eyes."

A tall, thin man steps forward. Dressed entirely in green ribbons and leaves, he sways back and forth like one of the giant hemlocks of this forest. Father Nature, he declares himself to us.

He collapses in a heap on the ground and addresses us in a weak voice. "I have been too long buried, too long quieted and ignored. I am weak from lack of attention. No one calls out my name these days. Please hear me—I live in this fertile soil. What power do you think gives rise to these great trees? I am moist and green; dark and fecund! Will you look on me? Will you see me?"

A few in the circle are willing to offer this spectacle wide-open eyes of innocence and trust. "Yes," they shout, "we see you."

"Do you see me!?"

Others join in, "Yes, we see you."

The Green Man grows before our eyes—or perhaps *because* of our eyes, as if our attention were the sunlight that calls him forth. Back on his feet he entices us to dance with him. A kind of vegetarian square dance erupts that sends his leaves flying. "It's the Jolly Green Giant!" shouts one who has locked elbows in a do-si-do twirl. His call unleashes a barrage of the loving irreverence that commonly circulates between men who have come to trust each other. The spirit of high play is set free. Is this playfulness also a gift of the Green Man's return to our lives?

The dance at times moves in the revelry of a carnival. Among playful freeform dancing come a series of shorter enactments. Our village bards come forth to distribute the fruits of their labors. To the rolling sound of the drum, we hear from Lives His Vision, this short tale:

Once upon a time, before there was time, a Seeker was born.
One who came to quest for the meaning of life. Down through the
eons of eternity he continued his search.
He looked in the high places
He looked in the low
And in between on the misty flats
He wandered to and fro.
But he found not the meaning of life . . .
Then he looked to his children
And he turned to his career
He searched out women
Hoping that they might hear.
But he found not the meaning of life . . .
He looked to the past
For what might have been.
He looked to the future
For what might still be.
But he found not the meaning of life . . .
And then on the side of a mountain near a swift running stream,
he learned to listen for the silence that followed the sound—
moving into the now is where the gift is found.

The Green Man returns with some leaves of verse:

Feed me wisdom,
forget the thin gruel of knowledge.
Cook it long, through many seasons;
through bitter winds of winter, through sour decay of autumn,
through salty passion of spring, through sweet nectar of summer,
My soul is hungry!
And knowledge, tasteless
without the slow simmering movement of the sea.
Let my victory come by way of defeat—
the feet of many dancers.

Mystery hold me,
Spirit ferment me,
God drink me, and be
Drunk of me!

And a man who walks with Coyote spirit comes forth with some old bones he has picked up along the way:

I am not afraid
to sing and dance.
When I enter the sweat lodge
crawling on my hands and knees
I am a child of mother earth
proclaiming "we are all siblings."
But I am not a sexless child,
a neuter inferior
of the devouring mother.
I have hair on my balls.
My cock thrusts out and up.
I am the Sky Father's Son!
The Father and I are one,
and I am brother to all things.
The fire-rocks and the hot sage-steam
are my sisters-equals.
I emerge from the "sweat"
challenge to honor and embrace the world,
to wed and bed
the Father's gift to me.
Mother, yes, and sister.
But spouse now:
mate, bride, wife.
And this Long Dance
is our wedding night!
Call me NIKA.
No, I am not afraid
to sing and dance.

The dance continues. By now we are well into the night. The arching tail of the Great Bear, Ursa Major, has swung some twenty degrees to the west in the course of our dance. That places us well beyond midnight. The energy of the dance has also descended beyond its midpoint. The novelty that spurred our initial vigor has worn off. The outer wheel of dancers turns with sluggish resolve.

And in this downturning there is one of us who feels this dance more as ordeal than celebration. Painted head to toe in white Kabuki makeup, he wanders among us as a ghost. His resistance to the dance becomes a dance with its own strangely compelling power:

> *There I am—white, angry, self-conscious, and cold as shit, slapping my cold feet on the cold ground. The men's dances are a blur of abstractness I can't relate to at all. I only want to huddle by the fire. From time to time, trying to look like I am dancing, I inch my way over to the bonfire.*
>
> *When I finally reach my limit of cold, boredom, and anger, I decide to take the center of the circle for my Vision Dance. Once there, I just stand silent, eyes closed, breathing deeply.*
>
> *I open my eyes and find myself back in my solitude site, standing in the center of my Medicine Wheel. I cry out for the sun to emerge from the gray clouds. I close my eyes again and wait. Next I hear rushing water. I open my eyes and see I am standing again on the rock where I had performed my dances during the threshold time. I chant "I am the middle, not the beginning, not the end." Placing my hand on my heart, I silently affirm my purpose: "I want to celebrate the man I have become, who is part of all creation." Now I see the sun setting in the west. I chant and dance and draw in its radiant energy. I feel peace in my soul, and simple joy in my heart.*
>
> *This time when I open my eyes, I am again in the here and now—the Vision Dance circle, at night, surrounded no longer by trees but by a ring of men's faces. I feel more alone now than I did during three days and nights by myself. Dazed, I leave the circle and walk numbly toward the fire. I have no idea whether I actually spoke or moved the whole time I stood in the center of the circle. I feel empty and cold.*

The dance goes on and on, the night gets colder, and the group's energy is lagging. The guides are everywhere—producing a flute, energizing the drumbeat, initiating a new chant—doing everything to keep the dreaded dance going. Why do I stay?

If only my smoldering rage would keep me warm!

—TRUE HEART

More logs are laid on the fire, releasing a shower of sparks into the pitch-black sky. Delighted by the beauty of this primitive fireworks display, the fire keeper stirs the coals some more, coaxing more heat and another fountain of sparks. An impromptu chorus gathers around the display. From within the growing chorus, a man chants the words of a Passamaquoddy song:

For we are the stars.
For we sing.
For we sing with our light.
For we are birds made of fire.
For we spread our wings over the sky.
Our light is a voice.
Our light is a voice. . . .

A soulful, Gregorian-like chant begins to form as each man sings a word or phrase and plays it off the others. It's a song that rises from the belly, and comes of age in some deep caverns of heart, before it pours like fine wine into the night sky. And it must be that Dionysus himself joins us now, for there is some impulse that leads us to drink long and deeply of this spirit, that warms us against the chill of night and exhorts us not to sober too soon. We offer up a rich mead of male voice to the Mystery of our surround.

And so, the dance continues. . . .

Sam carries the Witness Wand to our waiting center. In a prayerful manner he raises the Wand to rouse the attention of both worlds. A familiar breeze suddenly stirs the tops of the overarching hemlocks. It picks up from nowhere and disappears in a slow haunting sizzle that carries the ear to a deeper silence. Often

before, this same breeze has befriended us as we gathered in reverent word or gesture.

Sam asks us to perform a ritual anointing. Having had no
way to predict a need for sacramental oils, he has prepared an
anointing unction using whatever oil-based materials were on
hand: a god-awful concoction of poison ivy cream, insect repel-
lents, and burn ointments. He asks that we pray for him and
anoint him for strength and courage to answer the call he was
given by Coyote in the cave of his solitude. He has been called
to the contemporary equivalent of a shamanic vocation. He
clearly struggles with making his calling public, but there is
nothing in this man that appears to turn him away from trouble.
He removes his clothing and stands vulnerable to the confirming hands that anoint him, head to toe, with this reeking mess of
greenish black goo. Whatever this ritual may lack in form, it
makes up for in spirit.

Sam then calls on each man to bear witness to his vow in the
ancient way. He explains:

> In the Book of Genesis, Abraham entrusts a servant with a special
> mission: to go back to the homeland to procure a wife for Abraham's
> son. Before the servant departs, Abraham makes the servant swear
> faithfully to fulfill the mission. What I wish to call your attention to
> is how the servant makes his vow.
>
> Abraham says to him, "Put your hand under my thigh and swear
> by the God of heaven and earth that you will do as I have said." And
> it is recorded that the servant indeed "did put his hand under Abra-
> ham's thigh and swore to him."
>
> Now the Hebrew word translated here as "thigh" is yarek, which
> in other contexts is often translated as "loins."
>
> "Put your hand under my loins and swear . . . " Even today in a
> courtroom we swear to tell the truth or take a solemn oath by putting
> our hand on something sacred. In those days it wasn't a book.
>
> Is there a connection between words like testament, testify, testi-
> mony, and testicles? Apparently there is: testicles comes from the
> Latin word for "witness." Originally, to bear testimony meant to
> hold another man's balls and swear to him!

One by one, each man of this circle looks Sam straight in the eye as he holds him by the *yarek* and says, "I bear witness to your vow."

The anointing complete, Sam once again takes up the Witness Wand and sends his voice in all directions:

Through earth in me, O Mystery, be!
And be, O Double Round, my mystery!
I am alive, you see, I am alive
and all the world is with me.
To the Great Mystery
I lift my heart in thanks.
Scavenger is my name;
I am Scavenger of the Sacred Mysteries.
As I walk the earth on behalf of all,
my power goes out to heal the land.
Sacred is every step I take. . . .

By now, most of the men have danced with the Witness Wand in one way or another. I sound a hearty blast with the steer-horn trumpet, announcing that closure of the dance is near.

The signal inspires another man to seize the opportunity to call on these men for help. He picks up the Witness Wand and stands before us.

On his face is painted a mask with one eye looking outward and one eye looking inward. The initiate declares that he wants to reclaim his body as part of the Earth's body. He asks for a second birth, a symbolic enactment of his willingness to consciously accept the sacredness of matter—starting with the celebration of his own physicality. So we are to be the birth canal that gives him passage from the male womb of this dance ground into an acceptance of greater life.

He asks us to form two lines facing each other, and to lock arms low to the ground. We kneel close to the earth and stretch our arms across to form a long tunnel. He crawls on his belly beneath the resisting arms. His brothers have committed themselves to his passage and so we do not make it easy. We give him the gift of trouble. This is something that men can do well for each other. It is part of our way of loving. Let his commitment be tested. Let him reach down deep for the desire that will see him to the far end of this passage. If he falters, we will urge him on, but our arms will remain strong against his back. We have faith in him and so we press harder.

He squirms through the tunnel a few inches at a time, breathing hard and fast. The harder he fights, the stronger our resistance. Someone whispers, "Don't work so hard." And another, with a twinkle in his eye, offers, "Trust the Force, Luke!" The male birth canal roars with laughter, causing our grip to loosen, giving him an easier time of it. Our initiate catches on quickly and immediately begins to offer us instruction in Lamaze breathing. The sight of us all reverently chanting "Breathe! Push! Push!" in the middle of a forest, in the dead of night, with a poor sweating brother at our mercy—well, it pushes us all over the edge. And while we hold our bellies, our brother breaks free. A broad grin erupts from his face, now covered with sweat-moistened mud. A new joy does indeed inhabit his body.

But the initiatory spirit, it seems, is not yet through with him. We circle close around him, a few layers deep, and begin to rock him back and forth between us. We then gather him in our arms and lift him above our heads, offering him spread-eagle to the sky. As if he were our own man-child, we introduce him to the heavens.

Welcome to this Body,
Welcome to this Earth,
Welcome to this Manhood,
Sacred are they all.

We then lower him to stand once again on the Earth, to stand on his own two feet, as do we all in a new way. For some part of each of us was held aloft tonight. Some part that can now feel the strong hands of the generations of men who stand behind us. Hands that have tested us cruelly at times, hands that have touched us with loving firmness, hands that have worked with

what was given to them, hands that commend us to walk now—
to do our best with the life given to us.

"As I share my vision," Tony will later write, "and as those looking on help me enact it, it becomes alive inside me. I find that as I
dance, I lose my normal perceptions and became entranced with
the interaction of those around me, and the realness of the
images. At the completion of the dance I feel intensely uplifted
and truly different, as if an inner weight has been lifted and in its
place deep insight and a divine type of joy have been imparted."

Bill remembers the dance as a "challenge almost harder than
any other—the challenge to say with my body what my mind had
experienced. It was in the doing of the Vision Dance that I knew
something of what had happened. The dance helped reveal the
experience, and thus it enabled me to reenter the mystery and the
gift of my solitude time."

"That night I danced the dance," remembers Ross. "I gave that
dance my all. All my rage. All my anger. All my heart wounds.
All my joy and love of life. I danced my oldest disappointments
and my newest discoveries. I danced to the point of exhaustion
and past it. I danced till I was sure I'd collapse and didn't. I
danced till I felt like a man, an initiated man. I felt the authority
that flows not from my accomplishments nor my personality but
simply from my being a human being on this Earth. I have
danced the dance."

Wayne helps guide us toward closure with his poem "Dancing
Ground."

I own a life, only lightly;
a borrowed gift,
to dance a day and die away
to give away, like winter on the wheel.
A moment in time
to invite my true self forward.
Come out! Come out!
it is safe here, here at the center of the universe
A patch of ground, bare earth

dancing ground,
space of blood and soil
and tears
Men's blood, men's tears.
Birthing ground
earth passage, in the circle, always moving,
the circle, the dance,
among men
Pregnant with truth, no mother but each other.
Come out! Come out!
Here at the center of the world.
Brother's pain and joy shatters illusion
The trees witness, the water sings a death song,
boyhood, youth, stolen away
taken into the night, never to be seen or found.
Who is here now?
at the center of the world
Who names, who claims this life
what passion, what power,
what truth?
Show us your truth, O Man.
Dance, that your brothers may
know who you are
and share
your strength.

When all the men who wish to dance with the Witness Wand have done so, when we have given away all the songs and chants, when our prayers have mounted the wind and have been carried to the Four Directions, the beat of the big drum softens. We lift the drum from its stand, carry it to the center of the circle, and hold it above a flickering candle. The light of the flame fills the heart of the drum bringing a soft illumination to its skin. The steady pulsing beat fades like an echo. And it is finished.

The intensity of the dance then yields to the stillness of the night.

PART THREE

∿∿∿∿∿∿∿∿∿∿∿∿∿∿∿∿∿∿∿∿∿∿∿∿∿∿∿∿∿∿∿

THE ROAD HOME

We shall not cease from exploration
And the end of all our exploring
Will be to arrive where we started
And know the place for the first time.

—T. S. ELIOT

12

THE GIVEAWAY

Inside the Great Mystery that is,
we don't really own anything.
What is this competition we feel then,
before we go, one at a time, through the same gate?

—RUMI

TRANSLATION BY JOHN MOYNES AND COLEMAN BARKS

Often, as we wake, we are aware of having just experienced a beautiful or frightening or bizarre dream. Yet trying to recall images from that dream, so vivid just moments before, can be like trying to collect smoke in a sieve.

In the reincorporation phase of our Quest passage, we begin to emerge from a dreamscape of our own creation. We have journeyed beyond the realm of known borders, beyond that place where words turn back. Our task now is to return to live the dream. Our Vision Dance last night expressed that other reality in mythological terms to a circle of men who have trained themselves to speak this language.

Some of the men who awaken this morning do so with tattered remnants of the dance-dream still clinging to their skin—smeared face paint, torn ribbons, and feet caked with the dust of the dance ground. The throbbing pulse of the big drum still echoes in the bones.

This is our sabbath, a day of rest. Keeping this day open-ended honors the heart's need for contraction and stillness after a time

of intense energetic expansion. Just as the physical body incorpo-
rates the life-sustaining oxygen on the outbreath, the spiritual
body is likewise renewed in the process of giving away. Our ceremonial round reached a climax in last night's dance. We move
now from climax to completion. We breathe out the heady vapors
that have inspired us thus far. And at the bottom of that breath is
where I invite us to dwell today. We're not out of the woods yet.

A wide, a very wide, range of feelings moves through our collective heart this morning. Some men, having had enough of this
questing business, are eager to return to a regular life. Some still
thirst for every drop of awareness they can pour down their
throats. Some see the hours ebbing away and fret that they have
not completed all they have set out to do. And many of us will
find the diversity within the community living with equal vigor
inside.

Some of us sit alone beside the stream in contemplation. Others
write in their journals. Small groups enjoy the luxury of a pro-
longed breakfast around a smoky kitchen fire. Others cluster
around a favorite swimming hole. A small group of us is swept
into a whirlpool of competitive chatter that begins to turn faster
and faster. We have not enjoyed the banter of conversation since
we entered the sweat lodge more than four days ago. But after
having been sensitized to the silence for so long, many quickly
lose themselves in idle chatter that strays far from present reality.
Talk of favorite movies, television shows, and sports teams
erupts. Fantasies of our first meal back in town are shared as well
as who we plan to meet first, and how. The curtains to the window of the world we left behind have been suddenly thrown
wide open. Some relish the view, while others are devastated by
it. A new tension hovers like a thunderhead above the camp.

One man finally makes it rain. He confronts another: "Let's
stop polluting this sacred place with all this bullshit."

He's met with: "What's the big deal? Lighten up, man!"

Lightning flashes between them. Sides are drawn, and now
other players make their choices. It's the "Spiritual Purists
League" against the "Let's Party Crowd." The conflict that many
of us woke up with this morning, but couldn't quite name, is now

out-pictured where it's easier to see. Self-appointed spokesmen from both sides go at it for a while, becoming more and more entrenched in their positions. All the while, a greater part of the heart is being sacrificed to the ever-widening wide gulf between them.

Someone then steps into that gulf: "I got up this morning and noticed I could barely look any of you guys in the eyes," he says. "It was as if last night's dance was a way that men make love with each other—everyone putting his heart on the line. This morning I felt more opened up, but still a little protected, a little afraid. Part of me just wanted to split—you know, like after a one-night stand, head down the trail saying, 'It was great, guys, I'll call you later.'" A nervous laugh of identification ripples through the group, and he continues, "I see this whole battle as a question of how we're going to hang out with each other—now that the Quest is over—now that we've made some kind of man-love together. Now that I know I love you—now what?"

Within the silence that follows, the collective heart releases a sighing, resonant "Ahhhh . . . " This one has struck some chord of truth with his question. More of the universe circulates in that single *ah* than in all of the words we might spin around it. Some impulse brings us to our feet—perhaps, the impulse to simply honor the question. Standing in a loose circle, arms across each other's shoulders, our heads fall back, faces open to the sky. "Man Flower," someone whispers.

And so this meeting adjourns, refreshed by the thunderstorm and alerted to the wisdom of staying close to the heart today.

"I awake early," writes Ken in his journal on this sabbath morning.

> I am utterly and completely overwhelmed with regret, the despair of lost opportunities, the hopelessness of doing anything to change things now. It's too late! I have resisted much of this experience. Refused to relate to the man who calls himself Night Bear. Not learned to trust the male community. Failed to accept myself.
>
> But I also decide the Quest is not over. I go to the cooking fire. I bring my regrets but decide to leave my books and paper and pen in

the tent. No distractions. I choose to be present to the feelings and to the moment.

I spend perhaps an hour in this emotional space. Then Night Bear appears—my nemesis, the man who throughout this Quest has reflected parts of me I do not wish to see or accept. We dance, first with words. Tentatively seeking a rhythm, a connection. There are moments when we get close, but then a single word, a single nuance, drives us apart again. Then I remember the teaching that has led me to the most gold on this Quest: I need to venture to that place where words turn back. And so Night Bear and I dance, this time with our bodies. Our dance is part hugging, part wrestling. Suddenly he grabs me at the legs and neck and hoists me into the air! As he holds me up I am terrified. I trust no man to hold me safely. Yet I allow that feeling of fear to pass through me, and I release it. Then, without warning, he lets me go! Just before I hit bottom he lunges and catches me! Something moves inside me. I realize that I have placed myself into the hands of one I thought to be my enemy. Yet I learn about trust, of all things, from engaging with this man. And so, on this "day of rest," the entire purpose of my Quest is revealed to me.

For Twain, the morning also brings serendipitous insight.

I am all packed and anxious as hell to leave. I finally sit down by the stream and start to sob: "I've done my best!" The more I repeat these words, the more grief deepens in my gut—I feel as though I am vomiting it out.

Then the revelation hits: This whole Quest, before this community of men, I have been acting out my war within: a little boy's longing to be acknowledged by his father. "Daddy, I'm doing my best, can't you see?" Dad always "saw" my brothers—even if he "saw" them by abusing them. But I felt he never acknowledged my existence. With this revelation, healing begins. I know now I can let go of my child's demands and stop competing with other brothers/men for father's/God's attention.

And Marcus, who decided to leave the priesthood after twenty-one years, sits quietly by himself on the riverbank. He absent-

mindedly picks up a twig and consoles himself by rolling it between his fingers. Thoughts are rolling around his head as well. Doubts mostly. He is remembering how difficult it was for him to dance his vision last night. And although this morning he has been met by many confirming eyes that see him as more than equal to the task, he sits here now second-guessing his choice.

As I'm feeling the shape and nodes of this twig, I slowly become aware that my fingers are rubbing the main branch of the twig, not the short side branch. Through this simple act I come to finally accept the wisdom of my decision. My body, in its innate wisdom, confirms that my decision to leave the priesthood really lies along the main stem of my life. I now know I will go in that direction.

>>   <<

The mellowing light of late afternoon draws us back from our scattered sojourns together around the kitchen fire. We brew up pots of coffee and tea and swap stories of where the day has taken us. A lighthearted and convivial spirit moves between us.

The rest of the afternoon and evening will see us involved in more formal acts of letting go as we prepare to leave this place and the community we've shared. Later tonight, we plan to hold a ceremonial event known as the Giveaway. Following that we'll share a meal. The rest of the evening is set aside for a long council in which we give away all of the stories left to tell. The next day, following a closing council, we will break camp and make our way back to the world that lives on the other side of Guardian Rock. That is, if we live that long.

What lives in us now is this community, these woods, and the life force that circulates between us all. We will make plans, but we will also choose to let them go as soon as they are made. We still circle in the dance of here and now. We remind each other often, because we forget often. Right here is where life is. We ain't out of the woods yet!

Circulation is the guiding metaphor for our Giveaway. The

power of circulation—the movement of blood, water, air, and the life force itself—is what animates nature. Nature thrives so because it is continually giving away to itself.

We need to be reminded of this at the outset of our reincorporation work. Many teachers warn of the dangers of "spiritual materialism": clinging to vision, or to the specific conditions that brought vision, is just as misguided as hoarding material wealth. If who we are is not in circulation, then we are in a prison of our making. This withdrawal not only depletes us but our people as well. Once again, we'll find fear at the bottom of all this.

When we cling and hoard, it's out of fear. But as the Medicine Wheel reflects, fear will never put an end to winter or night or hot or cold, or whatever it is that currently threatens us. Hoarding summer will never make winter's passage any easier. To experience summer, we have to go through winter. This is not a mistake, this is part of the natural order and elegance of the universe.

And so, we will be able to truly leave this place, this community, only after we are willing to give away our attachments to it. If we cling to the beauty here, beauty dies here. This then is the paradox of the Giveaway ceremony: We shall own only what we are willing to give away.

The Giveaway Blanket lies before us on the dance ground. During the course of the afternoon, each of us has surreptitiously placed a gift on it. Some of the gifts are wrapped in paper, some in birch bark or in leather. One is covered by a plastic garbage bag.

The gifts differ dramatically in size and form, though all have a common power. For those who offer them, they represent an important event, process, or phase of life. For those who receive them, the objects will take on unpredictable significance.

Sitting in our circle around the blanket, we prepare ourselves once again to set sail on some unknown ocean; our ceremony is our vessel. I honor each man present for his willingness to loosen his grip on these gifts, and smudge the gifts with sweet cedar smoke to ritually set them free. A song begins to circulate among us. We then invite the eldest man present to push us offshore.

Richard walks slowly to the blanket and chooses an item

wrapped in the dusty white bark of a birch tree and tied with a ribbon of reed. It is a pair of army ID tags. As Richard lifts his hand for all to see, the tags jingle gently. Glints of candlelight reflect off the shiny surface. The chanting of the men who are witnessing in the outer circle grows soft. Tom, who offers this gift, stands before Richard. "There was a time in my life when I wore these tags every minute of every day," Tom says, allowing the men to witness the shaking in his voice. "Even after I left the service I kept these around my neck at all times. It was as if I were afraid to let go of my identity as a soldier, as a warrior. That identity had many sides: I was proud of my strength and bravery, but I was enraged at the toll it took on my body and my soul and ashamed of the pain I'd inflicted on others. I can now accept those conflicting sides as part of the wholeness of the experience. I surrender these tags as a sign of that acceptance and as a sign that I forgive myself." For Tom, the Giveaway releases him from a burden he has carried for years. For Richard, the gift of a warrior's identity reminds him that there are parts of himself that he has yet to explore. The coldness of the tags against his neck sends a shiver of fear through his body. But at the same time that shiver sends a message to another part of his being: "There is power to be found here. . . ."

Surprisingly, often a gift exchange occurs between two men who have seen themselves as antagonists. The Medicine Wheel reflects such coincidence as natural law: There is as much Eros in hate as there is in love.

On the first day of the Quest, Bob had felt an immediate and intense dislike for another man. Of course, it is this "enemy's" gift, a flint belt buckle, that the Giveaway asks him to walk home with. Bob—whose declared intention for the Quest was to struggle with his fears—reveals he has learned that his true enemy was not the man, but his *fear* of the man.

Greg spoke in many councils of his desire to be more open and receptive. He said he had sharpened his skills as an archer to fine precision, but was rarely able to be still long enough to be the target. Greg receives the Giveaway of a ceramic bowl. He claims it as an icon that confirms his choice to know himself as a vessel—as one who receives as well as gives.

Many times the gift reflects a man's choice to move forward into the next phase of his life. Sam gave away a rock he had taken from the grave of his spiritual guide, the Christian mystic Thomas Merton. "During the Giveaway I had the experience of letting go of everything that was of the first half of my life," he recalls. "The first half of my life was done and I would never be the same again."

David gives away a medal he had received in recognition of his work in organizing a special event during the Olympics. He's clearly proud of this achievement, but he now has his sight set on a new horizon. He tells the one who chooses his gift of his intention to let go of his attachment to this prior achievement so he can expand his vision. David passes the medal on with a blessing of support for the man who receives it and for the visions that live yet unseen in him.

Stalking my gift, I am drawn to a plastic shopping bag. Inside I find hundreds of decaying leaves. At the bottom of the leaves is a nondescript rock. Amusement and puzzlement battle to control my expression. The man who has been providing a drumbeat for this event stands. He has taken the name of Drum. "The bag means nothing," he says. "The leaves mean nothing. The rock means nothing. That's not the gift." He pauses—and hands me the drum he's been playing. "*This* is the gift," he smiles and lets out a coyote howl that echoes, even today, in my heart.

Wayne gives away a ceremonial rattle he has made out of hardwood and steer horn. He created it during a visit to his parents' home, where his father had a large collection of woodworking tools. "I have never been able to work with him on any project without huge difficulty and frustration," he says. "Yet I needed him to show me how to make what I pictured in my mind, and to teach me how to select and use the appropriate tools. It is a very special creation to me. For the first time, my father and I worked closely together. It was a joy! All the work was by my hand, but my hands were guided by my father."

The youngest man in the group steps to the blanket. During our journey, he has asked us to help him awaken his dormant qualities of decisiveness and commitment by calling him by the

name of Warrior. He reaches instinctively for a small package.
Inside is a medallion that acknowledges its owner as a veteran of
war. Young Warrior's eyes search the circle for the one who had
offered this gift. A big bear of a man, whom we have known as
Broken Walk, stands. "Perfect," he says, "read it."

"Vietnam Veterans against the War," says Warrior.

"There's a story that goes with that," continues Broken Walk,
"but very few people have been willing to listen to it."

*I volunteered to go to Vietnam when I was seventeen. When I got
home, two years later, I was pretty fucked up. I couldn't talk or nothing. I went to a veterans support group and all I could do was sit on
the floor and stare out the window. Then a couple of the other guys
came over and put their arms around me and said, "It's gonna be
okay. . . . It's gonna be okay." They gave me that badge, and I put it
on my chest.*

*For months after, we marched arm in arm up and down the East
Coast calling people's attention to what was really going on in Vietnam. We were treated to tear gas and riot sticks from the National
Guard and the tactical police. We went down to Florida, to the Repub-
lican National Convention, and marched there. I was given the flag to
carry during a march and the police were bearing down hard on us. I
got hit a couple times by their motorcycles and clubs but I was determined to carry that flag. And that's when my life turned around. I felt
a power, a greater power was there holding up that flag. I felt God
walking alongside me and I began to pull out of the nosedive I had
been in since I got back from Nam. I ended up bruised and in jail, but
I learned something that saved my life. I pass it on to you because you
want to know about these things. You've got that badge now.*

*There's a difference between being a soldier and being a warrior.
Don't ever get these two confused. When I was in the army I was a
soldier. I was a puppet doing whatever anybody told me to do, even if
it meant going against what my heart told me was right. I didn't
know nothing about being a warrior until I hit the streets and
marched alongside my brothers for something I really believed in.
When I found something I believed in, a higher power found me.
That's it. That's the story.*

And so the Giveaway continues until all the exchanges have been made. Gifts in circulation, stories in circulation, the life force always in circulation among those willing to touch and be touched. The Giveaway never ends, only our celebration of it. We have opened a door here that we do not hasten to close. And so our celebration continues.

The emptied Give-Away Blanket is now host to loaves of bread and wineskins of juice and wine. When we break bread together and pass the cup, is it not this same circulation of life that we celebrate? This ancient rite, which celebrates the mystery of our communion with life, is alive in this brotherhood. For we are here to keep the Feast in the best way we know how.

Now this juice and this wine—this *is* life's blood, soon to pass
through our veins. For this communion we give thanks. And we
make of our sharing of this wine a gesture of our willingness to share
our life's blood with others—to nourish each other so that we may all
grow. Our truth is our life's blood.
And this bread—this *is* life's body, soon to be part of our flesh. For
this communion we give thanks. This loaf is our community. Let us
stay within the fiery cauldron until we are well cooked—until we
emerge with the same humble and nourishing presence as this bread.
For soon the loaf of our community will be broken and passed
among others.

Our sabbath day concludes with a special meal, considerably more elaborate than our usual fare, and one touched with uncommon tenderness. Perhaps the intimate sharings of the Giveaway flavor this meal. Or perhaps it is the unspoken recognition that this meal places us on the closing turn of our time here. We break camp tomorrow. This is our last supper.

13

COMING HOME

*And the world cannot be discovered by a journey of miles,
no matter how long, but only by a spiritual journey, a
journey of one inch, very arduous and humbling and joy-
ful, by which we arrive at the ground at our feet, and learn
to be at home.*
— WENDELL BERRY, *THE UNFORESEEN WILDERNESS*

This summer morning awakens like most in these forested valleys. The ground mist slowly disappears into the sky, birds sing
their new song, the river flows as ever to the sea. But to this eternal choreography, we humans add the steps of our own colorful
dance with life—steps created from our awareness of beginnings
and of endings. This is just like all other mornings. Yet, it is also
our last morning together in this place.

The drum signal normally used to call us together finds the
men already milling about the dance ground, ready to begin the
closing circle that will turn us toward the world we left behind.
There is an eagerness here similar to that present the morning we
descended from the sunrise knoll and first faced this way. For we
are soon to be on the trail that leads past Guardian Rock, and that
trail always leads to adventure.

But fear, no stranger to moments like this, creeps around the
edges of our enthusiasm. It enters more than one heart present,
through holes left by doubt, impatience, and pride. Fear whispers, in a reasonable tone, to one man: "Whatever vision you

gained here is best left here because, after all, only these people
will ever be able to understand any of your experience—and you,
of all people, know the consequences of *not being understood*."
And to another, fear offers: "The planet's in pretty bad shape—do
you really think any of this stuff is going to *change the world?*"
Fear continues its rounds and finds another man: "You've had
your fun, now let's get back to the *real world*. . . ."

Yet even as our thoughts drift down the trail, a familiar serpen-
tine spirit suddenly reappears to turn my attention back to present. The breeze-that-arises-from-nowhere hisses through the treetops as if to say: "You're not out of the woods yet—stay awake!" I
heed its calling and ask us to gather once again around our
Medicine Wheel.

Someone has placed a carefully sawn slice of an old tree trunk
next to the eastern stone. My attention goes to the rings that rip-
ple outward from the center. I marvel at how much information is
stored in these tracings of the tree's passage through time. The
bands of differing widths and colors tell of times when there was
much rain and times when there was little. They reflect assaults
by fire and lightning, and onslaughts by insects. Recorded too are
the stories of the branches that grew and in their time fell, as all
our creations must do. As the rings clearly reveal, each year's
growth embraces all the previous years' experience and wisdom.

As we peer into the mirror of the Medicine Wheel, it too
reflects a world that has turned since we've been here. And in
that turning we realize that the ground at our feet—this place of
beauty and mystery—*has become our known world*. All our questing, all our penetration into the heart of what really matters, has
been yet another ring of our ongoing journey home.

The truth is we can never go *back*, only *onward*. There is nothing we lose by leaving this place, just as there is no way a tree can
lose the ring of its previous year's growth. Whatever sacredness
we have remembered here is part of us now. Whatever vision our
hearts have opened to lives inside, waiting only for its appointed
season. Whatever love we have known here needs nothing
beyond our self-remembering.

As we walk past the gateway of Guardian Rock toward our

towns and cities, we will enter a deeper part of the forest yet. This threshold gateway swings both ways and somehow manages always to open toward Home. Guardian Rock has apparently learned a few tricks from Coyote.

The Wheel is like a clear mountain lake this morning. Its waters are deep, its surface still. We peer into its depths and breathe across its quiet surface the question, our first and last question: Who am I?

The Medicine Wheel offers a parting gift to send us on our way:

It was a holy purpose that brought you into these woods, and it is an equally holy purpose that returns you. For you are men who have chosen to walk a path that leads between two worlds: a path with heart that places one foot in the physical world and one foot in the world of spirit. It is a path that leads through heaven and hell with equal regard. Be not afraid of what you find in either realm. You continue to seek perfect balance, and do honor your seeking because it is what keeps you on the path. But rest assured that you will not find balance through seeking— you find balance in who you are. Fear may temporarily cause you to forget who you are, but there is nothing in the world that can rob you of your richness.

So live your questions, stay attentive, and trust whatever comes. Living in your hearts, you are safe beyond the need for safety.

These reflections lead us into our final council. We pass the Talking Staff around with the question: "What lives in your heart now?" This time the Staff will move in the direction contrary to what we've been accustomed to. This practice reflects our intention to unravel this circle and release this vessel of brotherhood that a larger one may be formed. What is of most value is that which remains after the vessel is broken.

We say good-bye to the land and spirit that has served us well. We bid farewell to the men, some of whom we have come to know as true brothers. We acknowledge gifts given and gifts received and yearnings left unfulfilled. We may not know fully what societies embrace us now as kin or what mysteries we have embodied with such abandon as to escape our knowing. Nonetheless, we are here. The forest recognizes us. The trees bend toward our quiet conversation. The rocks have matched our will and tested our patience beyond what we could bear. And they are with us still.

Warrior, the youngest member of our clan, takes up the Talking Staff and speaks of the specific quality of manhood he admires in each of us present. He has stalked each man here closely and is grateful for the diverse modeling of manhood he has witnessed. Then Owl Heart, the eldest man, takes the Talking Staff and speaks of this journey as a ten-day contemplative prayer and of his delight to be able to celebrate the stage of life he has entered. Another man, Longing One, grieves his failure to allow anything of importance to touch him here. The Talking Staff continues to move around the circle evoking poems, prayers, promises . . .

Suddenly the river's song changes. A man across the circle whispers, "Look . . . upstream!" His glance show us where. For a moment our eyes struggle to penetrate the camouflage of foliage and the sparkles of sunlight glinting on the water. But then we see it: something, some creature, making its way down the center of the stream toward us.

It appears to be a fawn, a young spotted one, searching for something. Yet the stream has served up many apparitions during our time here: faces of departed loved ones, sounds of distant drumming, whispered callings of our names. This fawn—a visitor from this world or a reflection of some other?

It keeps coming, close enough now for our sight to confirm the deer-child as one of this world. Its slender legs find their way among the rocks and eddies. Its eyes are wide open, its ears upright and alert. The sudden appearance of this trembling creature has swept our minds clear of thought and brought our senses to full attention. We watch and wait.

The fawn comes closer still, until it stops in the river directly alongside our circle. It turns to face us. Any remaining armor falls from our hearts. Then, without hesitation, the fawn walks toward the riverbank, toward us. Its spindly legs grapple for purchase on the gravel slope until it gains a foothold. Bounding up onto solid ground, the fawn walks to the edge of our circle, pauses briefly, then nudges its way between Longing One and the man next to him to stand at the center of our Medicine Wheel.

And the world stops. The fawn stands dripping wet, impossibly unafraid, in the center of our collective heart.

What the fawn is looking for we will never know. What it finds is a refuge safe enough to trust its trembling heart to. A world of men. Imperfect and wholehearted men. In our midst, a part of each of us stands revealed: our homelessness, our vulnerability, our searching, our gentleness and strength, our willingness to step into the unknown . . .

My mind, in a desperate attempt to reassert itself, races between the two hemispheres of the brain looking for one to confidently host this event. No use. A crack has appeared between the worlds, and this gentle creature has led me through that crack. I suddenly find myself in a universe in which I truly belong. Tears stream from my soul, releasing the sorrow that accumulates in taking life for granted—those waters, mixed with the tender light of my return. I hear the word "epiphany" but I do not reach for it, for even its respectful tone forces this moment apart from all others. I feel in the fawn's vulnerable presence the invitation to hold to nothing, but to stand in the center of *every* moment with the open eyes and heart of this one. I let myself love outside of time for as long as I can bear before I reach out for that word once refused. In fear, I agree, this is an exceptional moment, apart from all others. In truth, the grace is unbearable.

And so I fall once again from the garden, from the moment that is all moments, from the immensity of the world-myself. But it lingers like a sweet fragrance around me. I can remember the full attention I gave to life and the full aliveness that life returned to me. I can remember the time I rested in the grace of the world and was free. I may not be able to live it fully, but I can remember it.

Call it vision, call it whatever you like—it is the experience of being fully alive. Not only as a receiver of life, but also as a giver of life. Somewhere within every man is a womb that bears life. Perhaps that womb is the heart. The world needs a man's heart.

Life-bearing hearts. Hearts that choose to remember what they cannot yet fully live.

The fawn turns to face the woods beyond our circle. This refuge of belonging is not its final destination. It knows that it cannot live within a moment frozen in time. Neither can our pilgrimage.

The fawn slowly turns its head to look into eyes that will no longer hold it to this place, and then disappears into the forest.

Its journey homeward continues . . . as does ours.

ACKNOWLEDGMENTS

My foremost and heartfelt thanks go to Ron Schaumburg, who approached me in the spring of 1991 with the invitation to collaborate on this project: for the enthusiasm and expertise he brought to the collection and distillation of notes, research, interviews, journal entries, and surveys from Quest participants, and for providing the sturdy loom on which the many voices in this book could be woven into tapestry.

I thank Ned Leavitt, friend, nemesis, agent, coach, and coconspirator in the Quest, for his skillful and passionate trail crossings between the northern forests and the canyonlands of Manhattan, for his willingness to wade in the troubled waters, and for his sustaining love of this work.

I am grateful to Tom Miller, for his initial act of faith in this book, and to my editor, Hugh Van Dusen, for his patient, spacious, and steadfast guiding of this book into the light of day.

I thank John Guarnaschelli, Sam Mackintosh, Molly Quarrier, and Tony Lysy for encouraging me to shoot from the hip and for their generous and honest feedback along the way.

To Chris Harding, Bob Frenier, Forrest Craver, and Dick Halloran for providing a forum for men's hearts to speak through *Wingspan:* I send prayers of thanks and support on behalf of all of us.

None of this would be possible without the love and forbearance of friends and family. I am grateful beyond measure to my wife, Indira Darst, who by her example was a constant reminder to let my heart sing and who encouraged me to finish the vision with as much Eros as it began. I give heartfelt thanks to the intrepid members of the 50/50 Club, the Soul Patrol, and to Richard Bachrach for challenging me to live the Quest at home and for loving guidance through thick and thin.

My deepest respect and gratitude go to the men who have journeyed with me on the Quest over the years. Their stories have been the lifeblood of the work. In addition to those already credited within the text, I acknowledge the following men, whose voices appear directly or indirectly in this book: Between Two Worlds, Dancing Owl, Vision Heart, Tony B., Blue Light, Donkey Eagle, Nysus, Roaring Mouse, Laz, Sundancer, Two Hawks, Defender of Children, Soaring Eagle, Jumping Mouse, Glowing Crystal Coal, Yisrael, Screaming Eagle, Fire Starter, Earthsky, Smiling Heart, Vision Man, Water Warrior, Turtle, Johnny's Father, Firefly, Silver Wolf, Summerwind, Tamaqua, Hummingbird Monk, Light Brother, Searching Eagle, and Dancing Owl. I honor you for your willingness to reveal what is written in your hearts.

Much of this Quest work has been shaped over the years by the skillful and committed service of my coguides and helpers. To Geoff Hubbell, Russell Comstock, Ned Leavitt, Michael Hetzel, and Peter Schell, my gratitude is beyond words.

This book has also provided me an opportunity to present the collective wisdom of all of my teachers. Their teachings are present throughout, though highly colored by my personal idiosyncrasies. In one way or another, they have all urged and guided me into the Trouble that leads to God. I send prayers of gratitude:

To my father, for whom my growing love and respect has taught me that manhood is not so much a destination, but a journey

To Hyemeyohsts Storm, for your writings that opened the door to the possibility of walking in good relation with all beings. To Sun Bear, Oh Shinnah Fast Wolf, and Charley Thom, for opening the door wider and challenging me to stand in my own native integrity

To Elizabeth Cogburn, who taught me forms and traditions, but more importantly called me to the dance as a dancer

To Delores LaChapelle, for your untamed scholarship and for

living in one place for so long

To Bert and Moira Shaw, for your Quest for the Word behind the words of the Guide's teachings

To Pat Rodegast, for opening the door between the worlds and allowing me to be touched by Emmanuel

To Emily Conrad-Da'oud and Susan Harper, for embodying your love of wilderness and guiding me to uncharted waters

To Natalie Goldberg, for teaching me to trust the pen held by no mind

To Robert Bly, whose immense generosity inspired me to give it all away, and made the way honest and beautiful with many songs

To Steven Foster and Meredith Little, keepers of the sacred fire that has warmed and illuminated the way for so many of us over the years

To Joseph Campbell, for his lively and generous celebration of the hero's journey

To the mountains, rivers, forests, and creatures of the Adirondacks that have so faithfully guided me to the sacrament of earth

I celebrate you all for your clarity and abandon in the face of the Great Mystery.

—Joseph Jastrab

Thanks to Dan Montopoli for suggesting a second book about men's work; Chris Harding for keeping *Wingspan* flying for so long; Sandy Choron for making things happen and making me laugh; Tom Miller for focusing the book and finding it a home; Ned Leavitt for helping us negotiate the boundaries between worlds; Hugh Van Dusen for his generosity, patience, and forbearance; Bud Clarke for carrying and nurturing the spark, for walking in the Beauty Way, and for holding the center together; Dan Barnett for teaching me the beauty of running water; Elliott Forrest for the gift of tea and healing; all the men who have quested with Joseph, especially those who responded to our questionnaire for contributing to this rich banquet of experience; my mother for starting me on this Earth Walk; Joseph Jastrab for trusting me with his story; and Susan, Sara, and Natania for allowing me to go off into the woods and for welcoming the one who returned.

—Ron Schaumburg

RESOURCES

Wingspan: Journal of the Male Spirit
8 Mt. Vernon St., #6
Dorchester, MA 02125
(617) 282-3521

Features articles with a mythopoetic perspective and interviews with leaders of men's conferences. National calendar of
men's events. Editor Chris Harding is an avid networker and is
available as a consultant for men's work referrals.

Way of the Mountain Center
P.O. Box 2434
Durango, CO 81302
(800) 578-5904

Publishes newsletter of hard-to-find books and other materials
on deep ecology, the spirit of place, and other earth-centered topics. Lively and thought-provoking reviews by the editor, Delores
LaChapelle.

Circles on the Mountain: A Journal for Rites of Passage Guides
Jennifer Massey
200 Beacon Hill Lane

Ashland, OR 97520
(503) 488-0908

Functions as a forum for dialogue among people offering
wilderness-based rites-of-passage work. Articles, interviews,
book reviews, and national Quest networking service.

Earth Rise Foundation
70 Mountain Rest Road
New Paltz, NY 12561
(914) 255-2782

Directed by Joseph Jastrab, offering Vision Quests, workshops,
and trainings for both men and women. Write for brochure and
list of events.